1/2 Cup Butter
1 " Sugar
1 Egg

1 Cup Unsweetened
Apple Sauce
Stir in 1 tsp Soda

1/2 tsp. Cloves
1 " Cinnamon
1 Cup Raisins
1 3/4 " flour
1 tsp Baking Powder
1 Cup Nuts

Frosting

1 1/2 Cups Confectioners Sugar
1 Egg
Butter size of Egg
Vanilla

till tender. Delicious.

BROWN BREAD—One and one-half cups so[illegible] sugar, [illegible] spoon s[illegible] ham flour. Mix well [illegible] rise one hour and bake in moderate oven.

Canton. MRS. A. O.

BRAN BROWN BREAD—One cup brown sugar 1 egg, 1-4 tablespoon salt, 2 cup Kellogg's bran, 1-2 teaspoon soda, 2 teaspoons baking powder, 1 cup flour, 1 cup sour milk, 1-2 cup raisins. Beat the egg, add sugar, beat again, add bran, raisins and sour milk. Sift together salt, soda, baking powder and flour and add to the above. Steam 3 hours in tightly covered can.

## Corn Oysters.

(This recipe takes the $1 prize.)

1 c of fresh RAW corn
1 egg
1/4 c flour
1 t salt
Little pepper

Grate corn from cob, add the slightly beaten egg and the flour and seasonings. Drop in small spoonfuls on a well greased griddle and fry to a golden brown color.

## Delicious Pudding.

One cup sugar, 1 tablespoon butter, 2 tablespoons flour, 1 lemon (grated rind), 1 cup milk, 2 eggs (spice).

Cream 1 cup sugar with a tablespoon of butter. Add 2 tablespoons of flour, spice (if desired) and grated rind of 1 lemon. One cup of milk and the beaten yolks of 2 eggs. Just before pouring into the baking dish stir in the stiffly beaten whites of eggs. Set dish in pan with hot water, and bake slowly. When it is done there will be a light, creamy souffle on top and a layer of creamy custard underneath.

Salem. ISOBEL WARD.

## Cream Slaw.

Whip one-half cup of heavy sweet cream until thick. Then add 1 1-2 tablespoons of sugar and salt, pepper, and celery salt to taste. Whip into this 1 cup of mild cider vinegar and beat until frothy. Have ready about 1-4 head of firm cabbage shaved fine. Mix altogether, chill and serve.

THELMA SCHROTH[illegible]

## Use Electric Oven to Bake "Mrs. Harding's Favorite Chicken Pie"

Use chicken or neck of veal. Cook thoroughly, until bones fall out if veal is used. Cut in small pieces. Peal a few small potatoes and 1 onion. Cook all in broth, and season the whole with salt and pepper to taste.

Make a rich pastry by using 1 1-2 pints of flour, 1-2 cup lard, 1 teaspoon salt, 2 [illegible]

A Collection of
Fine Food and Artifacts
from Generations of
Midwestern Women.

# Treasures of the Great Midwest

*Presented by the Junior League of Wyandotte & Johnson Counties in Kansas, Inc.*

First printing September 1995



Printed in the
United States of America

ISBN 0-9606412-1-1

Library of Congress Card Catalog
Number 95-77742

For information on ordering copies of cookbooks published by the Junior League of Wyandotte and Johnson Counties in Kansas, Inc., contact:

Cookbook Committee
JLWJC, Inc.
P.O. Box 17-1487
Kansas City, KS 66117-0487
913/ 371-2303
Fax: 913/ 371-3772

# About the Publisher

The Junior League of Wyandotte and Johnson Counties in Kansas, Inc. is an organization of women committed to promoting voluntarism and to improving the community through the effective action and leadership of trained volunteers. Its purpose is exclusively educational and charitable. The JLWJC reaches out to women of all races, religions, and national origins who demonstrate an interest in and commitment to voluntarism.

The JLWJC is committed to ensuring children have the opportunities and services essential for their physical, intellectual, emotional, mental and social growth and will advocate to see such opportunities and services are provided.

The proceeds realized from the sale of *Treasures of the Great Midwest* will be returned to the community through projects supported by the Junior League of Wyandotte and Johnson Counties in Kansas, Inc.

## Special Thanks

Title, Design, Art Direction
Anne Simmons
Willoughby Design Group

Photography
Scott Hepler,
Hepler Photography, Inc.

Styling by
Grace Knott

Food Styling
Vicki Johnson

Food Consultant
Lou Jane Temple

## Our Sponsors

Golden Heirloom
Halls

Crystal Heirloom
Farmland Foods

China Heirloom
CHUBB Group of Insurance Companies
DiCarlo Construction Company
Sally Blake Gille, Jennifer Gille Bacon, Sara Langston Bacon
The Lee Company

Linen Heirloom
A. Drue and Susan Jennings
DST Systems, Inc.
Executive Leadership Skills, Richard and Vicki Sherberger
Faultless Starch/Bon Ami Company
Mr. and Mrs. Kent Hobert, Carrie and Brian
KSHB TV 41
Margo Murray Humenczuk
Melvin M. and Alice Hawk
Spectrum Economics, Inc.
Sue Ann Fagerberg
Thompson Insurance Group, Inc.
Johnson County Bar Foundation
Burns Printing
Mr. and Mrs. Kirk W. Coen

## Cookbook Committee

Chairman
Nedra C. Hobert

Editor
Margo Murray Humenczuk

Recipe Standardization
Kellie L. Zych

Design Coordinator
Dawn R. Caspers

Funding Coordinator
Nancy W. Balsbaugh

Treasurer
Sally B. Jenkins

Promotion Coordinator
Lisa Ochs Coen

Testing Coordinators
Rita Z. Brungardt
Pamela Ostertag Carder
Janie DeGoler
Dawn M. Hightower
Miranda Iszory
Dianne D. Keller
Jo Ellen Kuckelman
Rene Ochs Morris
Betty L. Weeks
Gina R. Whitcomb-Shively

Sustaining Advisor
Alice Hawk

Board Liason
Marsha L. Oyer
Kathy Burke-Thomas

# Table of Contents

# Introduction

*Great times remembered in grandmother's kitchen.*

Travel with us to the times when the aromas, tastes, and flavors of our grandmothers' kitchens, steeped deep in our memories, come alive once again as we share the richness of their foods and families with current generations and those to come.

Remember with us the earthy aroma of pulling weeds in grandmother's garden, of hanging herbs up to dry, of enjoying a rich sage bread or comforting chamomile tea on a cold winter's evening. Remember spending rainy afternoons sorting through grandmother's button box, the clatter of the buttons of various textures and hues, finding a special treasure to admire or adorn the gown of a favorite doll. As we played, the familiar aroma of roast goose or Sunday beef roast, pungent vegetables, yeasty breads, and sweet cakes, pies and puddings filled the entire house.

As we sort through our grandmother's attic, the mother-of-pearl pins, calico dresses, crystal saltcellars, and treasured photographs bring back to mind the sensual aromas and flavors of her kitchen and the meals we shared there with our families. Our hobbies, too, return us to home; quilting, collecting, antiques and gardening awaken the hunger for the wholesome meals of our past. We yearn to bring back the closeness of the sacred family mealtime where hopes, dreams, concerns, and warm family times were shared.

The significance of the meal, so closely related to the time and love put into its preparation, is so easily lost in today's fast food society. Join us as we recreate the special mealtimes and memories of our past and introduce new recipes for today as well. Whether you choose to prepare a daylong labor of love such as our Traditional Christmas Goose, Herbed Corn Pudding, and Grandma's Potato Rolls or a do ahead Imperial Chicken with Lemon Pilaf, quick Cheddar Muffins, and fresh Garlic Green Beans, your family is sure to appreciate the special aromas and flavors of our collection of treasures from some of the finest kitchens in the Midwest. Join us in our celebration of the women whose artifacts and recipes we share with you in *Treasures of the Great Midwest*.

Sunday church service and potluck dinners are time honored traditions throughout much of the Midwest. Sharing food and fellowship nourishes the body and the soul. Wholesome food presented with elegance is the order of the day. Appetizers which are easily transported and look as lovely at serving time as they do right from the oven are always in demand.

Spinach Dip melds spinach, rich cheeses, and hot peppers to make a flavorful blend that is spicy and rich, appropriate for any occasion from a potluck buffet to an elegant cocktail party. Accompanied by spiced Pita Toast or cut breads of any kind, your guests are sure to return for more. They'll never guess how simple these appetizers are to prepare!

# Appetizers

## Hot Spinach Dip with Pita Toast

1 Tablespoon jalapeno peppers, chopped

¾ cup onion, chopped

2 tomatoes, chopped

10 oz. package frozen chopped spinach, thawed and squeezed dry

8 oz. cream cheese

2 cups Monterey Jack cheese, shredded

⅓ cup half and half

*Pita Toast:*

6 pita loaves (1 package)

2 teaspoons lemon pepper

2 teaspooons cumin, ground

½ cup butter, melted

reheat oven to 400°F. Grease an ovenproof dish. Mix all ingredients, pour into dish. Bake for 20 to 25 minutes or until bubbly. Serve with Pita Toast. Split pita loaves in half. Combine lemon pepper and ground cumin. Spread pita with butter, then sprinkle with lemon pepper and ground cumin mixture. Broil until crisp. Serve immediately.

This page generously sponsored by Mr. and Mrs. Gary Zych.

## Skewered Tortellini with Lemon Dip

1 cup creme fraiche, recipe follows
¼ cup grated Parmesan cheese
2 lemons, juiced, and zest, grated
3 cloves garlic, roasted, peeled and crushed
1½ lbs. tortellini
olive oil

ombine creme fraiche, Parmesan cheese, lemon juice, lemon zest and roasted garlic in small mixing bowl to make lemon dip. Set aside.

Bring water to boil in large stock pot. Add tortellini and cook al dente (do not overcook or it will fall apart when putting it on the skewer). Drain and sprinkle with olive oil. This will keep the tortellini from sticking together.

To serve, skewer two to three tortellini on 4-inch skewer. Serve hot with lemon dip.

## Creme Fraiche

2 cups heavy cream
2 Tablespoons buttermilk or sour cream

eat cream in heavy saucepan over low heat. Add buttermilk and mix well. Place in covered jar. Let sit at room temperature for 6 to 8 hours. Refrigerate at least 24 hours (36 is best) before serving.

**Makes 2 cups.**

## Sesame Shrimp

1½ lbs. large fresh shrimp
3 Tablespoons cornstarch
2 Tablespoons reduced-sodium teriyaki sauce
1 Tablespoon water
2 teaspoons fresh ginger
¼ teaspoon salt
⅓ cup sesame seeds, toasted
⅓ cup fine, dry bread crumbs
vegetable oil

eel shrimp and devein; set shrimp aside. Combine cornstarch with teriyaki sauce, water, ginger and salt; set aside. Combine sesame seeds and bread crumbs. Dip each shrimp into cornstarch mixture; coat with sesame seed mixture. Pour oil into a Dutch oven to a depth of 3 inches; heat to 365°F. Fry 8 to 10 shrimp at a time for one minute or until golden brown. Drain on paper towels.

Serves 8.

## Crab Rangoon

½ lb. fresh crabmeat, drained and chopped
½ lb. cream cheese, softened
½ teaspoon Worchestershire sauce
¼ teaspoon garlic powder
2½ to 3 dozen wonton wrappers
1 egg yolk, well beaten
oil for deep frying
hot mustard and/or sweet and sour sauce

ombine crabmeat, cream cheese, Worchestershire sauce and garlic powder in medium bowl and blend to a paste. Place heaping teaspoon on each wonton wrapper. Gather four corners of wonton wrapper together at top and moisten edges with egg yolk and pinch or twist gently together to seal. Heat oil in wok, deep fryer or electric skillet to 375°F. Add wontons in small batches and fry until golden brown (about three minutes). Remove with slotted spoon and drain on paper towels. Serve hot with sweet and sour sauce or hot mustard.

**Makes 30 to 36 appetizers.**

## Egg Rolls

½ lb. beef or pork, ground
1 teaspoon ground ginger
1 teaspoon salt
3 teaspoons onion, chopped
2 teaspoons wine or saki
2 teaspoons soy sauce
2 teaspoons cornstarch
oil
8 egg roll wrappers
sweet and sour sauce and/or hot mustard

ix all ingredients together except egg roll wrappers. Separate meat mixture into 8 equal portions and place on egg wrappers. Roll wrappers and fold tightly, wet edge and seal. Fry in hot oil until brown.

Serve hot with sweet and sour sauce and/or hot mustard sauce.

**Serves 8.**

## Hot Pepper Pecans

¼ cup butter or margarine
4 teaspoons soy sauce
1 teaspoon salt
12 shakes Tabasco sauce
2 cups pecans

elt butter and add soy sauce, salt and Tabasco. Pour over pecans. Toss well. Spread coated pecans on cookie sheet. Bake at 350°F for 30 minutes. Let cool on paper towels.

## Roasted Manila Clams with Smoked Bacon and Spinach

50 to 60 Manila clams
3 lbs. rendered smoked bacon
1 gallon fresh spinach, julienned
3 cups sweet vermouth
1 bunch fresh cilantro
2 cups water
1 Tablespoon salt
1 Tablespoon pepper

oss all ingredients together in a roasting pan and cover. Place roasting pan in a 450°F oven until clams open.

*Presented at Grand Street Cafe by Chef Michael*

## Picante Wheels

¼ cup cooked black beans
2 jalapeno peppers, seeded
1 whole pimento, seeded
1 teaspoon cumin
¼ bunch cilantro, snipped
¼ teaspoon salt, optional
2 8 oz. packages cream cheese, softened
2 (or more) 10-inch flour tortillas
salsa or picante sauce

ombine black beans, jalapeno peppers, pimento, cumin, cilantro and salt in a food processor with blade attachment and chop coarsely. Add cream cheese and blend until smooth. Spread mixture on tortillas, roll up and chill. Remove from refrigerator and cut into ½-inch slices. Serve with salsa or picante sauce.

## Salsa Supremo

2 15oz. cans stewed tomatoes
5 green onions
3 to 5 small fresh jalapeno peppers
1 Tablespoon fresh cilantro
3 cloves garlic
salt and pepper to taste

dd juice from tomatoes to food processor along with onions, jalapenos, cilantro and garlic. Puree. Check seasoning and add more if needed. Add tomatoes and pulse processor to desired chunkiness. Add salt and pepper to taste.

**Makes 2 cups.**

## Stuffed Mushrooms

32 large mushrooms
2 cloves garlic, crushed
¼ cup butter
¾ lb. bulk pork sausage or Italian sausage
½ to ⅔ cup seasoned dry bread crumbs
¾ cup grated Parmesan cheese
¼ cup fresh parsley, snipped
salt and pepper to taste
butter, melted

Clean mushrooms well. Remove stems from mushrooms and chop, reserving caps. Saute chopped stems and the garlic in butter in a small skillet over medium heat, until mushrooms are golden and tender, about 3 minutes. Add sausage and continue to saute, stirring constantly, until brown. Stir in bread crumbs, cheese, parsley, and salt and pepper to taste. Stuff each mushroom cap with about 1 tablespoon of the mixture. Set on baking rack. Drizzle melted butter over each mushroom cap. Bake or broil mushrooms for about 3 minutes, or until the filling begins to bubble and brown.

**Variations for fillings:**

Cream cheese and pork sausage
Bacon, onion, green pepper and bread crumbs
Artichoke hearts and blue cheese
Crabmeat, green onions and herbed cheese

## Asparagus Crepes Petite

*Crepes:*
3 eggs
1 cup all purpose flour, divided
⅛ teaspoon salt
1 cup milk
½ cup club soda
non-stick cooking spray

*Filling:*
1 lb. asparagus or 9 oz. frozen asparagus
5 oz. herbed cheese

Beat eggs in blender on low speed about 10 seconds or mix well with electric mixer. Add ½ cup flour with salt and mix well. Add remaining flour alternating with milk, and blend well. Transfer to a mixing bowl. Add soda and stir gently. Mixture should be the consistency of heavy cream.

Spray non-stick skillet with cooking spray. Heat until hot enough that sprinkles of water "dance" on skillet. Pour batter one tablespoon at a time to make crepes about 3 inches in diameter. Cook until edges of crepe are lightly browned. This may take less than a minute so make just a few at a time to start. Turn and cook the other side 20 to 30 seconds. Turn out of pan onto sheets of waxed paper. Crepes may be stacked with sheets of waxed paper between layers. Set aside.

Wash and trim asparagus. Cook in microwave or standing in boiling water until tender but slightly crisp. Cut off tips of asparagus to a length about ½ inch larger than the diameter of the crepe. Spread each crepe with herbed cheese. Place asparagus in center of crepe and roll. Arrange on serving plate with lemon slices or zigzag cut lemon halves. May be served chilled or at room temperature.

## White Grapes

white seedless grapes
8 oz. cream cheese, softened
4 to 8 Tablespoons confectioners' sugar
1 to 1½ cups coarsely chopped pecans

ix cream cheese and confectioners' sugar. The consistency should be stiff. Take 1 teaspoon of the cheese mixture in palm of your hand and wrap the cream cheese around the grape. If the mixture softens while working with it, refrigerate mixture until firm and then continue process. Set grapes on a plate. After all grapes are finished, roll in pecans and place on plate in freezer or refrigerator.

Refrigerate at least 2 to 3 hours before serving. May be served whole or cut in half. These can be made ahead and frozen for at least a week.

*A delightful treat for a hot summer afternoon!*

## Savory Artichoke Cheesecake

1 Tablespoon butter or margarine, softened
½ to ¾ cup fine dry bread crumbs
1 lb. cream cheese, softened
¾ cup feta cheese, crumbled, approximately 4 oz.
1 cup sour cream
3 large eggs
9 oz. package frozen artichoke hearts, thawed
½ medium red pepper, chopped
½ medium yellow pepper, chopped
½ cup green onions, sliced
1 large clove garlic, crushed
1 teaspoon dried tarragon leaves, crushed
½ teaspoon dried basil leaves, crushed
rye and pumpernickel toast points
fresh basil leaves and red pepper strips for garnish

reheat oven to 375°F. Grease inside of a 9-inch springform pan with softened butter. Sprinkle pan with bread crumbs to coat thickly; reserve remaining crumbs. Set pan aside.

Beat cream cheese until fluffy in large bowl of electric mixer. Add feta cheese, sour cream and eggs, and beat until smooth. Pat dry and finely chop artichoke hearts; add to bowl with cheese mixture. Beat in chopped peppers, onions, garlic, tarragon and basil until blended. Spoon into pan and spread evenly, being careful not to pull the bread crumbs into the mixture.

Bake for 35 minutes or until puffed and golden. Cool on wire rack to room temperature, then refrigerate three hours or overnight.

To serve, remove springform sides. Pat remaining bread crumbs onto side of cheesecake. Garnish with fresh basil leaves and red pepper strips. Serve with rye and pumpernickel toast points.

Serves 24.

## Coeur a la Creme

¾ lb. cottage cheese
8 oz. cream cheese, softened
½ cup sour cream
½ cup heavy cream, whipped
2 Tablespoons fresh dill, finely chopped
2 Tablespoons fresh parsley, finely chopped
2 Tablespoons fresh chervil, finely chopped, optional
2 Tablespoons fresh tarragon, finely chopped, optional
1 small scallion, finely julienned
salt and white pepper to taste

ombine cottage cheese, cream cheese and sour cream in mixing bowl and mix with electric mixer with flat beater attachment. Mix until smooth. Strain through a fine sieve two or three times. Fold in whipped cream and herbs, and salt and pepper to taste.

Line a mold with three layers of cheesecloth, letting the cloth overlap the edges. Put sprigs of fresh dill in the bottom of the mold and spoon in the cheese mixture, filling to the top (do not leave any extra space at the top). Fold the cloth over the cheese and refrigerate for at least one day.

Serve on cucumber rounds or with fresh vegetables.

## Pico De Gallo

2¼ lbs. plum tomatoes, finely chopped
1 large onion, finely chopped
¾ cup fresh cilantro, chopped
5 garlic cloves, minced
3 jalapeno chilies, seeded and minced
3 Tablespoons lime juice

ombine all ingredients in mixing bowl. Season with salt and pepper. Cover and chill at least 1 hour and up to 4 hours before serving. Serve with tortilla chips. Also perfect with enchiladas.

## Sherry Cheese Pate

2 3 oz. packages cream cheese, softened
1 cup shredded sharp cheddar cheese
¼ cup dry sherry
½ teaspoon curry powder
½ cup chutney
2 green onions, thinly sliced

ombine cream cheese, cheddar cheese, sherry and curry powder. Shape into a 5-inch circle on a serving platter and chill. Just before serving, spread chutney over cheese mixture and sprinkle with green onions. Serve with crackers.

Serves 12.

## Pizza Dough

1½ cups warm water, divided
2 teaspoons light brown sugar
2 packages dry yeast (4 teaspoons)
4½ cups unbleached all purpose white flour, divided
1 teaspoon salt
4 Tablespoons olive oil, divided

Measure ½ cup warm (not hot) water in a cup and add brown sugar. Dissolve both packages of yeast in water and sugar mixture. Set aside for at least 5 minutes. The yeast will become frothy during this time.

Sift 4 cups flour into a large mixing bowl with the salt. Make a depression in the middle of the flour and add 3 tablespoons olive oil and 1 cup of warm water. Add yeast mixture to flour mixture after 5 minutes.

Mix all ingredients in a large bowl with your hands, gather them together, and place them on floured surface. Knead dough for 8 to 10 minutes.

Rub a clean bowl with olive oil and place the kneaded dough in it. Moisten the top of the dough with olive oil. Cover bowl with a towel and place in a warm, draft-free place to rise. Let the dough rise for 1½ hours, remove and place on floured surface. Roll out dough for the pizza of your choice.

Place toppings on crust. Bake at 450°F for 25 to 30 minutes.

## Whole Wheat Pizza Dough

2 packages dry yeast (4 teaspoons)
1½ cups warm water, divided
2 teaspoons honey
4 cups whole wheat flour
1 teaspoon salt
4 Tablespoons safflower oil, divided

Dissolve the yeast in ½ cup warm water and add 2 teaspoons honey. Set aside for at least 5 minutes. Meanwhile, sift flour and salt in a mixing bowl. Make a depression in the center of flour mixture and add 3 tablespoons safflower oil and 1 cup warm water. Add yeast mixture to the flour and mix all the ingredients with your hands. Gather the dough together and place on floured surface. Knead dough, adding more flour if necessary. Knead for 8 to 10 minutes. The dough will be elastic and cohesive.

Place dough in a large oiled bowl. Brush the top of the dough with the remaining oil. Cover with a clean towel and put in a warm, draft-free place for 1½ hours. Punch down dough, place on a floured surface, and roll out dough for pizza.

Place toppings on crust. Bake at 450°F for 20 to 25 minutes.

## Florentine Pizza Dough

2 packages dry yeast (4 teaspoons)
¾ cup warm water
2 teaspoons light brown sugar
1 cup ricotta cheese
1 cup fresh spinach leaves, lightly steamed
4½ cups unbleached all purpose flour
1 teaspoon salt
4 Tablespoons olive oil, divided
1 egg

Dissolve yeast in the warm water and stir in brown sugar. Set aside for at least 5 minutes. Blend ricotta cheese and spinach leaves in a blender on high speed until smooth. Sift flour into mixing bowl with salt. Make a depression in the center of the flour and add 3 tablespoons olive oil, egg, spinach mixture and yeast mixture. Knead the mixture on a floured surface for 8 to 10 minutes or until the dough is uniformly mixed and elastic. Add more flour if necessary. Brush a large bowl with olive oil. Place dough in bowl. Brush the top of the dough with oil and cover with a clean cloth. Place the bowl in a warm, draft-free place for 1½ hours. Punch down dough, place on floured surface, and roll out dough for pizza.

Place toppings on crust. Bake at 450°F for 20 to 25 minutes.

**Variations for Pizza Toppings:**

Florentine—spinach, plum tomatoes, artichoke hearts, and mozzarella
Hawaiian—Canadian bacon, sliced pineapple, shrimp, Gruyere cheese, Parmesan cheese
Mexican—ground beef, jalapeno peppers, Mexican salsa, Monterey Jack and colby cheese
Italian—marinated chicken, fresh mushrooms, artichoke hearts, red onions, capers and Parmesan cheese

## Vegetable Pizza

1 large Boboli pizza crust
2 8 oz. packages cream cheese, softened
⅔ cup mayonnaise
1½ teaspoons dill
¾ teaspoons Beau Monde seasoning
¼ teaspoon garlic powder
toppings of your choice: broccoli, finely chopped cauliflower, finely chopped carrots, peppers, thinly sliced green onions

Preheat oven to 375°F. Bake Boboli crust for 10 minutes or until lightly browned. Set aside to cool.

Cream together cream cheese, mayonnaise, dill, Beau Monde and garlic powder. If possible, cover and refrigerate this mixture several hours or overnight to allow the flavors to blend. Spread mixture over crust. Top with desired amounts of the vegetables. Refrigerate covered, then cut into squares.

*The light versions of cream cheese and mayonnaise work very well.*

## Pizza Quatro Fromaggi

1 box frozen puff pastry
1 cup mozzarella cheese, grated
1 cup Monterey Jack cheese, grated
¼ cup Parmesan cheese, grated
¼ cup feta cheese, crumbled
1 Tablespoon oregano
olive oil to taste
1 Tablespoon green onion
black olives, if desired

Roll out one sheet of puff pastry to roughly fit a pizza pan. Bake it until lightly brown at an oven temperature specified by package directions.

Mix mozzarella, Monterey Jack, and Parmesan cheese and spread over crust. Dot with crumbled feta cheese. Sprinkle oregano on top and drizzle with olive oil. Add green onions and black olives as desired. Bake at 450°F until cheeses melt.

**Serves 8.**

## Bruschetta

3 large tomatoes, diced
2 Tablespoons fresh basil, chopped
2 teaspoons oregano
2 Tablespoons sweet onion, chopped
3 cloves garlic, minced
3 Tablespoons olive oil
salt and pepper to taste

Combine all ingredients. Cover and let flavors blend at room temperature one hour or more.

Serve on toast or Italian bread sliced 1 inch thick. Spoon tomato mixture on top.

**Serves 4.**

## Raspberry Cheese Ball

10 oz. sharp white cheddar cheese, grated
3 Tablespoons mayonnaise
scallions
raspberry preserves

Mix cheese, mayonnaise and scallions. Form into a ball and chill in wax paper.

Before serving, frost generously with preserves. Serve with crackers.

## Chicken and Ham Pinwheels

2 whole large chicken breasts, skinned and boned
⅛ teaspoon dried basil, crushed
⅛ teaspoon salt
dash pepper
dash garlic salt
4 thin slices fully cooked ham
2 teaspoons lemon juice
paprika

Rinse chicken and dry. Place one breast between wax paper and pound to ¼-inch thickness, repeat with remaining chicken.

Combine basil, salt, pepper and garlic salt and sprinkle on chicken. Place one slice of ham on each breast and roll up from long side. Place seam side down in baking dish. Drizzle lemon juice over chicken and sprinkle with paprika. Bake at 350°F for 30 minutes. Chill and slice thinly.

**Makes 24 to 30 appetizers.**

## Cucumber Tapa

2 1 lb. cucumbers, peeled if waxy
2 Tablespoons extra virgin olive oil
1 teaspoon sherry vinegar
2 oz. feta cheese, diced
¼ teaspoon salt, optional
pinch freshly ground black pepper
1 Tablespoon oregano leaves or
½ teaspoon oregano powder

Slice cucumber lengthwise and remove seeds. Cut 1 cucumber half into ¼-inch diced pieces and transfer into small bowl. Add olive oil, vinegar, feta cheese, salt and pepper and toss well to combine. Add oregano and toss again.

Use vegetable peeler to remove 1 or 2 long strips of cucumber flesh from underside of each cucumber half so they will not tip.

Divide cucumber and feta mixture among the cucumber pieces and stuff. Slice cucumber on a slight diagonal in 1-inch slices and serve immediately.

## Basil Tomato Dip

¼ cup sherry vinegar
2 Tablespoons Dijon mustard
1 Tablespoon red wine vinegar
1 Tablespoon olive oil
2 cups seeded, diced tomatoes, unpeeled
1 cup fresh basil, chopped
2 cloves garlic, crushed
2 Tablespoons grated Parmesan cheese

Combine all ingredients and serve with crackers.

## Cheesy Clam Dip

1 small onion, finely chopped
½ green pepper, finely chopped
3 Tablespoons butter
2 cans minced clams, well drained
4 Tablespoons ketchup
1 Tablespoon Worchestershire sauce
1 Tablespoon sherry
¼ teaspoon cayenne pepper
½ lb. processed cheese, melted

Saute onion and pepper in butter. Add clams, ketchup, Worchestershire sauce, sherry and cayenne pepper. Stir over medium heat until well blended.

Just before serving add melted cheese. Serve in chafing dish over low heat.

*Whole wheat crackers or tortilla chips go nicely with this dip.*

## Hot Cheese Triangles

¼ lb. feta cheese
8 oz. cream cheese, softened
2 Tablespoons beaten egg
8 oz. phyllo dough
½ cup unsalted butter, melted
¼ cup fine dry bread crumbs

Crumble feta cheese into bowl of electric mixer. Combine with cream cheese and egg and blend well. Chill mixture.

Place damp towel on counter and cover with wax paper. Unfold phyllo dough and place on waxed paper. Fold phyllo in half, with waxed paper and damp towel covering it. Keep covered until ready to use, to prevent drying. Remove one phyllo sheet and place on clean surface. Cut width wise into thirds. Brush top and bottom surfaces lightly with butter. Sprinkle top lightly with bread crumbs. Fold each section lengthwise in thirds to form section two inches wide. Place a teaspoonful of filling in top corner of one section. Fold corner to cover cheese mixture and make a triangle.

Fold flag fashion from left to right and right to left. Brush with butter to seal last edge. Repeat process until all phyllo dough and filling mixture has been used.

Place on buttered baking sheet and brush with butter. Bake at 400°F for 15 minutes or until golden brown. Serve immediately.

To Freeze: Cool on wire rack and transfer to plastic container. Freeze until ready to serve. Arrange frozen pastries on baking sheet. Reheat at 350°F for 10 minutes, until heated through.

**Makes 36 appetizers.**

## Creamy Mediterranean Dip

¾ cup mayonnaise
¼ cup sour cream
2 large roma tomatoes
2 Tablespoons dry basil
2 Tablespoons grated Parmesan cheese
2 teaspoons red wine vinegar
2 Tablespoons fresh lemon juice
½ teaspoon garlic powder

ombine all ingredients in food processor. Blend until smooth. Serve with wedges of pita bread.

**Makes one cup.**

## Marinated Tomatoes with Arugula, Blue Cheese and Fresh Herb Crostini

6 fresh tomatoes, blanched and peeled
1 cup extra virgin olive oil
⅓ cup balsamic vinegar
2 teaspoons fresh garlic, chopped
2 Tablespoons fresh herb blend, chopped
1 teaspoon salt
1 teaspoon pepper
4 oz. blue cheese
4 oz. arugula, julienned
1 baguette

ore tomatoes and drop in boiling water for approximately 20 to30 seconds. Remove tomatoes and chill immediately. Peel the tomatoes and cut in half. Combine olive oil, vinegar, garlic, herbs, salt, and pepper in a medium mixing bowl. Toss the halved tomatoes in the marinade and let stand in refrigerator for 2 to 3 hours.

Cut baguette into ½-inch thick slices, brush with olive oil. Sprinkle with fresh herbs and broil in oven to make crostini. Cover plate with julienned arugula and tomatoes. Sprinkle with blue cheese and serve with crostini on the side.

*Presented at Grand Street Cafe by Chef Michael Peterson.*

## Salmon Cream Spread

15½ oz. can salmon, drained and deboned with skin removed
8 oz. cream cheese, softened
1 Tablespoon lemon juice
2 teaspoons grated onion
¼ teaspoon salt
¼ teaspoon liquid smoke
pecans and/or snipped parsley

ombine salmon, cream cheese, lemon juice, onion, salt and liquid smoke. Mix well. Shape into a ball. Roll in pecans and/or parsley. Place in refrigerator or freezer to chill.

## Marinated Olives

6 oz. green olives, pimento or almond stuffed, drained
⅓ cup oil
¼ cup water
3 Tablespoons lime juice
1 Tablespoon cilantro, chopped
1 Tablespoon red pepper
1 Tablespoon cumin
1 clove garlic, minced

Combine all ingredients in a small saucepan. Bring to boil, reduce heat and simmer, covered, for 5 minutes. Remove from heat.

When cooled to room temperature, transfer olives to jars with tight fitting lids. Fill jars with cooking liquid. Chill 4 to 7 days before serving. Will keep in refrigerator four weeks.

## Sage and Cheddar Torte

12 oz. cream cheese
¼ cup fresh sage, chopped
1 cup shredded sharp cheddar cheese
¾ cup walnuts, chopped
2 Tablespoons milk

Blend all but two ounces cream cheese with sage. Blend half of remaining cream cheese with cheddar cheese. Blend remaining cream cheese with walnuts and add milk to ease mixing. Line a 2 cup mold with double thickness damp cheesecloth. Arrange whole fresh sage leaves in decorative pattern on bottom of mold. Add half cream cheese mixture, then add cheddar mixture, pressing gently between layers. Add walnut mixture. Smooth remaining cream cheese over walnuts, cover with edges of cheesecloth and refrigerate overnight.

Serve with baguette slices or bagel chips.

## Spinach Balls

2 packages chopped spinach, cooked and squeezed dry
2 small onions, finely chopped
3 cups packaged stuffing mix
6 eggs
¾ cup butter, melted
1 cup Parmesan cheese
1½ teaspoons garlic salt
½ teaspoon thyme
½ teaspoons pepper

Mix all ingredients together and shape into walnut size balls. Bake at 350°F for 20 minutes. Serve warm.

Can be frozen on cookie sheet after being baked. When frozen, remove from cookie sheet and place in plastic bag. When ready to serve, bake frozen at 325°F for 20 minutes or until heated through.

## Crabmeat Dip

8 oz. cream cheese, softened
1 Tablespoon milk
6½ oz. crabmeat
2 Tablespoons chopped onion
½ teaspoon horseradish, optional
¼ teaspoon salt
¼ teaspoon pepper
paprika

ix all ingredients except paprika in 1½ to 2 quart baking dish. Cook for 4 to 5 minutes in microwave on high power. Sprinkle with paprika before serving. Serve with butter crackers.

## Crabmeat Mousse

1 Tablespoon gelatin
¼ cup cold water
1 cup mayonnaise
2 Tablespoons flour
1 cup milk
1 cup fresh mushrooms, chopped
8 oz. cream cheese
¾ cup celery, minced
6¼ oz. can crabmeat, drained
1 teaspoon grated onion
1½ Tablespoons Worchestershire sauce

issolve gelatin in water. Combine flour with mayonnaise. Combine both mixtures in a saucepan with milk and mushrooms. Cook until thickened. Add remaining ingredients. Beat until mixture is smooth. Pour into mold and chill until firm. Remove from mold.

**Makes 4 cups.**

*Serve with crackers or breadsticks.*

## Jezabelle Sauce

8 oz. peach preserves
8 oz. apricot preserves
8 oz. pineapple preserves or ice cream topping
8 oz. horseradish
1 teaspoon dry mustard
1 teaspoon apple jelly
8 oz. cream cheese

ombine the peach, apricot and pineapple preserves (or pineapple ice cream topping) in a blender with the horseradish and dry mustard.

Right before serving add apple jelly. Pour over brick of cream cheese and serve as a spread for crackers.

Brunch with friends, a getaway without the children, peaceful moments at a bed and breakfast shared with someone special are memories enhanced with distinctive dishes especially for brunch.

Autumn brings bountiful crops of apples to Midwestern orchards. Flavors, textures, and colors as varied as the hues of the fall foliage are found in our versatile varieties of apples. No matter which variety of apple you select, our sweet Apple Pancakes are perfect for brunch on a crisp autumn day. Ideally suited for guests or for a special family meal, these spicy, warm apple pancakes are sure to please.

Try several of our favorite recipes for all the seasons of the year. Holiday Stollen with coffee by the fireplace in winter. Herbed Eggs Benedict rich with the herbs of our garden. Blueberry Coffee Cake made with berries picked as the summer sun rises. Join us anytime for brunch with your friends.

Beverages can bring a blend of flavors and colors to enhance a meal, buffet, brunch or dessert. Warm or cold, from a mug or fine crystal, select the perfect beverage to suit your fancy.

# Brunch & Beverages

## Apple Pancake

2 Tablespoons butter
2 Tablespoons sugar
1 teaspoon cinnamon
2 apples, pared, cored and thinly sliced
3 Tablespoons flour
¼ teaspoon baking powder
⅛ teaspoon salt
2 eggs, separated
3 Tablespoons milk
3 teaspoons sugar

Preheat oven to 400°F.

Melt the 2 Tablespoons of butter in an omelette pan. Mix together sugar and cinnamon and sprinkle over the butter. Place apple slices in pan and cook 5 minutes over low heat. Mix together flour, baking powder, salt, milk and egg yolks in a small bowl. In a separate bowl, beat egg whites with sugar until stiff peaks form. Fold egg yolk mixture into egg whites. Pour into pan and bake 10 minutes. Serve immediately.

Serves 1 to 2.

This page generously sponsored by 1995–1996 JLWJC Executive Committee.

## Blueberry Coffeecake

½ cup shortening
1 cup sugar
2 eggs
1 teaspoon vanilla
2¼ cups flour
1 Tablespoon baking powder
⅔ cup milk
2½ cups fresh or frozen blueberries
⅔ cup sugar
⅔ cup flour
½ cup margarine or butter
¼ teaspoon almond extract

Preheat oven to 350°F. Grease two 9-inch round cake pans. Beat shortening and 1 cup sugar until light and fluffy. Add eggs and vanilla; beat well. Stir together 2¼ cups flour and baking powder. Add to beaten mixture alternately with milk. Spread into prepared pans. Top each with 1¼ cups blueberries. Combine ⅔ cup sugar and ⅔ cup flour; cut in margarine and almond extract until crumbly. Sprinkle over blueberries. Bake 25 to 35 minutes. Cool slightly; cut into wedges.

**Serves 12 to 16.**

*Excellent for a brunch or served with coffee.*

## Sour Cream Coffeecake

3 cups flour
1½ teaspoons baking powder
1½ teaspoons baking soda
½ teaspoon salt
¾ cup butter
1½ cups sugar
3 eggs
2 teaspoons vanilla
1 pint dairy sour cream
¾ cup light brown sugar, packed
2 teaspoons cinnamon
1 cup walnuts, coarsely chopped

Grease and flour a 10-inch tube or Bundt pan. Mix flour, baking powder, baking soda and salt. Set aside. Cream butter with electric mixer until soft. Gradually add granulated sugar and beat well. Add eggs one at a time, beating thoroughly after each addition; add vanilla. Then add dry ingredients alternately with sour cream, mixing after each addition until smooth. Set aside. Mix brown sugar, cinnamon and nuts in a small bowl.

Preheat oven to 350°F. Put about ⅓ of the batter in the prepared pan. Sprinkle with ⅓ of sugar mixture. Repeat until batter and mixture are used. Bake for one hour. Let stand on cake racks about 5 minutes, then turn out of pan. Sprinkle with confectioners' sugar or glaze with favorite frosting.

**Serves 10 to 12.**

*Coffeecake can be served warm or cold for brunch. For an added touch, place fresh daisies in the center hole. This cake can be made in advance and frozen.*

## Herbed Eggs Benedict

1 whole egg
3 Tablespoons fresh lemon juice
1½ teaspoons Dijon mustard
1 teaspoon fresh dill, sage, basil or marjoram
½ cup butter, melted
½ cup cold butter, in pieces
8 oz. thinly sliced Canadian bacon or ham
1 teaspoon butter
4 eggs
boiling water
4 English muffins
lemon slices and parsley for garnish

ut 1 egg into blender or food processor with steel blade. Add lemon juice, mustard and herb of your choice. Process and slowly pour in warm melted butter. Add cold butter a piece at a time, processing until blended. Hollandaise sauce is runny, but thickens as it cools.

Keep Hollandaise warm over hot, not boiling, water. Put ham in skillet with butter and heat through, turning once. Crack eggs into boiling water without breaking yolks. Cook until whites are set, but yolks are still soft.

Top four muffin halves with layer of heated ham and a poached egg. Drizzle herbed Hollandaise over egg. Place remaining muffin half on side of plate and garnish with lemon slices and parsley sprigs.

**Serves 4.**

## Holiday Stollen

¾ cup raisins
½ cup candied fruit, chopped
⅓ cup dried currants
¼ cup rum
4½ to 4¾ cups all purpose flour, divided
2 packages (4 teaspoons) dry yeast
1 cup milk
½ cup butter
¼ sugar
1 teaspoon salt
2 eggs
2 Tablespoons grated orange zest
1 Tablespoon grated lemon zest
½ teaspoon almond extract
1¼ cups confectioners' sugar, sifted
few teaspoons milk or rum
½ cup slivered almonds

oak raisins, candied fruit and currants in rum. Set aside. Combine 1½ cups flour and yeast in a large bowl. Warm milk, butter, sugar and salt until 115 to 120°F, stirring constantly. Add milk mixture to dry mixture. Add eggs, zest and almond extract. Beat at low speed of electric mixer 1 minute. Scrape bottom and sides of bowl with a spatula. Beat on high speed 3 more minutes. Stir in fruit mixture, almonds and as much of the remaining flour as you can mix in using a spoon, not the electric mixer.

Turn dough out onto a lightly floured surface to knead in remaining flour. Knead 8 to 10 minutes or until smooth and elastic. Place dough into a buttered bowl, turn once to butter surface. Cover with a clean towel and let rise in a warm place until double, about an hour. Punch down dough; divide in half, cover and let rest 10 minutes.

Roll one half to make a 12 x 18-inch oval. Fold long side of oval to within ½ inch of opposite side; seal edge. Place on greased baking sheet. Repeat with remaining dough. Cover with a towel; let rise until double, 30 to 45 minutes. Bake in preheated 375°F oven 15 to 20 minutes. Cool on racks for a few minutes.

Combine confectioners' sugar and enough milk or rum to make a glaze of drizzling consistency. Drizzle over stollens while warm, sprinkle with almonds.

**Makes 2 loaves.**

## Blue Cheese Omelette with Parsley

4 eggs
2 teaspoons fresh parsley, chopped
2 Tablespoons water
salt and freshly ground pepper to taste
1 Tablespoon butter
3 oz. blue cheese, coarsely chopped
parsley sprigs

Whisk together eggs, parsley, water, salt and pepper. Heat the butter in a non-stick frying pan. When the butter bubbles, pour the egg mixture in all at once. Cook over a moderate-high heat for a few minutes, bringing the fork through the mixture to allow the unset egg to run through the edges.

When the omelette is set underneath but still creamy on top, scatter the cheese over the surface of the omelette. Leave for a few moments until the cheese begins to melt, then fold the omelette over.

To serve, slide onto a serving plate and garnish with parsley. Divide in half to serve.

Serves 2.

*This dish is quite simple, but very rich.*

## Sour Cream Muffins

1½ cups flour
1½ teaspoons baking powder
½ teaspoon baking soda
¼ teaspoon salt
¼ cup butter
1 egg
¾ cup sour cream
¼ cup milk
¼ teaspoon vanilla

Preheat oven to 400°F. Grease 12 cup muffin pan.

Mix flour, baking powder, baking soda and salt in large bowl. Cut in butter until mixture resembles coarse crumbs. Make a well in center of mixture. Beat egg in small bowl; add sour cream, milk and vanilla. Pour into well in flour mixture, mixing just until moistened. Spoon into greased muffin pan, filling each cup ⅔ full. Bake 15 minutes or until lightly browned. Makes 10 to 12 muffins.

**Variations:**

*Lemon Sour Cream Muffins:*
Combine and stir 2 tablespoons lemon juice, 2 tablespoons sugar and 2 teaspoons grated lemon peel into batter. Continue as directed.

*Nut and Brown Sugar Sour Cream Muffins:*
Combine and stir ¼ cup firmly packed brown sugar and ¼ cup chopped walnuts into batter. Continue as directed.

*Cinnamon Raisin Sour Cream Muffins:*
Combine and stir 2 tablespoons sugar, 1 teaspoon ground cinnamon and ¼ cup raisins into batter. Continue as directed.

## Potato Pancakes With Spicy Pepper Relish

*Spicy Pepper Relish:*

1 Tablespoon vegetable oil

1 jalapeno pepper, cored, seeded and minced

1 small yellow chili pepper, cored, seeded and minced

1 small mild red chili pepper, cored, seeded and minced

2 Tablespoons green onion, sliced

2 Tablespoons white wine vinegar

hot pepper sauce to taste

salt and pepper to taste

*Potato Pancakes:*

1 large egg

1 Tablespoon flour

¼ teaspoon salt

pinch black pepper

2 large potatoes (1 lb.), peeled, coarsley grated and set aside in bowl of cold water

1 to 2 Tablespoons butter

1 Tablespoon vegetable oil

o prepare relish, heat oil in a medium skillet. Add peppers and onion and saute over medium heat for about 3 minutes, until onions are transparent. Remove from heat and place mixture in a small bowl. Return skillet to heat and add vinegar to deglaze skillet. Pour vinegar into pepper and onion mixture. Let cool slightly and taste. Add salt, pepper and hot pepper sauce, as desired. Set aside.

Combine egg, flour, salt and black pepper in a mixing bowl and beat lightly. Drain potatoes and pat dry. Add potatoes to batter and toss until blended.

Heat oven to 200°F. Heat half of the butter and half of the oil in a large skillet over medium high heat until hot. Spoon one quarter of the potato mixture into the skillet and flatten into a 5-inch pancake. Spoon another quarter of the mixture into skillet, allowing a few inches between the 2 pancakes, and flatten. Cook over medium heat for 5 minutes or until bottoms are lightly browned. Turn with a spatula and cook until the other sides are lightly browned and potatoes are cooked through. Transfer pancakes to a baking sheet and place in oven to keep warm. Use remaining butter, oil and potato mixture to make 2 more pancakes. Spoon relish over each pancake and serve.

**Serves 4.**

## Peach French Toast

1 cup brown sugar

½ cup butter

2 Tablespoons water

2 lbs. fresh peaches, peeled & sliced

1 loaf French bread, 12 slices

5 eggs

1½ cups milk

1 tablespoon vanilla

eat sugar and butter in a small saucepan on low until melted. Add water and continue cooking until sauce becomes thick and foamy. Pour into 9x13-inch pan, cool 10 minutes. Place peaches on top of sauce and cover with bread placed close together. Blend together eggs, milk and vanilla and pour over bread. Refrigerate overnight. Bake for 40 minutes in a preheated 350°F oven. Loosely cover with foil last 10 minutes if mixture is browning too quickly.

**Serves 12.**

## Rhubarb-Strawberry Coffeecake

3 cups fresh or 13 oz. frozen rhubarb, cut in 1-inch pieces

16 oz. strawberries, sliced and sweetened

2 Tablespoons lemon juice

1 cup sugar

⅓ cup cornstarch

3 cups flour

1 cup sugar

1 teaspoon baking soda

1 teaspoon baking powder

1 teaspoon salt

1 cup margarine

1 cup buttermilk

2 eggs, slightly beaten

1 teaspoon vanilla

¾ cup sugar

½ cup flour

¼ cup margarine

Combine fruit in a saucepan and cook covered, about 5 minutes. Add lemon juice. Combine 1 cup sugar and cornstarch; add to rhubarb mixture. Cook and stir 4 to 5 minutes until thickened and bubbly. Cool.

Preheat oven to 350°F. Grease a 9x13x2-inch baking pan.

While filling is cooling; stir together the flour, 1 cup sugar, baking soda, baking powder and salt in mixing bowl. Cut in 1 cup margarine to fine crumbs. Set aside. Beat together buttermilk, eggs, and vanilla in a medium bowl; add to dry ingredients. Stir to moisten. Spread ½ of batter in baking pan. Spread cooled filling over batter in pan. Spoon remaining batter in small mounds over filling. Set aside. Mix ¾ cup sugar and flour; cut in ¼ cup margarine to consistancy of fine crumbs. Sprinkle crumbs over batter in pan. Bake for 40 to 45 minutes.

**Serves 24.**

*Absolutely heavenly topped with a little vanilla ice cream or frozen yogurt!*

## Sausage Grits

Preheat oven to 350°F. Grease a 9x13-inch baking dish.

Fry sausage. Drain on paper towels. Cook grits in boiling, salted water, stirring frequently, for 5 minutes. Add margarine and cheese. Stir until melted and remove from heat. Add milk, eggs and sausage. Mix thoroughly and pour into prepared pan. Sprinkle with paprika. Bake for 45 minutes.

**Serves 8 to 10.**

1 lb. hot bulk sausage

1 cup hominy grits

4 cups boiling water

1 teaspoon salt (optional)

½ cup margarine

¼ lb. garlic cheese, crumbled

½ cup milk

3 eggs, slightly beaten

paprika

*Serve with mixed fruit and muffins or as a brunch side dish. This recipe can be frozen for up to a*

## Smoked Ham and Potato Fritatta

2 medium boiling potatoes, unpeeled
10 large eggs
¼ cup fresh parsley, chopped
¼ cup fresh chives, chopped
3 Tablespoons olive oil
1 small onion, peeled and thinly sliced
¼ lb. smoked ham, thinly sliced and cut into 1-inch squares
½ cup Parmesan cheese
freshly ground pepper to taste

Place potatoes in a saucepan of lightly salted boiling water and boil until tender. Drain and set aside to cool. Break the eggs in a large mixing bowl and beat until well mixed. Stir in parsley and chives.

Preheat oven to 400°F.

Pour olive oil into a 2 quart square or oval baking dish and swirl to coat the sides and bottom evenly. Scatter the onion slices over the bottom of the dish and place in the oven for 10 minutes until the onions are softened and beginning to brown. Meanwhile, thinly slice the potatoes.

Remove baking dish from the oven and reduce oven temperature to 350°F. Arrange ham in a single layer on top of the onions. Arrange potatoes in one layer over the ham. Pour in the eggs and sprinkle the cheese evenly over the top. Season with pepper.

Return the baking dish to the oven and bake 25 to 30 minutes or until the eggs are set and the fritatta is puffed and lightly browned on top. Serve hot or cold.

Serves 6.

## Herbed Biscuits

1½ cups sifted all purpose flour
3 teaspoons baking powder
¼ teaspoon salt
¼ teaspoon cream of tartar
1 teaspoon sugar
½ teaspoon dried dill
2 Tablespoons fresh chives
1 cup half and half

Preheat oven to 450°F.

Sift flour, baking powder, salt, cream of tartar and sugar together into a medium bowl. Stir in dill and chives; mix well. Pour in cream all at once; stir with fork only until dough rounds up into a ball. Turn dough onto a lightly floured surface; knead only a few strokes. Gently pat or roll out dough to ½ to ¾ inch thickness. With a 2½-inch biscuit cutter, cut straight down into dough, being careful not to twist cutter. Place on an ungreased cookie sheet; bake for 10 to 12 minutes.

Makes 8 biscuits.

## Cornmeal Pancakes with Maple Butter

⅔ cup cornmeal

⅓ cup flour

2 teaspoons baking powder

½ teaspoon salt

1 teaspoon cinnamon

1½ Tablespoons sugar

1 egg

1¼ cups milk

3 Tablespoons butter, melted

*Maple Butter:*

⅔ cup maple syrup

½ cup butter, softened

Combine cornmeal, flour, baking powder, salt, cinnamon and sugar in a mixing bowl. In another bowl, beat the egg lightly, then beat in the milk. Make a well in the center of the dry ingredients and slowly stir in the egg mixture. Add the melted butter and stir just until smooth. Do not overbeat.

Preheat a greased griddle until a few drops of cold water bounce when dripped on it. Ladle about 3 tablespoons of batter onto the griddle for each pancake. Do not crowd the griddle or pancakes will run together. Cook until bubbles appear on the surfaces, and undersides are golden brown, 2 to 3 minutes. Turn with a spatula and cook until the undersides are lightly browned. Remove pancakes from the griddle and keep warm. Serve with maple butter.

To make maple butter, simmer maple syrup in a small saucepan and over medium heat for 7 to 10 minutes until it is reduced to ½ cup. Remove from heat and let cool to lukewarm. Add softened butter and stir until creamy and well blended.

**Makes 12 pancakes.**

## Oatmeal Waffles

¾ cup old fashioned rolled oats (do not use quick cooking or instant)

1¼ cups water

3 Tablespoons butter

1¼ cups flour

1 Tablespoon sugar

1½ teaspoons baking powder

½ teaspoon baking soda

½ teaspoon salt

½ teaspoon cinnamon

2 large eggs

1 cup buttermilk

n a medium saucepan, combine oats with water. Bring to a simmer over medium heat and cook, stirring frequently, for 3 minutes. Remove from heat and stir butter into hot oatmeal until melted.

Sift the flour, sugar, baking powder, baking soda, salt and cinnamon into a mixing bowl. In another bowl combine eggs and buttermilk and beat lightly. Stir oatmeal into egg mixture. Add oatmeal mixture to dry ingredients and stir until well blended, do not overbeat.

Preheat waffle iron until hot.

Cook waffles according to waffle iron manufacturer's directions, using about ¾ cup batter for each 8-inch waffle.

**Makes 4 8-inch waffles.**

*Serve with blueberry preserves, real maple syrup, or topped with yogurt.*

## Tarragon Crepe Nests with Baked Eggs

*Crepes:*

½ cup flour

⅛ teaspoon salt

⅛ teaspoon freshly ground white pepper

½ cup whole milk

3 Tablespoons water

1 large egg

1 large egg yolk

1 Tablespoon fresh tarragon, chopped or 1 teaspoon dried tarragon

1½ Tablespoons butter, melted

*Baked eggs:*

8 large eggs

salt and black pepper to taste

3 Tablespoons butter, melted

fresh tarragon, chopped

ombine flour, salt and white pepper in a large mixing bowl. Make a well in the center of the dry ingredients. Combine milk with 3 tablespoons of water and gradually stir into the dry ingredients. Beat the whole egg and the egg yolk together lightly in a small bowl. Add eggs to batter, along with the tarragon and butter. Stir until ingredients are blended. Let batter rest for 1 to 2 hours before making crepes.

To make the crepes, heat a lightly greased 5-inch to 5½- inch crepe pan over a medium-high heat until beads of water sizzle when dropped onto the surface. Stir crepe batter, then ladle 1½ to 2 tablespoons batter into the pan and swirl to coat surface completely. Let cook until bottom of crepe is lightly browned, 30 to 45 seconds. Turn onto a wire rack to cool, then stack on a plate between layers of waxed paper to prevent from sticking together. Continue until all the batter is used, adding more butter to the pan as needed. These crepes can be made in advance and kept in the refrigerator overnight or frozen until needed. Makes 14 to 16 crepes.

Preheat oven to 350°F.

Ease 1 crepe into each of 8 generously buttered, standard size muffin tins, gently ruffling edges. Bake in the center of the oven for 8 minutes. Break an egg into each crepe cup and season each egg with butter and black pepper. Bake for 7 to 9 minutes, or until whites of eggs are set but yolks are still runny. Remove from the oven and using both hands, lift crepe cups from muffin tins onto serving plates. Drizzle a teaspoon of butter over each egg and garnish with tarragon. Serve immediately.

**Serves 4 to 8.**

## Basil Poached Eggs

3 Tablespoons basil vinegar

2 Tablespoons fresh basil or 1 teaspoon dried basil

4 large eggs

fresh basil for garnish

ill a large skillet with 3 cups of water or enough to make a poaching bath at least 1 inch deep. Add vinegar and basil. Bring this to a simmer over medium-low heat.

Break each egg into a small cup, then carefully slide each into the simmering liquid. Simmer gently for about 2 minutes, or until whites are set, spooning the hot liquid over eggs to lightly firm yolks. Using a slotted spoon, remove eggs from liquid and garnish with a sprig of fresh basil. Serve warm.

**Serves 4.**

*This is easier to make if egg poaching molds are used. Terrific with a side of Canadian bacon. May also be made with marjoram or tarragon.*

## Spinach Souffle

2 oz. butter or margarine
4 oz. fresh spinach leaves, washed, trimmed and chopped
8 oz. button mushrooms, finely chopped
1 clove garlic, crushed
3 Tablespoons flour
7 fluid oz. whole milk
salt and freshly ground pepper to taste
8 oz. Gruyere cheese, grated
3 eggs, separated

Melt the butter in a large saucepan, add the spinach, mushrooms and crushed garlic. Stir over high heat for 1 to 2 minutes. Stir in the flour and cook for 1 additional minute.

Remove from heat and stir in the milk and seasoning. Return to heat and bring to a boil, stirring constantly and cook for 1 minute. Remove from heat and beat in 7 oz. of the cheese followed by the egg yolks.

Whisk the egg whites until stiff but not dry. Fold lightly into the sauce mixture. Spoon into a 2½ pint greased souffle dish and sprinkle the remaining cheese over top of the mixture.

Bake at 375°F for about 40 minutes or until nicely browned and just set. When it is just set, it will jiggle slightly, but not be loose. Serve at once.

**Serves 6 to 8.**

## Swedish Nut Cake

2 eggs
2 cups sugar
20 oz. crushed pineapple, with juice
1 teaspoon vanilla
1½ teaspoons baking soda
2 cups flour
½ cup pecan pieces

Preheat oven to 350°F. Spray 9x13-inch pan with non-stick cooking spray. Cream eggs and sugar. Add pineapple, vanilla and baking soda. Mix. Add flour and pecans. Batter will be thin. Pour into prepared pan. Bake until center comes clean with toothpick, approximately 25 to 30 minutes. Cool. Top cake with cream cheese frosting to create a rich dessert, or serve without frosting as a terrific coffeecake.

## Cream Cheese Frosting

½ cup margarine
8 oz. cream cheese, softened
1 teaspoon vanilla
1 lb. confectioners' sugar
½ cup pecan pieces

Cream margarine and cream cheese. Add vanilla and then confectioners' sugar. Mix in pecans or sprinkle them over the top.

Frost cake with cream cheese frosting.

## Heartland Danish Rolls

4 cups all purpose flour
2 eggs
1½ teaspoons salt
½ cup sugar
½ lb. butter (¼ lb. frozen, ¼ lb. softened)
½ cup milk, scalded and cooled
½ cup water
2 oz. cake yeast
1 teaspoon lemon juice or ¼ teaspoon lemon rind, grated
egg wash (1 egg mixed well with 2 Tablespoons water)

Mix all ingredients except frozen butter and egg wash. Stir until blended well and forms a sticky dough. Place in greased covered container and put in refrigerator overnight or for at least two hours.

Remove bowl from refrigerator and place dough on floured board. Gently roll out into rectangle about 12x18-inch. Grate ¼ of frozen butter into middle third of dough. Fold end ⅓ over grated butter. Grate butter over end you have just laid over the middle ⅓ and fold remaining end over grated butter. Roll out gently to 12x18-inch and repeat process.

Roll out and cut rectangle into 18 one-inch strips, one at a time. (Cut rectangle into 12 one-inch strips if you prefer larger rolls.) Twist dough as you form a circle tucking dough at the very end of the circle under the roll. Place on a greased cookie sheet. Allow to rise until double in bulk. Using your fingers, make a flat circle in the middle of the roll. Place filling in the recessed circle. Brush the exposed dough with egg wash. Place in 375°F oven for about 17 minutes or until dough is lightly browned. Remove from oven and immediatley drizzle glaze on browned rolls. Freezes well.

**Makes 18 small or 12 large rolls.**

**Fillings:**

Canned pie filling—any flavor
Cherry pie filling or blueberry spread over a mixture of 3 oz. cream cheese mixed with 2 tablespoons sugar
Streusel—¼ lb. butter combined with 1 cup flour and 1 cup sugar
Any jelly—plain or with streusel topping
Pecan praline—1 tablespoon flour mixed with 2 tablespoons dark brown sugar, chopped pecans (about 2 tablespoons), 2 tablespoons softened butter, and 1 teaspoon light corn syrup

**Glaze:**

1 tablespoon melted butter mixed well with ½ cup confectioners' sugar, 1 teaspoon milk, ½ teaspoon vanilla and a dash of salt

## Spinach Quiche

5 eggs, beaten
1 cup whipping cream
½ cup milk
½ teaspoon black pepper
⅓ cup onion, chopped
½ cup frozen chopped spinach, thawed and dried
8 slices crisply cooked bacon, crumbled
8 oz. Swiss cheese, grated
1 unbaked 9-inch deep dish pastry shell

Preheat oven to 400°F. Beat eggs and mix well with cream and milk. Stir in remaining ingredients except pastry shell. Fit pastry shell into quiche pan. Pour egg mixture into pastry shell. Place quiche on foil lined cookie sheet and bake for 40 to 45 minutes. Let stand 15 minutes before serving.

**Serves 6.**

## Wassail

6 cups apple cider
1 cinnamon stick
¼ teaspoon nutmeg
3 Tablespoons fresh lemon juice
2¼ cups unsweetened pineapple juice
¼ cup honey
1 teaspoon lemon zest, grated

Bring the cider and cinnamon stick to a boil, then cover and reduce heat. Simmer for 5 minutes. Add the rest of the ingredients and simmer 5 more minutes.

**Makes twelve 6 ounce servings.**

*This is a great cold weather drink, especially around the holidays. This can be served hot with apple or pineapple chunks, orange or lemon slices, or all of these floating in the wassail. A splash of rum may also be added.*

## Champagne Punch

12 oz. can frozen orange juice concentrate, thawed
6 oz. frozen lemonade, thawed
6 cups water
750 milliliter bottle champagne
frozen ice ring, if desired
1 cup fresh strawberries, if desired

Chill the ingredients. All ingredients may be mixed ahead of time except the champagne. When ready to serve, pour ingredients, including champagne, into punch bowl. Float the ice ring and fresh strawberries in punch if desired.

**Makes 2½ to 3 quarts, or 15 to 16 servings.**

*Strawberries can also be frozen in the ice ring for a more festive presentation.*

## Almond Tea

6 almond tea bags
1½ cups sugar
¾ cup fresh lemon juice
6 cups boiling water
6 cups cold water
1½ teaspoons almond extract
1½ teaspoons vanilla extract
mint sprigs

Place tea bags, sugar and lemon juice in large container then add the boiling water. Steep 10 minutes. Add remaining ingredients and chill. Use mint sprigs for garnish.

**Serves 12.**

*A refreshing treat for light lunches, showers and brunches.*

## Cranberry Punch

½ cup sugar
1 cup water
1 teaspoon whole cloves
3 cinnamon sticks
2 cups cranberry juice
2 cups apple cider
2 to 3 cups burgundy wine or 2 to 3 cups gingerale

Boil first 4 ingredients for 5 minutes, strain and cool. Set aside. Mix together the cranberry juice and cider in a large punch bowl. Add sugar, water and spice mixture. Add your favorite burgundy or 2 to 3 cups gingerale. Stir gently to mix. Serve chilled or over ice.

Makes twelve 6 ounce servings.

## Cranberry Cordial

3 cups ground cranberries, ground in food processor
3 cups sugar
2 bottles dry white wine (*e.g.* Sauvignon Blanc)

Mix all ingredients together until sugar is completely dissolved. Put the mixture in sterilized jars and refrigerate for 22 days. Strain before serving.

Makes 3 quarts.

*Serve at Thanksgiving or put in decorative jars to give away at the end of a party as a gift.*

## Sangria

1 large orange
1 large lemon
⅛ teaspoon cinnamon
⅛ teaspoon nutmeg
sugar to taste
1½ oz. brandy
1 fifth claret
1 cup club soda, chilled

Cut 2 thick slices from the center of the orange, then from the center of the lemon. Remove the seeds from all slices and set slices aside. Squeeze the juice from the remaining parts of the orange and lemon and strain into a 2 quart container. Add the spices, sugar, brandy, claret, orange and lemon slices and mix well. Cover and let stand for 1 hour. Pour the claret mixture and soda into a large decanter or serving pitcher. Pour over ice in tall, chilled glasses and garnish each glass with a fruit slice. White Bordeaux wine may be used instead of claret, if desired.

## Champagne Kir

½ cup cassis or black currant syrup

2 bottles champagne, chilled

12 to 14 thin curls of lemon zest

Pour 2 teaspoons cassis into each champagne flute. Fill glasses ¾ full with champagne. Drop a curl of lemon zest into each glass.

**Makes 12 to 14 drinks.**

## Tequila Champagne Punch

2 quarts white wine, chilled

2 6 oz. cans frozen pineapple juice concentrate, reconstituted with water

750 milliliters tequila, chilled

2 750 milliliter bottles champagne, chilled

2 quarts soda water, chilled

strawberry halves or orange slices

In a punch bowl combine wine, pineapple juice and tequila. Just before serving, add champagne and soda water. Float fruit in punch or freeze in ring.

**Makes 2 gallons.**

## Ramus Fizz

ice

6 oz. can frozen lemonade concentrate

6 oz. gin

6 oz. half and half

1 teaspoon vanilla

¼ cup pasteurized egg product

Fill a blender with ice. Pour ingredients over the ice and blend until smooth.

**Serves 4.**

## Lemonade

2 cups sugar

2½ cups water

1 cup fresh mint leaves, crushed

6 lemons, juiced

1 lime, juiced and rind, grated

oil sugar and water together for five minutes in a medium saucepan. Pour over mint leaves and brew for one hour. Strain. Add juice of lemons, grated rind and juice of lime. Let stand until cold. Use ⅓ cup of syrup to each cup of water plus ice.

**Serves 8 to 10.**

## Frothy Fruit Smoothie

⅓ cup apple juice

⅓ cup skim milk

1 Tablespoon wheat germ

2 teaspoons honey

3 Tablespoons nonfat dry milk

2 Tablespoons bran

2 ice cubes

dd all ingredients, in order, to a blender and blend until frothy. Drink cold.

*This is both a healthy and delicious drink.*

## Freshly Brewed Tea

fresh, cold water

½ to 1 teaspoon of your favorite tea leaves for every 6 oz. cup of tea

tea ball

earthenware teapot

eat the fresh, cold water to a rolling boil. Fill the teapot with hot tap water to warm and remove water. Add ½ to 1 teaspoon tea leaves for each cup of tea to tea ball and place the tea ball in the teapot. The tea ball should be no more than half full. Pour boiling water over the tea, cover and steep for 3 to 5 minutes. To serve, pour into teacups.

*Serve hot with lemon, cream and sugar as accompaniments. For iced tea, pour over ice in tall glasses. Serve with a wedge of lemon or sprig of mint.*

Grandma's Potato Rolls were always the highlight of any holiday meal. Each time Grandma would spend the day preparing her always perfect potato rolls. At mealtime, as the family raved about her special rolls, Grandma would always fret that they'd have been better if she'd done just one or two little things differently.

We always chuckled about Grandma the perfectionist who never thought her fabulous rolls were quite as good as they should be. As the years went by and I moved away, I tried to make Grandma's Potato Rolls, and try as I might, they wouldn't turn out quite right. A call to Grandma revealed her secret; grease your hands with butter, don't flour them when preparing the rolls.

Now that Grandma is unable to make her special rolls and I've taken over the official duty, I find myself fretting each time about the one thing I should have done differently, even when the rest of the family insist the rolls are as good as Grandma's.

# Breads & Grains

# Grandma's Potato Rolls

1½ cups Idaho potatoes, cooked and mashed
⅔ cup solid shortening
½ cup sugar
1 teaspoon salt
4 eggs
2 cakes yeast (6 packages dry yeast, 13½ teaspoons)
½ cup lukewarm potato water
1 cup milk, scalded (let cool to lukewarm)
6 to 8 cups all purpose flour
butter

Butter a large bowl, set aside.

Cook and mash potatoes, add shortening, sugar, salt, and eggs. Cream well. Dissolve yeast in lukewarm potato water, add to lukewarm milk and then add to potato mixture. Mix well. Add 3 cups flour and beat 3 minutes. Add enough flour to make a dough you can handle (not stiff). Knead about 10 minutes. Place kneaded dough into buttered bowl and turn to butter top. Cover with a towel and allow to double.

Working with buttered hands divide dough into three equal parts, shape as desired, place in a greased pan and allow to rise until double.*

Preheat oven to 400°F. Brush with butter and bake.

**Makes 36 rolls.**

**To form twists:* Divide each third into 12 pieces. Shape each piece by rolling the dough into a 10-inch strip, forming a figure 8 and twisting the dough to form a rectangular roll. Place dough into a greased cake pan. Bake for 15 to 20 minutes.

**To form snails:* Roll each third into a 12-inch rope, divide into 12 pieces. Roll each piece into a 12-inch strip. Press one end of a strip to a greased cookie sheet; wind strip around itself; tuck other end underneath. Bake for 12 minutes.

**To form fan-tans:* Roll one third of dough into 15x8-inch rectangle. Spread with butter. With sharp knife, cut dough lengthwise into 5 (1½-inch) strips. Stack strips; cut into 12. Place cut side up in greased, 2½-inch muffin tin. Bake for 12 minutes.

**To form cloverleaf:* Divide each piece into three small pieces and roll into balls. Place the three balls into 2½-inch muffin tins. Bake for 12 minutes.

This page generously sponsored by Catering by Gina.

## Refrigerator Potato Rolls

1 cup mashed potatoes
⅔ cup solid shortening
½ cup sugar
2 Tablespoons salt
2 eggs
1 package dry yeast (2¼ teaspoons)
½ cup lukewarm water
1 cup milk, scalded (let cool to lukewarm)
6 to 8 cups all purpose flour

ombine potatoes, shortening, sugar, salt and eggs in large mixer bowl. Beat until smooth. Dissolve yeast in lukewarm water. Add yeast mixture and lukewarm milk to potato mixture. Add 3 cups flour and beat 3 minutes at medium speed. Add enough flour to form a stiff dough, turn out on floured board and knead about 10 minutes. Place in greased bowl, turn to grease top. Cover with towel and let rise until double in bulk.

Knead dough down, again grease top, place in bowl, cover and store in refrigerator. About 2 hours before serving, divide dough into two equal parts, then divide into 12 pieces. Shape dough* into desired dinner rolls. Let rise and bake.

**Makes 24 cloverleaf rolls.**

*See shaping instructions under Grandma's Potato Rolls.

*Great do ahead recipe for the busy cook on the go.*

## Lemon Loaf

¾ cup margarine
1½ cups sugar
3 eggs
2¼ cups plus 2 Tablespoons flour
¼ teaspoon salt
¼ teaspoon baking soda
¾ cup buttermilk
grated rind of 1 lemon
¾ cups nuts, chopped (optional)

*Glaze:*
juice of 1 lemon
½ cup sugar

reheat oven to 350°F. Grease and flour a 9x5-inch loaf pan.

Cream margarine and sugar in a large bowl and beat in eggs. Sift dry ingredients together and add to batter, alternating with buttermilk. Mix well. Stir in grated lemon rind and nuts. Pour into 9x5-inch loaf pan. Bake at 350°F for 1 hour. (Bake at 325°F for 1 hour and 15 minutes if a glass pan is used.) While loaf is baking, prepare glaze by stirring together lemon juice and sugar. Allow mixture to stand until sugar dissolves. After removing loaf from pan, pierce top of loaf with a cake tester in several places and spoon glaze over loaf. Allow to cool; then slice to serve.

**Makes 1 loaf.**

## Swiss Egg Braid

1½ cups milk
½ cup butter
2 packages dry yeast (4½ teaspoons)
½ cup warm water (105° to 115°F)
2 eggs
½ cup sugar
2 teaspoons salt
6 to 7 cups all purpose flour

*Glaze:*
1 egg, beaten
poppy seeds

Scald milk, add butter and let it melt in the milk.

Dissolve yeast in warm water adding a pinch of sugar.

In a large mixing bowl, beat the eggs, add sugar, salt and yeast mixture. When milk mixture is cool, stir it into egg mixture. Gradually add flour, beating well after each addition. Add last of flour by hand. Turn dough onto a floured board and knead for 5 minutes or until dough becomes smooth and elastic. Place dough in a well greased bowl and cover. Allow to rise until doubled in size, 1 to 2 hours.

Gently punch dough down and place on a floured board to shape. To braid: Divide dough in half. Divide each half into 3 12-inch lengths. Place on a greased cookie sheet and braid. Cover and let rise until doubled in size, about 1 hour.

When ready to bake, brush loaves with egg glaze and sprinkle with poppy seeds. Bake in a preheated 350°F oven for 35 to 40 minutes. Remove from cookie sheet and cool on a rack.

**Makes 2 loaves.**

*This bread freezes well.*

## Buttermilk Wheatberry Bread

| *Ingredient* | *1 pound loaf* | *1½ pound loaf* |
|---|---|---|
| water, 75°F to 85°F | 1 cup | 1½ cups |
| powdered buttermilk | 3 Tablespoons | 5 Tablespoons |
| honey | 2 Tablespoons | 3 Tablespoons |
| whole wheat flour | 2 cups | 3 cups |
| bread flour | ½ cup | ¾ cup |
| wheatberries, cooked | ¼ cup | ½ cup |
| wheat gluten | 1 Tablespoon | 2 Tablespoons |
| salt | 1 teaspoon | 1½ teaspoons |
| butter | 1 Tablespoon | 1½ Tablespoons |
| dry yeast | 1 teaspoon | 1½ teaspoons |

Soak ½ cup dry wheatberries in a saucepan in 2 cups of water overnight. Simmer for 35 to 45 minutes. Allow to cool. Cooked wheatberries may be kept in the refrigerator for one week.

Add ingredients to breadmaker in order suggested by manufacturer. Use whole wheat cycle (longest cycle) and light color setting. Bake according to manufacturer's instructions.

*1995 Kansas Festival of Breads Champion for the Bread Machine Category. Used with permission. Wheatberries can be purchased in natural foods stores.*

## Magi Bread

½ cup butter or margarine
1 cup granulated sugar
2 eggs
1 teaspoon vanilla extract
2 cups all purpose flour
1 teaspoon baking soda
pinch of salt
1 cup mashed bananas (about 3)
11 oz. can mandarin orange segments, drained
6 oz. chocolate pieces
1 cup shredded coconut
⅔ cup sliced almonds
½ cup maraschino cherries, chopped
½ cup dates, chopped
confectioners' sugar

Preheat oven to 350°F. Grease two 7½ x 3¾-inch loaf pans.

Cream butter with sugar, add eggs and vanilla; beat until fluffy. Sift flour with baking soda and salt; add alternately with mashed bananas. Stir in mandarin oranges, chocolate pieces, coconut, ½ cup sliced almonds, cherries, and dates. Pour into loaf pans. Sprinkle remaining almonds on top of each loaf. Bake for 1 to 1¼ hours. When cool, sieve confectioners' sugar over top of each loaf.

**Makes 2 loaves.**

## Whole Wheat Walnut Baguettes

¼ cup warm water (105° to 115°F)
2 packages dry yeast (4½ teaspoons)
2 cups warm water
3 Tablespoons oil
3 Tablespoons honey
1½ cup whole wheat flour
¾ cup wheat germ
1½ Tablespoons salt
4 to 5 cups all purpose flour
1 cup walnuts, chopped
1 egg white, lightly beaten

Combine the ¼ cup warm water and yeast in a large mixing bowl. Let stand 5 to 10 minutes until foamy. Stir in 2 cups water, oil, honey, whole wheat flour, wheat germ and salt. Mix well for about 5 minutes.

Gradually add the flour until batter is thick. Add walnuts. Dough can either be kneaded with a dough hook or by hand. Knead about 10 minutes until smooth and elastic. Place dough in greased bowl and cover.

Let dough rise until doubled in volume, about 1½ hours. Punch dough down and divide into 2 pieces. For baguettes: flatten dough into a rectangle, roll into a cylinder and place in greased baguette pans. For round loaves: form dough into 2 balls and place on a greased cookie sheet. Cover with towel and let rise 45 to 60 minutes until dough has doubled in size.

Preheat oven to 400°F. Brush loaves with egg white and place in middle of oven. Place a shallow pan of boiling water on the lower rack.

Bake 35 to 45 minutes or until loaves sound hollow when tapped. Remove loaves from pan and let cool on rack.

**Makes 2 loaves.**

## Povatica

4 packages dry yeast (9 teaspoons)
1 teaspoon sugar
1¾ cups lukewarm water, divided
⅓ cup powdered milk
1 egg, beaten
5 cups flour, divided
⅓ cup sugar
1 heaping teaspoon salt
¼ cup butter, melted

*Nut filling:*
1½ cups butter, melted
1 cup water
½ cup powdered milk
1½ lbs. English walnuts, ground
3 cups sugar
½ teaspoon salt
2 eggs, beaten

Dissolve yeast and 1 teaspoon sugar in ½ cup lukewarm water. Beat 1¼ cups lukewarm water, powdered milk and egg with an electric mixer. Add 1 cup flour and beat. Add yeast mixture and 1 cup flour and continue mixing. Add ⅓ cup sugar and salt, beat. Gradually mix in 1 cup flour. Add melted butter. Gradually add 1½ cups flour (use ½ cup flour to knead dough). Knead well and set on a floured cloth in a warm place. Brush the top with oil, cover and let rest at least 1 hour.

Prepare nut filling by combining the water and powdered milk in a separate pan; scald the mixture. Add milk to walnuts and stir. Mix in butter. Stir in sugar and salt. Add eggs and stir well.

Cover a 38x60-inch table with a white cloth (a sheet will do), being sure that the cloth is larger than the table. Lightly flour the cloth. Place risen dough on the center of the cloth. Pull dough gently until it forms a rectangle approximately 28x38 inches. The dough should be paper thin. If it tears, pull it together and patch it. Spread the filling evenly, but thinly, on the dough. Cover every inch of dough. Form dough in roll by lifting the end of the cloth and rolling the dough evenly over and over and over. Do not work too rapidly. Divide the roll in two. Fold each roll in to a "U" shape and place in greased 9x5x2-inch loaf pan. Brush with beaten egg.

Bake at 350°F for 1 hour and 15 minutes. Let cool in pans for ½ hour. Loosen on sides with knife and take out of pans. Place on cooling rack.

**Makes 2 loaves.**

## Carrot Bread

7/8 cup water
3 cups bread flour
3 Tablespoons sugar
½ teaspoon salt
1½ Tablespoons powdered milk
1½ Tablespoons butter or margarine
1½ to 2½ teaspoons quick rise dry yeast
1 cup carrots, finely shredded

Place ingredients including carrots into the bread machine in the order recommended by the manufacturer (carrots can be added with the flour) and process according to the instructions included with your machine.

**Makes a 1½ lb. loaf.**

## Orange Crunch Muffins

2 teaspoons grated orange zest
¼ cup sugar
¼ teaspoon water
1⅓ cups all purpose flour
3 Tablespoons sugar
3 teaspoons baking powder
½ teaspoon salt
1 egg, beaten
1 cup milk
3 Tablespoons margarine, melted
1 cup nugget cereal

Preheat oven to 400°F. Grease or paper line a 12 cup muffin tin.

Combine orange zest, ¼ cup sugar and water to make a crumbly topping. Set aside.

Mix flour with 3 tablespoons sugar, baking powder and salt. Combine egg and milk, add to flour mixture. Add margarine and mix to moisten. Fold in cereal. Fill muffin tins ⅔ full and sprinkle with topping. Bake for 15 to 20 minutes.

**Makes 12 muffins.**

## Blueberry Muffins

1½ cups all purpose flour
1 cup sugar
1½ teaspoons baking powder
9 Tablespoons butter
1 egg
½ cup evaporated milk
½ teaspoon vanilla
1 cup fresh blueberries

Preheat oven to 350°F. Spray 12 medium muffin tins with non-stick spray or line with paper liners.

Mix flour, sugar and baking powder. Add 8 tablespoons of the butter and cut in until crumbly. Set aside ½ cup of the crumbly mixture for topping. Add egg, milk and vanilla, and mix. Fold in blueberries. Spoon into muffin tins. Mix ½ cup of crumbly mixture with 1 tablespoon of butter and sprinkle over muffins.

Bake 20 to 30 minutes.

**Makes 12 muffins.**

## Bagels

2 packages dry yeast (4½ teaspoons)
1½ cups warm water (105° to 115°F)
4½ to 5 cups bread flour
3 Tablespoons sugar
1 Tablespoon salt
1 Tablespoon sugar (to be used in boiling)

Dissolve yeast in warm water (stir water while adding yeast to prevent clumping). Let stand five minutes. Combine about half the flour with 3 tablespoons sugar and salt in a large bowl. Add the yeast mixture and beat well with a wooden spoon or electric mixer for a minute or two, to work the gluten in the flour. Slowly add the rest of the flour, just enough to make the dough lose its wet look, until it's too stiff to stir.

Turn out onto a lightly floured surface and knead about 6 to 8 minutes, adding only as much flour as needed, and adding the flour about a tablespoon at a time, as you knead.

Cover; let rest 10 minutes. Cut into twelve portions, shaping each into a smooth ball. Using your thumb and forefinger, punch a hole into the center of each ball, and pull gently to make a two-inch hole in the middle. Place on a greased baking sheet. Cover; let rest 10 to 20 minutes.

Broil five inches from heat about two minutes on each side. Do not brown.

Heat one gallon water and 1 tablespoon sugar to boiling. Boil four to five bagels at a time in simmering water for 30 seconds on each side. Drain on a wire rack.

Place bagels on a lightly greased baking sheet and bake at 375°F 25 to 30 minutes, until slightly browned.

**Makes 12 bagels.**

**Variations:**

*Rye bagels:* Substitute 1¼ cups rye flour for 1¼ cups white flour. Add 2 teaspoons caraway seed to the mixture when yeast is added. Let the dough rise for one hour before shaping. Halfway through baking, brush the bagels with an egg wash (egg whites and water) and more caraway seeds.

*Whole wheat bagels:* Substitute 1¼ cups whole wheat flour for 1¼ cups white flour. Let the dough rise for one hour before shaping.

*Herb bagels:* Add 2 teaspoons dried marjoram, or 1 teaspoon dried dill, or 1 teaspoon tarragon or ½ teaspoon garlic powder to the dough when you add the yeast mixture is added.

*Poppy seed or sesame seed bagels:* Before baking brush bagels with an egg wash; sprinkle with poppy or sesame seeds.

*Cinnamon raisin bagels:* Add 1 tablespoon sugar and 1½ teaspoons cinnamon to the flour mixture. During kneading, add ½ cup dark raisins.

## Zucchini Bread

3 eggs
1 cup applesauce
1 teaspoon vanilla
1 cup crushed pineapple, drained
2 cups zucchini, peeled and shredded
3 cups all purpose flour
(½ cup less if using packaged mix frosting)
1¼ cups sugar
¼ teaspoon baking powder
1 teaspoon salt (optional)
1 teaspoon baking soda
1 teaspoon cinnamon
1 container pecan coconut frosting
(packaged mix may be substituted)

Preheat oven to 350°F. Grease a Bundt pan or 2 9x5-inch loaf pans or 4 to 5 small loaf pans.

Mix together eggs, applesauce and vanilla in large bowl. Stir pineapple and zucchini into mixture. Sift together the dry ingredients and then add to zucchini mixture. Stir frosting into mixture. Bake 70 minutes for Bundt pan; 60 minutes for regular loaf pans or 40 minutes for small loaf pans. Test with a toothpick prior to end of baking time. Cool 30 minutes in pan; then turn out and serve sliced.

*Optional glazing:* Beat together 1 cup confectioners' sugar, 1 to 3 tablespoons milk, and 1 tablespoon melted margarine.

## Eggnog Bread

3 cups all purpose flour
¼ cup sugar
4 teaspoons baking powder
½ teaspoon salt
½ teaspoon nutmeg
1 egg, beaten
1¾ cups canned or dairy eggnog
½ cup cooking oil
½ cup pecans, chopped
½ cup golden raisins

*Frosting:*
½ cup sifted confectioners' sugar
2 to 3 teaspoons eggnog

Preheat oven to 350°F. Grease a 9x5x3-inch loaf pan.

In a large bowl stir together flour, sugar, baking powder, salt and nutmeg. Combine egg, eggnog and oil; add to the dry ingredients, stirring until just combined. Stir in the nuts and raisins. Turn into greased loaf pan. Bake for 60 to 70 minutes. Cover with foil after 50 minutes if bread browns too quickly. Cool in pan for 10 minutes. Remove bread from pan; cool on a wire rack. Wrap bread. Store overnight. To serve, stir together confectioners' sugar and enough eggnog to make a glaze of drizzling consistency. Drizzle over bread.

**Makes 1 loaf.**

## Kolache (Nut Rolls)

5 cups all purpose flour
1 cup margarine
1 package plus 1 teaspoon dry yeast (3¼ teaspoons)
¼ cup warm water
3 eggs
1 cup sour cream
filling for Kolache (see below)

Cut margarine into flour in a large bowl until margarine is the size of small peas. In a separate bowl dissolve yeast in warm water. Add eggs, sour cream, and yeast mixture to the flour. Let stand covered in bowl about 10 minutes. Keep warm. Divide dough into 8 equal portions. Sprinkle sugar liberally over rolling board. Roll dough into a rectangle until about ¼-inch thick. Fill as desired by spreading filling thinly over surface of dough. Roll similar to jelly roll from smaller side, tucking ends under roll. Place on jelly roll pans or French bread pans that have been covered with baking paper. Bake at 350°F about 20 to 30 minutes until slightly browned. When cooled, slice to serve. Makes 80 servings, 8 long rolls, 10 slices per roll.

**Filling for nut rolls:**

Mix together 2 pounds ground walnuts, sugar to taste (approximately 1 cup) and warm milk. Add milk a little at a time until you reach a spreadable texture. Two pounds of walnuts will fill 8 rolls.

**Filling for date and nut rolls:**

Spread ⅛ of a can or jar of date filling on rolled out dough. Mix together 1 pound ground walnuts and sugar to taste (approximately ½ cup). Sprinkle nut mixture on top of date filling. This mixture will fill 8 rolls.

A jar or can of apricot or poppyseed filling can be used in place of the date filling.

## Dill Bread

1 package dry yeast (2¼ teaspoons)
¼ cup warm water
½ cup small curd cottage cheese
1 egg
3 Tablespoons butter or margarine, softened
1 Tablespoon sugar
2 teaspoons dill weed
½ teaspoon salt
2 to 2¼ cups all purpose flour

Dissolve yeast in warm water. Heat cottage cheese until lukewarm. Stir together all ingredients except flour in a large bowl. Add flour and stir to form a soft ball. Knead by hand until well mixed. Cover bowl with a towel and allow to rise for 1 hour, or until double in size. Punch down and place in a greased 9x5-inch loaf pan. Cover and let rise again until bread is almost to the top of the pan. Preheat oven to 350°F. Bake for 40 to 45 minutes or until cake tester inserted in middle comes out clean. Remove from pan and cool completely before slicing.

**Makes 1 loaf.**

## Double Whole Wheat Bread

2 packages dry yeast (4½ teaspoons)
1 cup warm water
⅓ cup honey
2 cups milk
¼ cup margarine
1 Tablespoon salt
5 cups whole wheat flour
¼ cup wheat germ
3 cups all purpose flour

Sprinkle yeast in water; stir in 1 teaspoon honey. Stir until yeast dissolves. Let stand undisturbed until bubbly and double in volume (about 10 minutes).

Combine remaining honey with milk, margarine and salt in a small saucepan; heat until margarine melts. Pour into large bowl; cool to lukewarm. Stir in yeast mixture. Stir in whole wheat flour and wheat germ. Add enough all purpose flour to make a soft dough.

Turn out onto lightly floured surface. Knead until smooth and elastic (about 10 minutes) using only as much flour as needed to prevent sticking. Place in large buttered bowl. Cover with towel and let rise until double (about 1 hour).

Punch down dough; turn onto lightly floured surface and knead a few times. Invert bowl over dough and let rise 10 minutes.

Divide in half and knead each a bit. Shape into 2 loaves and place in buttered 9x5x3-inch pans. Let rise again until double, about 45 minutes.

Preheat oven to 400°F. Bake for 40 minutes or until bread is browned and sounds hollow when tapped. Remove from pans to wire rack to cool.

**Makes 2 loaves.**

## Cranberry Orange Bread

1 cup cranberries, coarsely chopped
½ cup nuts, chopped
1 Tablespoon orange zest, grated
2 cups all purpose flour
1 cup sugar
1½ teaspoons baking powder
1 teaspoon salt
½ teaspoon baking soda
2 Tablespoons shortening
¾ cup orange juice
1 egg, well beaten

Preheat oven to 350°F. Grease and flour a 9x5x3-inch loaf pan.

Combine cranberries, nuts, and orange zest. Set aside. In a large mixing bowl combine flour, sugar, baking powder, salt and baking soda. Cut in shortening with a pastry blender or two knives. Stir in orange juice and egg just until dry ingredients are moistened. Fold in cranberry-nut mixture. Pour into prepared loaf pan. Bake 60 minutes or until a wooden pick inserted into center comes out clean.

Cool in pan on a rack for 15 minutes. Remove from pan, cool completely. Store tightly wrapped. Best if left tightly wrapped overnight before serving.

**Makes 1 loaf.**

## Pasta with Avocado and Garlic

2 Tablespoons butter
4 cloves garlic, finely chopped
2 Tablespoons all purpose flour
1⅓ cups milk
½ teaspoon ground black pepper
¼ teaspoon salt
8 oz. package dried pasta (preferably penne)
2 small ripe avocados
1 Tablespoon lemon juice
¼ cup sliced natural almonds, toasted

Melt butter in a 1 quart saucepan over medium heat. Add garlic and saute 3 minutes. Add flour, stirring until blended, and cook 3 minutes. Whisk in milk and cool until thickened and smooth, stirring occasionally, about 4 minutes. Reduce heat to very low; add pepper and salt and cook 10 minutes. Remove white sauce from heat and set aside 5 minutes.

Meanwhile, cook pasta following package directions and drain thoroughly.

Just before serving, peel, halve and pit avocados; cut into ½-inch chunks. Stir avocado chunks and lemon juice into white sauce until mixture turns a pale green. Avocados should still be in chunks.

To serve, toss hot pasta with avocado mixture; transfer to serving platter or 4 individual plates and top with almonds.

**Serves 4.**

## Roasted Vegetable Pasta

2 lbs. leeks, quartered lengthwise, with some green
¼ cup olive oil
¼ cup defatted chicken broth
2 Tablespoons fresh thyme leaves
1 Tablespoon coarse salt
black pepper, coarsely ground
6 ripe plum tomatoes (1 lb.) sliced in ¼-inch rounds
2 yellow squash, sliced in ¼-inch rounds
½ cup pitted black olives
⅓ cup Italian parsley, chopped
1 lb. fettuccine, cooked al dente

Preheat oven to 400°F.

Place leeks in a shallow roasting pan and drizzle with olive oil and chicken broth. Sprinkle with thyme, salt and pepper. Cover with foil and bake for 30 minutes. Remove foil; add tomatoes, squash and olives. Bake, uncovered, for 45 minutes more or until vegetables are tender, tossing vegetables once or twice.

Remove vegetables from oven and toss with parsley and cooked pasta in a large bowl. Serve hot or at room temperature.

**Serves 6.**

## Linguine with Garlic and Balsamic Vinegar

6 Tablespoons olive oil

8 large cloves garlic, cut into ¼-inch dice

1 lb. linguine

1 to 1½ cups Parmigiano-Reggiano, freshly grated

8 to 10 Tablespoons balsamic vinegar blended with 1 teaspoon brown sugar

eat 3 tablespoons olive oil in a large skillet over medium heat. Add the garlic and lower the heat to the lowest possible setting. Cook, covered, for 5 minutes. Uncover and continue cooking over the lowest heat for 8 minutes or until the garlic is barely colored to pale blonde and very tender. Stir it frequently with a wooden spatula. Do not let the garlic turn darker as it will bitter.

As the garlic braises, prepare the linguine, cooking it to al dente. Before draining the pasta, spoon 3 tablespoons of the cooking water into the cooked garlic.

Remove the garlic from the heat and add the pasta. Add the remaining olive oil and toss. Season with salt and pepper. Gently toss the cheese with the pasta. Turn the pasta into a heated serving bowl. As you serve the pasta sprinkle each plateful with a teaspoon or so of the vinegar.

**Variation:**

Add 1 cup coarsely chopped fresh basil leaves to the braised garlic a few seconds before tossing it with the pasta. Let the basil warm and its aroma blossom, then remove from heat and add pasta, followed by olive oil and cheese.

**Serves 4.**

## Asparagus-Pasta Stir Fry

1 lb. fresh asparagus, trimmed

½ cup onion, sliced

1 clove garlic, minced

2 Tablespoons vegetable oil

2 Tablespoons soy sauce

1 teaspoon ginger root

½ teaspoon Worcestershire sauce

⅛ to ¼ teaspoon red pepper flakes

6 oz. vermicelli or angel hair pasta, cooked and drained

iagonally slice asparagus into 1½-inch to 2-inch pieces. In a large skillet or wok stir fry asparagus, onion and garlic in oil until crisp-tender. Add soy sauce, ginger root, Worcestershire sauce and red pepper flakes, and mix well. Add cooked pasta and stir fry until thoroughly heated and evenly mixed.

**Serves 6.**

## Pasta with Smothered Onion Sauce

2 Tablespoons butter
3 Tablespoons olive oil
1½ lbs. onions, sliced very thin (about 6 cups)
salt
black pepper, freshly ground
½ cup dry white wine
2 Tablespoons chopped parsley
⅓ cup grated Parmesan cheese
1 to 1½ lbs. pasta (spaghetti is recommended)

Put the butter, the olive oil and the onions in a large saute pan. Cover and turn the heat to very low. Cook for at least 45 minutes, until the onions become very soft. Uncover the pan, raise the heat to medium high and cook the onions until they become colored to a deep dark gold. Any liquid the onions may have shed will now boil away.

Add salt and liberal grindings of pepper. Bear in mind that onions become very sweet when cooked in this manner and need an adequate amount of seasoning. Add the wine, turn the heat up and stir frequently while the wine bubbles away. (May be cooked ahead to this point; reheat and toss with pasta to complete dish.) Add the parsley, stir thoroughly and take off heat. Toss with cooked, drained pasta, adding the grated cheese. While tossing, separate the onion strands somewhat to distribute them throughout the pasta. Serve immediately.

**Serves 4.**

## Barley Pine Nut Casserole

1 cup pearled barley
4 Tablespoons butter
¼ to ½ cup pine nuts
1 cup onion, chopped
½ cup fresh parsley, minced
½ cup chives, minced
¼ teaspoon salt
¼ teaspoon pepper
2 cans beef broth
parsley for garnish

Preheat oven to 375°F.

Rinse barley in cold water and drain well. In frying pan, lightly toast pine nuts in 2 tablespoons of the butter. Remove from pan and set aside. In a large pan add remaining butter, onions and barley; cook until lightly toasted, remove from heat. To this mixture add the pine nuts, parsley, chives, salt and pepper. Spoon the mixture into a 1½ quart casserole. Heat broth to boiling and add to barley mix. Bake for 1 hour and 15 minutes.

**Serves 8.**

## Noodles Parmesan

1 lb. noodles
½ cup butter or margarine
½ cup grated Parmesan cheese
2 Tablespoons chives, chopped
2 Tablespoons parsley, chopped
2 eggs, slightly beaten
2 cups milk

Prepare noodles according to package directions.

Preheat oven to 300°F. Drain noodles and put in a large mixing bowl. Add butter and toss lightly with a fork until is evenly distributed. Place one third of noodles in a deep baking dish. Sprinkle with half of the cheese, chives and parsley. Layer the second third of the noodles in the dish. Sprinkle with the remaining cheese, chives and parsley, and end with the final layer of noodles. Combine eggs with milk and pour over casserole.

Recipe can be prepared ahead to this point and refrigerated until 30 minutes before baking. Bake for 40 to 45 minutes until firm.

**Serves 8.**

## Mushroom Wild Rice

½ cup butter or margarine
2 Tablespoons onion
2 Tablespoons green pepper
½ to 1 cup sliced almonds
1 cup wild rice
½ pound fresh mushrooms, sliced
2½ cups chicken broth

Preheat oven to 350°F.

Melt butter and saute onion, green pepper until onion is translucent. Add almonds during the last minute of saute time (to keep from burning). Mix all ingredients and put in a greased 1½ quart casserole.

Bake uncovered for 1 hour or until broth is absorbed.

**Serves 4 to 6.**

## Lemon Rice

1 cup uncooked rice
2 Tablespoons butter or margarine
2 cloves garlic, minced
1 teaspoon grated lemon peel
¼ teaspoon pepper
2 cups chicken broth
2 Tablespoons fresh parsley, chopped

In a large saucepan combine all ingredients except parsley. Bring mixture to a boil, stirring once or twice. Lower heat to simmer and cover with a tight fitting lid. Cook for 15 minutes, or until liquid is absorbed. Stir in parsley.

**Serves 4 to 6.**

## Vegetable Couscous

1½ cups couscous
½ cup raisins
1 teaspoon turmeric
2 cups boiling water
⅔ cup almonds, sliced
15 oz. can chick-peas, rinsed and drained
3 scallions, thinly sliced
2 medium tomatoes, halved, seeded and diced
11 oz. can mandarin oranges
½ cup red pepper, thinly sliced
⅓ cup fresh lemon juice
⅓ cup olive oil
2 cloves garlic, minced
grated zest of 1 orange
2 Tablespoons fresh basil, minced or 2 teaspoons dried
½ teaspoon salt
freshly ground black pepper to taste
green-leaf lettuce

Place the couscous, raisins, and turmeric in a large bowl, then pour the boiling water over them and stir well. Cover with foil or a large platter and let sit 5 minutes. Fluff with a fork, cover again, and let sit 10 minutes.

Stir in the almonds, chick-peas, scallions, tomatoes, mandarin oranges, and red peppers.

Combine the lemon juice, olive oil, garlic, orange zest, basil, salt and pepper, beat to blend. Pour over the couscous mixture and toss. Cover and chill at least 30 minutes, or up to 24 hours, before serving. Serve mounded on leaves of green-leaf lettuce.

Serves 8 to 12.

## Cajun Rice

2 cups uncooked rice (preferably converted)
2½ cups stock (fish or shrimp stock)*
1½ Tablespoons onion, finely chopped
1½ Tablespoons celery, finely chopped
1½ Tablespoons green pepper, finely chopped
1½ Tablespoons unsalted butter
½ teaspoon salt
⅛ teaspoon garlic
pinch of white pepper
pinch of ground red cayenne pepper
pinch of black pepper
*may substitute fish bouillon

Preheat oven to 350°F.

In a 9x5x2½-inch loaf pan, combine all ingredients and mix well. Cover pan snugly with foil. Bake until rice is tender, about 1 hour 10 minutes. Foil may be removed after one hour if a lot of liquid remains.

Serves 8.

We lived on 10 acres about 20 miles from downtown in an area our relatives referred to as "out in the boonies". It was, in reality, the beginning of the change from farmland to suburb, despite the herd of cows from the Belle Vernon Dairy residing across the street.

Even though my mother did not drive, we went into town to grocery shop one day a week. In the summer months, we depended on garden vegetables, wild berries, grapes and apples to round out our meals.

After a cold, snowy winter, the first shoots of lettuce from my mother's garden were a welcome treat. The tender sweet lettuce and baby spinach were a welcome change from those strong, dark, dandelion greens we ate to make do until the lettuce was big enough to pick. About the same time the wild strawberries would begin to ripen; just a few at first, a treat to be treasured and eaten on a special occasion.

As shown in our Strawberry-Romaine Salad, those first springtime salads were arranged with great care, each one a work of art. The tender leaves of the lettuces, mild flavor of baby spinach, sweetness of strawberries and rich crumbles of Gorgonzola combine in a tapestry of beauty to the eye and palate.

# Salads

## Strawberry Romaine Salad

1 cup vegetable oil
¾ cup sugar
½ cup red wine vinegar
2 cloves garlic, minced
½ teaspoon salt
½ teaspoon paprika
½ teaspoon ground white pepper
1 large head romaine lettuce
1 head Boston lettuce
1 lb. fresh baby spinach
1 pint strawberries, hulled and sliced
4 oz. Gorgonzola cheese, crumbled, about 1 cup
½ cup chopped walnuts, toasted

ombine oil, sugar, vinegar, garlic, salt, paprika and white pepper in jar. Cover tightly and shake vigorously.

Wash all greens well. Tear romaine and Boston lettuce into bite size pieces. Arrange torn lettuce, spinach, strawberries, cheese, and walnuts on individual salad plates. Pour desired amount of dressing over salad.

Serves 12.

*Extra dressing may be stored in refrigerator; great on other salads.*

This page generously sponsored by Dr. R. Wayne and Joyce Thompson.

## Swedish Potato Salad

2½ to 3 pounds boiling potatoes
3 Tablespoons olive oil
1 Tablespoon red wine vinegar
¼ teaspoon salt
pepper to taste
2 to 3 medium carrots, scraped, trimmed and cut into ½-inch cubes
1 cup frozen peas, thawed
1 large Granny Smith apple, cored and chopped
1 medium red bell pepper, chopped
1 small Vidalia onion, chopped
salt and freshly ground black pepper to taste

*Sour Cream Horseradish Dressing:*
½ cup mayonnaise
½ cup sour cream
1 to 2 Tablespoons prepared horseradish
salt and pepper to taste
fresh lemon juice

Prepare sour cream horseradish dressing: Combine mayonnaise, sour cream and horseradish, stir until well blended. Season with salt and pepper to taste. Refrigerate until ready to use.

Boil potatoes in a large pot, in water to cover until tender. Drain and cool, then peel and cut into small cubes. Place potatoes in a large bowl and set aside. Combine oil and vinegar in a jar and shake until well blended. Add salt and a generous amount of pepper. Add to potatoes and toss lightly to mix. Set aside at room temperature.

Cook carrots in boiling water to cover until just tender, drain. Add carrots, peas, apples, red bell pepper and onions to potato mixture and toss lightly. Add sour cream horseradish dressing and toss to mix. Refrigerate prior to serving.

Serves 6.

*Horseradish and vegetables add an unusual twist to the traditional favorite.*

## Wilted Greens

6 cups fresh garden leaf lettuce
4 scallions, thinly sliced

*Bacon Dressing:*
8 slices bacon
⅓ cup cider vinegar
1 Tablespoon honey
1 teaspoon salt
⅛ teaspoon pepper

Place leaf lettuce and scallions in a large wooden bowl. Cut bacon into julienne strips and brown. Turn off heat and quickly stir in vinegar, honey, salt and pepper. Pour dressing over greens and toss. Let stand 10 minutes, toss again and serve.

Serves 6.

## Cucumber Salad

4 cucumbers, peeled and thinly sliced
1 yellow onion, thinly sliced
¾ cup sugar
½ cup water
1 cup white vinegar
1½ teaspoons dried dill

Mix sliced cucumber with the yellow onion. Combine the sugar, water, white vinegar and dill in a small sauce pan. Bring mixture to a boil. Pour over the cucumber and onion and chill.

Serves 6.

## Salad Nicoise

¾ lb. fresh green beans, cut into thirds
1 teaspoon salt
2½ to 3 lbs. very small new potatoes
crisp lettuce leaves
2 7 oz. cans tuna packed in oil, drained and flaked
2 large ripe tomatoes, cut into wedges
2 hard cooked eggs, cut into wedges
1 large cucumber, peeled and thinly sliced
10 to 12 anchovy fillets, soaked in milk, drained and split lengthwise
2 Tablespoons green onions, chopped
¼ cup Italian black olives or Greek olives, halved and pitted

*Vinaigrette:*

2 Tablespoons fresh lemon juice
1 clove garlic, crushed
6 Tablespoons olive oil
salt and freshly ground black pepper to taste

Add green beans and salt to 1 quart rapidly boiling water. Return to a boil and cook beans until just tender, about 15 minutes. Transfer to very cold water using a slotted spoon and let cool completely. Drain thoroughly and toss with ¼ cup vinaigrette. In a second pot, cook potatoes in boiling water until tender but not falling apart. Drain and cut into wedges while still hot. Place in bowl and toss with remaining vinaigrette.

Arrange lettuce on 4 to 6 large salad plates. Place a mound of tuna in the center of each. Arrange beans and then potatoes around each mound of tuna. Surround potatoes with tomato wedges, egg wedges, and cucumber slices. Top each mound of tuna with anchovy filets and sprinkle with green onions and olives for garnish.

Serves 4 to 6.

Vinaigrette:

Combine lemon juice, garlic salt and pepper in a small bowl. Whisk in olive oil.

## Herb Bean Salad

3 cups cooked or canned small white beans
1 cup cucumber, pared, seeded and diced
1 cup sweet red pepper, diced
2 Tablespoons celery, chopped
2 Tablespoons green onions, chopped
2 Tablespoons parsley, chopped
¼ to ½ lbs whole tender green beans
6 cherry tomatoes, halved
lettuce leaves

*Herb Dressing:*
¼ cup lemon juice
¼ cup white wine vinegar
1 Tablespoon fresh basil, chopped
1½ teaspoons fresh thyme
1 Tablespoon honey
1 Tablespoon Dijon mustard
½ teaspoon grated lemon zest
½ teaspoon salt
1 small clove garlic, minced
⅛ teaspoon black pepper
½ cup olive oil

ombine white beans, cucumber, red pepper, celery, green onions and parsley. Toss well with ½ cup herb dressing. Let stand 1 hour at room temperature.

Snap ends of green beans and steam about 2 minutes or until crisp-tender. Pour 2 tablespoons dressing over green beans while they are still warm and toss. Arrange white bean mixture, green beans and tomatoes on lettuce lined salad plates. Serve with additional dressing.

**Serves 6.**

**Herb Dressing:**

Combine all ingredients except oil. Whisk until honey is well blended. Gradually beat in oil until slightly thick.

**Makes 1 cup.**

## Waldorf Salad

2 eggs
¼ cup sugar
Dash of salt
2 Tablespoons lemon juice
⅔ cup whipped cream
2 cups chopped apples
1 cup pineapple chunks
1 cup grapes, cut into halves
2 bananas, sliced
½ cup pecans, chopped
½ cup celery, chopped

eat eggs slightly. Add sugar, salt and lemon juice and cook in top of double boiler until thick, stirring constantly. Cool.

Fold whipped cream into cooled egg mixture. Combine apples, pineapple, grapes, bananas, pecans and celery and fold into dressing.

**Serves 6.**

*Unusual lemony dressing makes this a unique touch to an old favorite.*

## Sauerkraut Salad

15 oz. can sauerkraut
½ cup carrots, shredded
¼ cup onions, chopped
½ cup celery, cut in ¼-inch diagonal slices
⅓ cup green pepper, diced
⅓ cup plus 1 Tablespoon sugar
¼ teaspoon fresh black pepper
¼ teaspoon celery seed

While in can, cut sauerkraut into smaller pieces with knife. In a medium sized bowl, combine all ingredients and mix well. Cover and chill overnight.

Serves 6.

## Citrus Wheat Berry Salad

1 cup wheat berries
¼ teaspoon salt
½ cup orange juice
½ cup raisins
2 teaspoons sherry vinegar
1 Tablespoon grainy mustard
2 Tablespoons virgin olive oil
freshly ground black pepper to taste
½ cup oranges, peeled and chopped
¼ cup fresh pineapple, chopped
1 teaspoon orange zest, grated
½ cup scallions, thinly sliced
¼ cup mint leaves, thinly sliced
6 mint sprigs for garnish

Boil 2 cups of water, add wheat berries and salt. Simmer over low heat until tender approximately 1½ to 2 hours. May add more water if needed to prevent kernels from burning. Drain wheat berries and set aside to cool.

Soak raisins in ½ cup of orange juice for 15 minutes. Transfer 2 tablespoons of the raisin-soaking liquid to a large bowl. Add vinegar and mustard. Slowly whisk in oil and season to taste with black pepper.

Combine dressing, wheat berries, oranges, pineapple, orange zest, raisins, scallions, and sliced mint. Stir until ingredients are well mixed. Serve with fresh mint sprigs for garnish.

Serves 4 to 6.

## Creamy Cole Slaw

1½ lbs. (12 cups) cabbage, shredded
1 teaspoon salt
⅔ cup sugar
⅓ cup vinegar
1 cup whipping cream

Shred cabbage in a blender or food processor. Refrigerate, covered, for several hours. Mix salt, sugar, vinegar and whipping cream with electric mixer just until blended. Be sure not to overmix. Let stand for 30 minutes. Toss dressing with cabbage and serve.

Serves 8 to 12.

## German Potato Salad

4 lbs. red potatoes
6 slices bacon, diced
½ cup sugar
3 Tablespoons flour
2 teaspoons salt
¼ teaspoon pepper
1 cup cider vinegar
1 cup water
4 green onions, sliced

Boil potatoes in their skins until just tender. Drain and cool slightly then peel and cut into thin slices. Fry bacon in large skillet until crisp. Remove from drippings. If necessary, add more bacon fat to make ½ cup drippings. Blend sugar, flour, salt and pepper. Stir into bacon drippings to make smooth paste. Add vinegar and water. Boil 2 to 3 minutes. Stir constantly. Combine sauce, potatoes and onions in skillet. Cover with a tea towel (not a skillet lid) and let stand at room temperature 3 to 4 hours. Sprinkle with crisp bacon just before serving.

Serves 10 to 12.

*Best served at room temperature or reheated before serving.*

## Red Bean and Brown Rice Salad

16 oz. can red beans, rinsed and drained
1½ cups cooked brown rice, preferably cooked in chicken broth
1 cup cucumber, peeled, seeded and diced
1 cup tomato, seeded and diced
½ cup green pepper, chopped
½ cup celery, chopped
3 Tablespoons fresh parsley, cilantro, basil or dill, chopped
2 Tablespoons green onion, sliced
thyme sprigs for garnish

*Mustard Vinaigrette:*

⅓ cup white wine vinegar
1 Tablespoon olive oil
2 teaspoons Dijon style mustard
1 teaspoon sugar
½ teaspoon garlic salt
⅛ teaspoon pepper

Whisk all vinaigrette ingredients together until well mixed. Makes ½ cup.

Combine beans, rice and ¼ cup vinaigrette. Mix well and let stand at least 1 hour at room temperature. Add cucumber, tomato, green pepper, celery, herbs and green onion. Mix well. Spoon into a serving bowl and garnish with thyme.

Serves 8.

# Oriental Chicken Salad

4 chicken breast halves, boneless and skinless
1 large head green leaf lettuce
2 11 oz. cans mandarin oranges, drained
1 cup alfalfa sprouts
1½ cups fresh snow peas
1 cup cashews
1 cup chow mein noodles

*Glaze:*
¼ cup white wine
½ teaspoon ginger
¼ teaspoon garlic powder
¼ teaspoon black pepper
1 teaspoon paprika
1 Tablespoon lemon juice
2 Tablespoons Teriyaki sauce
2 teaspoons soy sauce
2 Tablespoons margarine
1 Tablespoon brown sugar

*Poppy Seed Dressing:*
½ cup sugar
1 teaspoon dry mustard
1 teaspoon salt
1 Tablespoon grated onion
5 Tablespoons white wine vinegar
1 cup vegetable oil
1½ Tablespoons lemon juice

Combine glaze ingredients in medium skillet over medium heat, cooking until bubbly. Add chicken and cook until all liquid is absorbed and chicken is well coated with glaze. Set aside.

Tear lettuce into bite-size pieces and divide among four plates. Arrange ¼ cup sprouts in "nests" in center of each plate. Divide oranges and snow peas and sprinkle each on lettuce around sprouts. Divide chicken and place on top of sprouts. Sprinkle ¼ cup cashews and chow mein noodles over each salad. Serve with Poppy Seed Dressing.

Serves 4.

**Poppy Seed dressing:**

Mix sugar, dry mustard, salt, onion, and 2 tablespoons vinegar. Add oil slowly, in thin stream, constantly beating with electric mixer. Add lemon juice and remaining vinegar and beat until thick. Stir in poppy seeds. Store in refrigerator. Serve at room temperature.

## Spicy Black Bean and Rice Salad

15 oz. can black beans, drained and rinsed
½ cup celery, chopped
½ cup green onion, chopped
1 cup plum tomatoes, chopped
1 Tablespoon fresh cilantro, chopped
3 teaspoons rice vinegar
2 teaspoons olive oil
1 teaspoon hot pepper sauce
½ teaspoon freshly ground black pepper
1 cup cooked rice

Combine the beans, celery, green onion, tomatoes and cilantro in a large bowl; set aside.

In a jar, mix together the vinegar, olive oil, hot pepper sauce and black pepper. Cover and shake vigorously. Pour marinade over bean mixture and stir gently to mix. Sprinkle cooked rice over all and stir well. Cover and chill 6 to 8 hours.

Serves 8.

*A colorful dish, perfect for entertaining. May be prepared a day in advance if desired.*

## Mandarin Orange Salad

½ head romaine lettuce, torn into pieces
½ head iceberg lettuce, torn into pieces
11 oz. can mandarin oranges, drained
1 cup celery, sliced or chopped
2 Tablespoons balsamic vinegar
¼ cup almond oil
2 Tablespoons fresh parsley, chopped
⅛ teaspoon Tabasco sauce
½ teaspoon salt
⅛ teaspoon freshly ground black pepper
4 Tablespoons sugar
½ cup sliced almonds

To caramelize almonds, melt sugar in a small cast iron skillet and stir in almonds. Quickly spread in shallow pan to cool.

Combine lettuce, oranges and celery in a large salad bowl. In a small bowl, whisk together balsamic vinegar, almond oil, parsley, Tabasco sauce, salt and pepper to make dressing. Set aside.

When almonds have reached room temperature, toss salad with dressing and garnish with caramelized almonds.

Serves 8.

## Curried Salmon Bulgur Salad

1 lb. salmon, cooked and deboned
½ cup onion, chopped
2 Tablespoons vegetable oil
1 Tablespoon curry powder
1 cup bulgur wheat
2 cups water
2 Tablespoons fresh parsley, chopped
lettuce leaves
tomato wedges
carrot curls
pickle fans
black olives

In a 2 quart sauce pan, saute onion with oil for 5 minutes or until tender. Add curry powder and bulgur and saute for 1 to 2 minutes, stirring continuously. Add bulgur mixture to 2 cups water. Bring to boil and simmer, covered, on medium heat for 20 to 25 minutes or until liquid is absorbed. Add salmon and parsley; toss lightly. Turn mixture into container; cover and chill.

Serve mounded on crisp lettuce leaves; garnish with tomato wedges, carrots curls, pickle fans and olives.

**Serves 4.**

*For variety try adding ½ cup sliced, toasted almonds, ½ cup cooked peas or ½ cup sliced red or green*

## Cauliflower Cole Slaw

1 head romaine lettuce
1 head iceberg lettuce
½ to 1 head cauliflower, grated
1 cup freshly buttered and toasted bread crumbs

*Garlic Dressing:*
1 cup mayonnaise
1 clove garlic, crushed
1 Tablespoon lemon juice
2 Tablespoons Parmesan cheese
salt and pepper to taste

Tear romaine and iceberg lettuce into bite size pieces. Combine greens with cauliflower . Lightly toss with Garlic Dressing. Sprinkle with bread crumbs.

**Serves 10 to12.**

## Antipasto

1½ lbs. new potatoes
2 carrots, cut into thin 1-inch strips
2 cups broccoli florets
4 oz. provolone cheese, cut into strips
2 oz. pepperoni, thinly sliced
1 cup pitted black olives
½ cup olive oil
½ cup white wine vinegar
2 Tablespoons parsley, snipped
2 Tablespoons dried oregano
1 teaspoon dried thyme
¼ teaspoon red bell pepper

Cook potatoes for 20 minutes in lightly salted boiling water. Add carrots for last 5 minutes. Drain and cool slightly. Cut potatoes into quarters. In a large bowl combine potatoes, carrots, broccoli, olives, and pepperoni. Set aside.

Mix oil, vinegar, parsley, oregano, thyme and red pepper in a jar. Mix well. Add cheese to vegetables, pour marinade over all. Refrigerate 4 to 24 hours. Stir occasionally to distribute marinade. Drain well and serve on a plate lined with lettuce leaves.

Serves 10 .

## Tabbouleh

Soak the bulgur in water for 30 or 40 minutes then drain well. Combine the bulgur, onions, parsley, mint, tomato, cucumber and garlic. Add the oil and lemon juice; then salt and pepper to taste. Allow to stand at least 30 minutes to develop flavors. Garnish with fresh mint leaves or serve in a lettuce lined bowl.

Serves 6 to 8.

1 cup bulgur (cracked wheat)
⅓ cup green onions, chopped
1½ cups fresh parsley, chopped
½ cup fresh mint, chopped
1 tomato, seeded and cut into ½-inch dice
½ cucumber, peeled, seeded and cut into ½-inch dice
1 clove garlic, finely minced
3 Tablespoons olive oil
3 Tablespoons lemon juice
salt and freshly ground pepper to taste
fresh mint leaves for garnish
lettuce for garnish

## Layered Fruit Salad

6 oz. package softened cream cheese
8 oz. carton strawberry yogurt
1 Tablespoon sugar
2 teaspoons lemon juice
2 cups whipped cream
2 Tablespoons amaretto
2 cups fresh blueberries
3 ripe peaches, sliced
2 cups strawberries, sliced
2 cups green grapes
20 oz. can pineapple chunks, drained
2 Tablespoons sliced almonds

ombine cream cheese, yogurt, sugar and lemon juice. Beat until smooth. Add whipped cream and amaretto. Continue beating until smooth and thick. Refrigerate.

Spoon 1/3 of the topping mixture into the bottom of a large bowl. Layer blueberries, peaches, and strawberries. Spoon in 1/3 of the topping mixture. Layer grapes and pineapple. Finish with remaining topping. Sprinkle with sliced almonds.

Serves 20.

## Frozen Fruit Cups

12 oz. frozen orange juice concentrate, thawed
12 oz. water
1 cup sugar
16 oz. can pineapple tidbits, drained
16 oz. can apricots, drained and diced
6 bananas, diced
1 cup maraschino cherries, chopped
1 cup miniature marshmallows, chopped (optional)
1 cup pecans, chopped (optional)

old all ingredients gently together. Line 32 muffin cups with paper liners. Spoon in salad and freeze. When frozen, remove from muffin tin and store in freezer bag. Remove individual salads as needed a few minutes before serving. Remove paper liner and serve.

Serves 32.

## Spinach Salad

Rinse spinach and tear into small pieces in a large bowl. Add tomatoes, red onion, artichoke hearts, cheese, bacon and eggs. Toss well.

**Dressing:**

Mix bacon drippings, tarragon vinegar, lemon juice, sugar and Worcestershire sauces together while drippings are still warm. Add dressing to salad just before serving.

**Serves 6.**

*Excellent with grilled meats and crusty bread. Serve with red wine (Cabernet Sauvignon).*

1 lb. fresh spinach
2 medium tomatoes
½ red onion, chopped
1 large jar marinated artichoke hearts
½ cup Monterey Jack cheese, shredded
6 strips cooked bacon, crushed
3 hard boiled eggs, sliced

*Dressing:*

½ cup warm bacon drippings
¼ cup tarragon vinegar
2 Tablespoons lemon juice
1 Tablespoon sugar
¼ teaspoon Worcestershire sauce

## Vegetable and Pasta Toss

1½ cups shell macaroni
2 cups broccoli florets
1 cup cauliflower florets
1 cup fresh mushrooms, sliced
6 oz. can artichoke hearts, drained, rinsed and chopped
1 cup pitted ripe olives, sliced
½ cup green onion, chopped
¾ cup Italian dressing
1 medium avocado, seeded, peeled and sliced
1 medium tomato, seeded and chopped

*Italian Salad Dressing:*

2 Tablespoons white vinegar
⅓ cup extra virgin olive oil
½ teaspoon Dijon mustard
1 Tablespoon parsley, finely chopped
2 teaspoons fresh tarragon, finely chopped or 1 teaspoon dry tarragon, crumbled
2 teaspoons minced chives
2 teaspoons dried basil
½ teaspoon salt
¼ teaspoon freshly ground pepper

Cook macaroni according to package directions; drain. Rinse with cold water, drain well. In a large bowl combine macaroni, broccoli florets, cauliflower florets, sliced mushrooms, artichoke hearts, ripe olives, and chopped green onion. Toss with Italian dressing. Cover and chill several hours. At serving time, toss vegetable mixture with avocado and tomato.

**Makes 12 to 16 servings.**

**Italian Dressing:**

In a small bowl whisk the vinegar, mustard, salt and pepper together. Add the olive oil and beat again. Stir in the fresh or dried herbs. Makes about ¾ cup.

## Chinese Cabbage Salad

2 heads Napa cabbage, shredded
1 small bunch green onions, diced
11 oz. can mandarin oranges, drained
6 Tablespoons butter
1 seasoning packet from Ramen noodles
½ cup slivered almonds
2 packages Oriental Ramen noodles
¼ cup sesame seeds

*Dressing:*

½ cup oil (1 tablespoon of which may be sesame seed)
¼ cup sugar
3 tablespoons red wine vinegar
1 Tablespoon soy sauce

Combine Napa cabbage and green onion. Add mandarin oranges and toss together. Melt butter in skillet. Mix in seasoning packet, slivered almonds, Ramen noodles (break up noodles) and sesame seeds. Brown lightly and set aside to cool.

In a small bowl whisk dressing ingredients together. Pour over cabbage mixture and toss in browned noodle mixture.

Serves 12 to 14.

*Best if served immediately. Can be prepared a day ahead and mixed together just prior to serving. Excellent for a special lunch.*

## Spicy Chicken Salad Stuffed Rolls

2 cups cooked chicken, diced
2 cups cheddar cheese, shredded
8 oz. cream cheese
4 oz. can green chilies, chopped
3 Tablespoons green onion, chopped
1 teaspoon ground cumin
1 teaspoon chili powder
1 teaspoon red pepper
6 medium hard rolls

In a large bowl mix together chicken, 1½ cups cheddar cheese, cream cheese, chilies, green onion, cumin, chili powder and red pepper. Cut out small top out of each roll and hollow out. Fill rolls with mixture. Sprinkle remaining cheddar cheese on top of each roll. Place on baking sheet and bake at 375°F for 7 to 9 minutes.

Serves 6.

## Fresh Tomato Salad with Basil Vinaigrette

3 ripe tomatoes, thinly sliced
1 red onion, thinly sliced
4 large lettuce leaves

*Basil Vinaigrette:*
¼ cup extra virgin olive oil
3 Tablespoons red wine vinegar
Salt and freshly ground black pepper to taste
¼ teaspoon dry mustard
⅛ teaspoon sugar
2 Tablespoons parsley, chopped
2 Tablespoons fresh basil, chopped

Blend the oil, vinegar, salt, pepper, mustard and sugar together in a jar. Shake to blend. Gently stir in the parsley and basil.

Place a leaf of lettuce on each of the four plates. Arrange the tomatoes and onion slices overlapping of one another in a circle on the lettuce. Top with the dressing.

Serves 4.

*Great way to serve fresh tomatoes from the garden—very pretty. For a variety try the dressings which follow.*

## Blue Cheese Dressing

1 cup sour cream or plain yogurt
1 Tablespoon white wine vinegar
2 Tablespoons crumbled blue cheese
salt and pepper to taste

In a medium bowl, combine sour cream and vinegar and blend thoroughly. Fold in blue cheese. Add salt and pepper to taste.

## Soy Sesame Dressing

1 Tablespoon sesame seeds
½ cup peanut oil
1½ Tablespoons oriental sesame oil
2½ Tablespoons red wine vinegar
½ teaspoon tamari soy sauce
1 clove garlic, pressed
salt and freshly ground black pepper to taste

Toast sesame seeds over medium-high heat until they begin to smoke, approximately 3 minutes. Shake the pan around while the seeds are cooking to toast them evenly. Pour the seeds into a small bowl to cool. Combine all the remaining ingredients in a jar and shake till well blended. Add sesame seeds and shake again then chill until ready to serve.

## Spinach and Goat Cheese Salad With Balsamic Vinaigrette

4 cups tightly packed spinach leaves

½ small head radicchio

1 oz. mild, unseasoned goat cheese, or fresh feta cheese, crumbled

¼ teaspoon cracked pepper

*Balsamic Vinaigrette:*

1 large shallot

¼ cup hot water

2 Tablespoons balsamic vinegar

1½ Tablespoons extra-virgin olive oil or walnut oil

1 Tablespoon fresh or 1 teaspoon dried basil

⅛ teaspoon ground black pepper

tack and roll up 12 spinach leaves. cut roll crosswise into ½-inch wide strips. Repeat until all spinach has been cut. Roll up radicchio leaves and cut crosswise into ½-inch wide strips. In a large bowl, toss radicchio and spinach with vinaigrette. Divide among 4 chilled plates; sprinkle with cheese and cracked pepper.

**Balsamic Vinaigrette:**

Combine shallot, hot water, balsamic vinegar, olive oil, basil and ground black pepper in a food processor fitted with a chopping blade. Process vinaigrette until smooth.

## Taffy Apple Salad

1 large can crushed pineapple

2 cups mini-marshmallows

2 Tablespoons flour

½ cup sugar

½ teaspoon vinegar

1 egg

5 to 6 large apples, chopped with peel

12 oz. Spanish peanuts, chopped

8 oz. whipped cream

rain pineapple and save syrup. Mix pineapple and marshmallows together, refrigerate.

In a sauce pan, whisk together pineapple syrup, flour, sugar, vinegar and egg. Heat slowly until bubbly. Refrigerate.

After pineapple mixture and syrup mixture have chilled, mix syrup mixture, pineapple mixture, apples and nuts together. Fold in whipped cream.

**Serves 10.**

*Helpful hint: Chop apples last to keep from browning.*

A favorite food in parts of the Midwest is a hearty, thick stew of readily available vegetables and meats called burgoo. Burgoo is made of tomatoes and other vegetables, meat, sometimes squirrel or rabbit, and plenty of seasoning. Burgoo varies from family to family and kitchen to kitchen depending on the tastes of the cook and family members.

After a vacation in the South and a taste of gumbo in New Orleans, Aunt Virginia started experimenting with her recipes. The result was a Catfish Burgoo which would rival any gumbo in the South. Using the catfish so bountiful in the Midwest, a blend of garden vegetables, home-grown herbs and spices and a sprinkling of shrimp imported from the coast, the new burgoo was created. Widely acclaimed as the best burgoo in the county, Catfish Burgoo is bound to be a favorite, no matter where in the country you live.

# Soups & Stews

## Catfish Burgoo

1 slice bacon, chopped
2 Tablespoons flour
1 large onion, chopped
1 red pepper, cored and cut into ½-inch dice
1 green pepper, cored and cut into ½-inch dice
1 teaspoon garlic, minced
¾ teaspoon salt
¼ teaspoon freshly ground pepper
¼ teaspoon thyme
⅛ to ¼ teaspoon ground red pepper
14½ oz. can chicken broth, plus enough water to equal 3 cups
1 cup frozen okra, sliced
1 cup canned tomatoes, drained and chopped
1 cup green onions, chopped
1 lb. catfish fillet, cut into 1½-inch chunks
8 oz. medium shrimp, peeled and deveined
3 cups cooked long-grain rice, optional

Cook bacon in a large, heavy Dutch oven over medium heat until crisp. Drain onto paper towels. Reduce to medium-low heat and stir flour into drippings and cook. Stir frequently until mixture is a deep golden brown, approximately 12 to 15 minutes.

Stir in onion, diced green and red peppers, garlic, salt, pepper, thyme and ground red pepper. Cover and cook, occasionally stirring, until vegetables are tender, about 10 minutes. Stir in broth, okra, tomatoes, and green onions. Return to a simmer and cook, covered, until mixture is thickened and vegetables are tender, 10 to 15 minutes. Stir in the catfish and shrimp; cook until fish is opaque, 5 minutes more. Stir in bacon. May be served with biscuits or over long-grain rice.

Serves 6.

**This page generously sponsored by The Ellis Family.**

## Black Bean Soup

16 oz. dry black beans
1 Tablespoon oil
1 large onion, diced
1 large clove garlic or 1 Tablespoon garlic powder
1 large green pepper, diced
15 oz. can tomato sauce
1 teaspoon salt
½ teaspoon pepper
1 large can tomatoes

oak beans overnight. Drain and rinse. Add 8 cups water and heat to boiling. Boil 3 minutes and remove from heat. Let stand 1 hour. Saute onion, garlic and green pepper in oil. Add to beans. Add remaining ingredients. Heat to boiling. Reduce heat to low and simmer 2 hours.

**Serves 6 to 8.**

*The flavor is just as savory as the cooking aroma.*

## Flint Hills Mushroom and Wild Rice Soup

1 cup wild rice
1 teaspoon salt
½ lb. bacon, diced
¾ cup onion, chopped
¾ cup celery, chopped
⅓ cup green pepper, chopped
¾ cup butter or margarine
1 cup all purpose flour
1 teaspoon salt
⅛ to ¼ teaspoon white pepper
4 cups milk
1 lb. fresh mushrooms, chopped fine
2 cups chicken stock
2 Tablespoons sherry
2 oz. jar pimentos, diced
½ lb. fresh mushrooms, sliced
1 pint half and half
⅓ cup almonds, toasted and set aside

our boiling water to cover rice and let stand 20 minutes. Drain and repeat two more times. The last time add salt and cook until tender. Drain and set aside.

Cook bacon and drain on paper towel. Saute onion, celery and green pepper in reserved drippings.

Make a mushroom sauce by melting butter in a saucepan over low heat. Blend in flour, salt and white pepper. Add milk all at once. Cook quickly, stirring constantly until mixture thickens and bubbles. Place finely chopped fresh mushrooms in a container and cook in microwave for 2 minutes, stir, and cook 2 more minutes. Stir in the cooked mushrooms, and the liquid, into the sauce mixture. Pour mushroom sauce, stock, sherry, pimento, bacon, vegetable mixture and rice into a soup kettle. Bring to a simmer. Add fresh mushrooms and continue to simmer for 5 minutes. Add half and half and heat through. Sprinkle almonds on top.

3 cans of mushroom soup may replace the mushroom sauce of butter, flour, salt, pepper, milk and 1 lb. mushrooms.

**Serves 6 to 8. Serves 8 to 10 if serving in mugs.**

*This robust soup combines contrasting colors, textures and flavors to make a sensational cold weather entree.*

## Basic Chicken Stock

4 lb. hen
1 lb. chicken wings
2 Tablespoons salt
4 peppercorns
5 quarts water
½ bay leaf
pinch of thyme
6 green onions, with tops
2 stalks celery, with leaves and cut in 2-inch pieces
3 cloves
1 large onion, studded with the 3 cloves
salt and pepper to taste

Place the chicken, salt, peppercorns and water in a stock pot. Bring to a boil over medium heat, removing residue from the surface. Cover the pot and reduce heat. Simmer for 1 hour, skimming frequently. Add remaining ingredients, cover, and cook approximately 2½ hours. Skim off fat. Season to taste with additional salt and pepper. Remove chicken and vegetables from stock. Strain stock through wet muslin. Chill and remove fat before using. This recipe can be made in advance and frozen.

**Makes 4 quarts.**

## Oriental Soup

3 cans chicken broth, defatted
6 cups water
1 teaspoon hot oil
¼ onion, chopped
1 clove garlic, sliced in half
¼ teaspoon ground ginger
several rings of sliced green pepper
1 large celery stalk, sliced
2 chicken breasts, skinned and sliced diagonally oriental style
frozen oriental stir fry vegetables
dash of pepper
salt or soy sauce to taste
cilantro to garnish

Add all of the ingredients to a slow cooker on high setting for a couple of hours, or low setting all day so they simmer. About 15 to 30 minutes before serving, add stir fry vegetables and let simmer until vegetables are crisp-tender. If desired add salt or soy sauce and pepper to taste right before serving.

Fresh vegetables may be used in place of frozen.

*A good soup to come home to after a day's work.*

## Fresh Corn and Zucchini Chowder

1 Tablespoon butter or margarine
1 cup onions, chopped
2 cloves garlic, minced
3 cups (6 ears) fresh corn kernels, divided
14½ oz. can chicken broth
1 tomato, seeded and diced
1 cup zucchini, diced
¼ cup whipping cream
2 Tablespoons fresh basil, julienned
2 Tablespoons fresh chives, minced
2 Tablespoons fresh parsley, snipped
salt and freshly ground pepper to taste

Melt butter in a large saucepan over medium heat. Add the onions and garlic. Cover and cook until the onions are tender, approximately 3 minutes. Stir in 2 cups of the corn and the chicken broth. Bring to a boil then reduce heat. Simmer, covered, for 5 minutes. Puree soup in a blender in small batches and return each batch to the saucepan. Add remaining 1 cup corn, tomato and zucchini. Cover and simmer 5 minutes. Remove from heat and stir in cream, basil, chives and parsley. Season with salt and pepper to taste.

**Serves 4.**

*Serve soup in warm bowls. A great way to utilize fresh vegetables and herbs from a summer garden.*

## Mexican Corn Stew

1 cup dry pinto beans
1 teaspoon olive oil
1 cup onion, chopped
1 Tablespoon garlic, minced
¼ cup jalapeno peppers, chopped
½ cup carrot, thinly sliced
½ cup celery, thinly sliced
2 red peppers, seeded and diced
3 Tablespoons cilantro, minced
6 cups vegetable stock
16 oz. package frozen corn
2 teaspoons cumin
2 teaspoons coriander
½ teaspoon cayenne pepper

Soak beans overnight in cold water. Drain and add to slow cooker. Heat olive oil in large skillet over medium-high heat. Add onions and garlic and saute until onions are soft, 3 to 5 minutes. Add jalapeno peppers, carrots, celery and red peppers. Cook 3 minutes. Add to slow cooker. Add cilantro, stock, corn, cumin and coriander. Cook on low until beans are tender and stew is thick, about 6 to 8 hours. Stir in cayenne pepper.

**Serves 8 to 10.**

*Serve with tortilla chips.*

## Boeuf Bourguignon

3 Tablespoons all purpose flour
½ teaspoon salt
½ teaspoon freshly ground pepper
3 lbs. lean, boneless beef chuck, cut into 1½-inch cubes
2 Tablespoons vegetable oil, divided
2 cups onion, chopped
½ cup carrot, peeled and chopped
1 teaspoon garlic, minced
2 cups Burgundy wine
1½ cups beef broth
1 Tablespoon tomato paste
1 Tablespoon fresh parsley, chopped
½ teaspoon thyme
1½ cups water
16 pearl onions, peeled
6 slices bacon, diced
8 oz. small fresh mushrooms

ombine flour, salt, and pepper in large bowl. Toss beef with flour mixture, shaking off excess flour. Heat half of the oil in large non-stick skillet over medium-high heat. Add 6 to 8 pieces of beef to skillet and brown well on both sides. Using a slotted spoon, move beef to large Dutch oven. Repeat with remaining beef, adding remaining oil as needed. Reduce heat to medium. Add onions and carrot to skillet and cook until softened, about 3 minutes. Add garlic and cook until fragrant, about 30 seconds. Pour in wine and cook 2 minutes, scraping up browned bits from the bottom of the pan. Add mixture to Dutch oven along with broth, tomato paste, parsley and thyme. Reduce heat to low and simmer, covered, until beef is almost tender, approximately 1½ hours.

Bring water to a boil in a large saucepan. Add onions and cook over medium heat. When almost tender, add bacon and cook for 2 more minutes. Drain and return onion mixture to pan. Cook, stirring occasionally, until onions are lightly browned. Add mushrooms, onions, and bacon to stew. Simmer uncovered until meat is tender, about 30 minutes.

Serves 8.

*A hearty beef stew, best if made a day in advance.*

## Chicken Vegetable Soup

3 lbs. chicken, cut up
2 quarts water
2 cups carrot, diced
2 cups celery, diced
6.25 oz. instant seasoned long grain wild rice
8 oz. fresh mushrooms, sliced
1 yellow onion, diced
½ cup butter

ook chicken in about 8 cups of water over medium-high heat until tender. Remove chicken from stock to cool. Skim fat and residue off of the stock. Add carrots and celery to stock and cook until tender. Add rice and seasoning packet that comes with the rice. Continue to cook over medium heat. Saute mushrooms and onion in the butter. Add to the stock. Skin and bone chicken and cut into small pieces. Add to the stock.

Serves 6 to 8.

## Corn Belt Chowder

1 Tablespoon butter

2 Tablespoons olive oil

2 teaspoons jalapeno pepper, finely minced or
1 dried chili pepper, crumbled

1 medium onion, finely minced

2 Tablespoons flour

6 to 7 cups chicken stock

2 10 oz. cans of whole kernel corn or
3 large ears of fresh or frozen corn, cooked and scraped

1 small zucchini, finely diced

1 small red pepper, cored and finely diced

salt and freshly ground black pepper to taste

12 medium sized fresh or frozen shrimp,
cooked, peeled and diced (optional)

½ cup heavy cream (optional)

pinch of freshly grated nutmeg or cayenne

cilantro, chives and parsley, finely minced for garnish

Heat butter and oil in a heavy 3 quart saucepan. Add the jalapeno pepper and onion and saute over medium heat until the onion is soft and starts to brown. Add flour and blend thoroughly, making sure that the flour does not burn. Immediately add 6 cups of stock and corn and whisk until the soup comes to a boil. If desired, ¾ cup of the corn can be set aside to put in soup later. Reduce heat and simmer for 15 minutes. Remove from heat. When the soup is cool, pour into a food processor and puree until smooth. Return it to the saucepan and reheat. Add zucchini, red pepper, salt, black pepper, shrimp and reserved corn. Simmer until vegetables are soft, about 15 minutes. If soup is too thick, add remaining stock. Add cream, if desired, and heat through. Top with spices and herbs.

**Serves 8 to 10.**

*For a thicker soup, use less chicken stock and fewer jalapenos. Cheddar muffins make an outstanding accompaniment to this soup.*

## Classic Clam Chowder

½ cup butter

1 medium onion, chopped

5 to 6 stalks celery, chopped

8 Tablespoons flour

2½ quarts half and half

¼ lb. salt pork cut in ¼-inch cubes

3 cups cooked red or new potatoes,
cubed with skins on

4 cans minced clams and liquid or
½ lb. clams, shelled and rinsed

½ cup chicken stock

1 teaspoon Worchestershire sauce

salt and pepper to taste

white pepper to taste

Melt butter, saute onion and celery. Add flour and brown. Slowly add cream until flour dissolves and thickens. Add remaining ingredients and put in a slow cooker for 4 hours. Season with salt and pepper.

**Serves 8.**

*Great for large family gatherings, informal luncheons or Sunday night dinner.*

## Kansas Bean Soup With Swiss Chard

1 lb. dried white beans, cannellini or great northern
2 lbs. chuck arm roast, cut into ½-inch cubes
beef soup bone
1¾ teaspoons salt, divided
½ teaspoon freshly ground pepper, divided
2 Tablespoons olive oil, divided
3 cups onions, chopped
3 cups carrot, peeled and chopped
2 cups celery, chopped
2 cloves garlic, minced
1 Tablespoon fresh thyme or ½ teaspoon dried thyme, chopped
1 bay leaf
2 teaspoons fresh rosemary, chopped
2 smoked ham hocks (1½ lbs.)
8 cups water
2 14½ oz. cans chicken broth
14½ or 16 oz. can tomatoes, drained and coarsely chopped
8 cups Swiss chard, sliced, or spinach, torn

Rinse and clean beans. In large bowl, cover beans with 2 inches water and soak overnight. (To quick soak: Combine beans with water to cover by 2 inches in large saucepan and bring to boil. Boil for 2 minutes, cover and let stand 1 hour.) Drain and set aside.

Sprinkle beef and beef bone with ¼ teaspoon of the salt and ¼ teaspoon of the pepper. Heat 1 tablespoon of the oil in large Dutch oven over high heat. Add beef and bone 5 or 6 pieces at a time and cook until browned on all sides. Transfer to a plate. Heat the remaining 1 tablespoon oil in Dutch oven over medium high heat. Add onions, carrots, and celery. Cover and cook, stirring occasionally, until vegetables are tender, about 10 minutes. Stir in garlic, bay leaf, thyme and rosemary, cooking 30 seconds. Return beef and bone to Dutch oven. Add drained beans, ham hocks, water, chicken broth, remaining 1½ teaspoons salt and remaining ¼ teaspoon pepper. Bring to a boil. Reduce heat and simmer partially covered for an hour.

Stir in tomatoes. Simmer until beans and meat are tender, about 30 minutes more. Remove ham hocks and cool. Cut meat into ½-inch pieces and return meat to soup. Discard all bones and bay leaf. Skim fat and return soup to a simmer, stir in chard and cook until chard is tender, about 10 minutes.

Serves 12.

*A very hearty soup with lots of flavor. Can be made ahead of time and refrigerated up to 2 days.*

## French Beef Stew

3 lbs. rump roast, cut into chunks
3 carrots, diced
1 lb. jar whole pearl onions, drained
20 oz. can tomatoes, including all liquid
20 oz. can tiny peas
1½ Tablespoons salt
1 can beef consomme soup
½ cup white wine
4 Tablespoons minute tapioca
1 Tablespoon brown sugar
½ cup prepared bread crumbs
1 bay leaf
pepper to taste

Combine all ingredients in a large Dutch oven or pot. Cover and bake at 250°F for 6 to 7 hours. This may also be cooked in a slow cooker on low for 6 to 7 hours.

**Serves 6.**

*The longer it simmers, the better the taste. Great served with sourdough rolls.*

## Red Pepper Soup

4 to 5 large red peppers
3 medium cloves garlic
1 Tablespoon butter
2 large leeks, chopped
3 cups chicken stock
salt and pepper to taste
3 Tablespoons dry sherry

Cut peppers into 4 or 5 sections. Clean out seeds and flatten sections, skin up on an aluminum foil covered cookie sheet. Broil until skins begin to blacken, remove peppers and immediately place in cold water. Remove skins.

Slice leeks and soak in cold water for 20 minutes. Lift leeks out of water to rinse and remove sand. (Be sure to lift out leeks rather than pouring water off leeks. Discard sandy water.) Crush garlic cloves. Melt butter in large pot and cook leeks and garlic until juices are released, about 5 minutes. Uncover, add the chicken stock, season with salt and pepper and simmer for 30 minutes. Place skinned pepper pieces in leek and chicken stock for the last 15 minutes of cooking. Cool stock slightly. Strain solids from stock and set aside. Food process all solids until smooth, approximately 45 seconds. Gradually add stock through feed tube of food processor to desired thickness; thicker is better. Remove processed soup to large pan and stir in sherry to taste. Let soup reheat slightly. Should be served at room temperature.

For garnish, top soup with a large tablespoon of sour cream and cross a few slices of lime peel on top.

**Serves 4 as a first course.**

*A light soup, perfect for brunch or served with a salad.*

## White Chili With Salsa Verde

*Salsa:*

2 cups fresh tomatillos, coarsely chopped (approximately 8 oz.)

½ cup onion, chopped

½ cup fresh cilantro or parsley, chopped

1 pickled jalapeno pepper, finely chopped

1 clove garlic, minced

½ teaspoon dried oregano

2 to 3 Tablespoons lime juice

*Soup:*

5 cups chicken stock

1 teaspoon cumin seed

4 chicken breast halves (1½ lb.)

olive oil flavored cooking spray or 1 teaspoon olive oil

1 clove garlic, minced

1 cup onion, chopped

16 oz. package frozen white shoepeg corn

2 4 oz. cans diced green chilies, not drained

1 teaspoon cumin

2 to 3 Tablespoons lime juice

15 oz. can cannellini or great northern beans, drained and rinsed

⅔ cup tortilla chips, crushed

1½ oz. (⅔ cup) Monterey Jack cheese, shredded

Combine the first 7 ingredients in a bowl and mix well. Refrigerate 30 minutes to blend flavors. Makes about 2½ cups.

Combine stock and cumin in a large saucepan and bring to a boil. Add chicken and reduce heat to low. Cover and simmer 20 minutes or until chicken is tender. Remove chicken from bone and cut into 1-inch pieces. Return chicken to saucepan. Spray medium skillet with cooking spray or rub with olive oil and heat over medium heat. Add garlic, cook and stir one minute. Remove from pan and add to chicken mixture. Add onions to skillet, cook and stir until tender. Add onion, corn, chilies, cumin and lime juice to chicken mixture. Bring to a boil. Add beans and cook until heated. Place about 1 tablespoon each of tortilla chips and cheese in 8 individual soup bowls. Ladle hot soup over cheese. Top with salsa.

**Serves 8.**

*Great for a family since varying amounts of salsa can be added for different tastes.*

## French Onion Soup

5 cups onions, thinly sliced
½ cup butter
3 cans (10½ oz. each) condensed beef broth
3¼ cups water
1¼ teaspoons Worcestershire sauce
1 teaspoon sugar
½ teaspoon salt
dash liquid hot pepper sauce
1 cup white wine
8 slices French bread
½ cup butter, melted
1½ cups Swiss cheese, shredded

Saute onions in ½ cup butter in a 4 quart saucepan, for 15 minutes or until tender and golden brown. Stir in beef broth, water, Worcestershire sauce, sugar, salt and hot pepper sauce. Cover and cook over moderate heat, about 45 minutes. Blend in wine and heat to serving temperature.

Preheat oven to 350°F. Dip both sides of bread slices in melted butter. Place on cookie sheet and toast for 10 minutes. Turn and toast 5 more minutes or until lightly browned. Top each bowl of soup with a bread slice and Swiss cheese. Microwave until cheese bubbles.

## Southwest Stew

6 slices bacon, diced
1 lb. pork, cut in 1-inch chunks
flour
1½ cups corn
4 medium zucchini, coarsely chopped
2 medium green peppers, coarsely chopped
1 large red onion, finely chopped
3 tomatoes, coarsely chopped
¼ lb. fresh mushrooms, sliced
2 Tablespoons cilantro, chopped
salt and pepper
1 teaspoon Worcestershire sauce
8 oz. can tomato sauce
3 cloves garlic, minced
1 teaspoon peppercorns, crushed
1 teaspoon chili powder
ground cumin, to taste
oregano, to taste
2 green chili peppers, chopped

Fry bacon in a large pot. Remove and drain on paper towels, saving bacon drippings. Dredge pork in flour and brown over medium heat in bacon drippings. Stir in corn and zucchini and saute for 1 to 2 minutes over medium heat. Drain. Add chopped peppers, onions, tomatoes, mushrooms, and cilantro. Season with salt and pepper and Worcestershire sauce. Combine tomato sauce with garlic, peppercorns, chili powder, cumin, oregano and chili peppers. Stir into meat and vegetable mixture. Cover and simmer over low heat until juices are absorbed, approximately 2 hours. Stew should be thick.

## Lamb Ragoût

1½ cups dried chick peas or garbanzo beans
water
5 teaspoons vegetable oil, divided
1 cup onions, chopped
2½ lbs. boneless lamb shoulder, cut into 1½-inch cubes
4 cloves garlic, minced
1 teaspoon salt
¾ teaspoon freshly ground pepper
½ teaspoon thyme
1 bay leaf
2 14½ oz. cans chicken broth
35 oz. can tomatoes, chopped and liquid reserved
1 lb. turnip, peeled and julienned
12 oz. carrot, peeled and julienned
10 oz. frozen lima beans
parsley for garnish

Rinse and clean chick peas. Place peas in a large bowl and cover peas with 2 inches of water. Soak overnight. Drain and set aside. To quick soak: Boil chick peas for 3 minutes, remove from heat and allow to stand for one hour. Heat 2 teaspoons of the oil in large skillet over high heat.

Add onions and cook until tender, approximately 5 minutes. Transfer to a large stock pot. Heat remaining 3 teaspoons oil in same skillet over high heat. Add ⅓ of lamb to the skillet and brown well on all sides. Transfer lamb with a slotted spoon to the broth pot. Repeat with remaining lamb. Add 2 cups water to skillet and simmer over high heat for 1 minute. Add pan juices to broth pot. Stir in soaked chick peas, garlic, salt, pepper, thyme, bay leaf and chicken broth. Bring to a boil. Reduce heat, cover and simmer for 1 hour. Skim occasionally. Add tomatoes with liquid, turnips, carrots and lima beans. Cover and cook for 30 minutes more or until lamb and chick peas are tender. Sprinkle with parsley.

**Makes 10 servings.**

Can use 1½ cups potatoes, diced, in place of chick peas.

*This flavorful, hearty soup is especially good on a cold day.*

## Football Stew

2 lbs. stew beef
2 or more potatoes, quartered
2 carrots, quartered
2 stalks celery
1 onion, sliced
15 oz. can tomatoes
1 bay leaf
salt and pepper to taste

Arrange ingredients in an ovenproof baking dish. Cover and bake at 250°F for 5 to 6 hours.

**Serves 4.**

## Indian Summer Soup

3 medium onions, chopped
1 lb. ground beef or cubed stew meat
1 clove garlic, minced
3 cups beef stock or broth
28 oz. can tomatoes
1 cup celery, sliced
1 cup potatoes, diced and peeled
½ cup lentils (optional)
1 cup carrots, sliced
1 cup green beans, trimmed and cut
12 oz. canned corn, drained
1 cup dry red wine
1 Tablespoon fresh parsley, chopped
½ teaspoon dried basil
1 Tablespoon salt
¼ teaspoon dried thyme
freshly ground pepper

Cook onions, beef and garlic together in Dutch oven over medium heat until beef is browned. Drain grease completely and add remaining ingredients. Bring to a boil. Reduce heat and simmer for 1 hour. Season to taste.

**Serves 6.**

*This recipe can also be made in several days in advance and frozen for several weeks. Instead of seasoning with salt, use lemon juice for no-salt cooking.*

## Taco Soup

1 lb. ground chuck
1 onion, chopped
1 package (1¼ oz.) taco seasoning or 2 Tablespoons taco seasoning
1 to 1½ cups water
16 oz. can tomato juice
16 oz. can kidney beans
16 to 17 oz. can whole kernel corn and liquid
8 oz. can tomato sauce
14 to 16 oz. can hominy
4 oz. can chopped green chilies
1 package dry ranch salad dressing mix
sour cream
cheddar cheese or Monterey Jack cheese, grated
corn chips
salsa

Brown beef and onion. Add remaining ingredients through ranch dressing and cook on low until piping hot. Serve over corn chips in individual bowls and top with sour cream, cheese, additional chips or salsa.

**Serves 6 to 8.**

## Artichoke and Mushroom Soup

2 Tablespoons onion, chopped
¾ cup mushrooms, thinly sliced
3 Tablespoons butter
2 Tablespoons flour
1½ cups chicken stock
2½ cups half and half
16 oz. can artichoke hearts, drained and diced
salt to taste
cayenne pepper to taste
Beau Monde seasoning to taste

Saute onions and mushrooms in butter for 5 minutes. Stir in flour and cook slowly for 2 minutes. Slowly add stock and half and half. Stir with whisk over low heat to thicken. Stir in artichokes and seasonings, to taste.

**Serves 4 to 6.**

## Black Olive Gazpacho

2 cups chicken stock
½ cup plain yogurt
½ cup sour cream
½ cucumber, peeled, seeded and chopped
½ red bell pepper, seeded and chopped
½ green bell pepper, seeded and chopped
½ cup black olives, sliced
¼ cup green onions, chopped
2 Tablespoons fresh parsley, chopped
salt and white pepper to taste
Worcestershire sauce and hot pepper sauce to taste

Whisk together chicken stock, yogurt and sour cream in a large bowl. Add chopped vegetables and seasonings and refrigerate. Check seasonings before serving. Serve chilled.

**Serves 6.**

*A refreshing first course for a summer luncheon.*

## Spicy Chicken Gumbo

3 lb. chicken, skinned and quartered
2 Tablespoons vegetable oil
¼ cup all purpose flour
2 cups onions, chopped
¾ cup green pepper, chopped
1 rib celery, chopped
2 cloves garlic, minced
1 teaspoon salt
¼ teaspoon thyme
⅛ teaspoon ground red pepper (optional)
8 oz. smoked garlic sausage, halved lengthwise and sliced ¼-inch thick
10 oz. frozen cut okra, thawed
3 to 6 cups cooked rice, depending on serving size desired (½ to 1 cup rice per serving)

lace chicken in deep skillet with enough cold water to cover. Bring to a boil and cook 2 minutes. Reduce heat, cover and let simmer 20 minutes. Strain stock into a large bowl and set aside. Remove chicken. When cool enough to handle, remove meat and tear into large pieces, discarding skin and bones.

Heat oil in large Dutch oven over medium heat. Add flour and cook, stirring constantly, until mixture browns, about 15 minutes. Add onions, green pepper and celery. Cook, stirring occasionally, until vegetables are tender-crisp, about 10 minutes. Add garlic. Stir in 4 cups reserved chicken stock. Add chicken meat, salt, thyme, and red pepper. Bring to a boil and simmer 10 minutes. Add sausage and okra and continue to cook until okra is tender, about 12 to 15 minutes. Serve over rice.

**Serves 6.**

*Great Super Bowl party soup served with breadsticks.*

## New Orleans Gumbo

4 Tablespoons butter
4 Tablespoons flour
1 cup onion, chopped
1 cup celery, chopped
1 lb. okra, sliced
2 cups canned tomatoes, drained
5 cups chicken or fish stock
1 cup tomato liquid
5 bay leaves
3 cups raw shrimp, deveined
1 dozen crab, scaled
2 dozen oysters
2 Tablespoons parsley, chopped
salt and pepper to taste
dash of cayenne pepper
2 Tablespoons gumbo file

elt butter in saucepan. Add flour, saute onions and celery until light brown. Add okra and cook about 30 minutes, stirring often. Stir in tomatoes and gradually add chicken or fish stock and tomato liquid. Add bay leaves, shrimp, crab, oysters, parsley, salt, pepper and cayenne pepper. Cover and simmer 1 hour, stirring often. Stir file powder into gumbo just before serving.

**Serves 6.**

*Canned seafood can be substituted for fresh. Serve with French bread and Caesar salad.*

# American Posole

1 lb. posole, washed well or 2 15 oz. cans white/yellow hominy

6 cups cold water

2 to 3 medium onions, coarsely chopped or 4 to 5 Tablespoons dried onion, chopped

4 large cloves garlic, peeled and crushed or 2 Tablespoons garlic salt

4 Tablespoons cooking oil

3 lbs. pork shoulder, boned and cut in ¾-inch cubes

1 teaspoon oregano leaf, crumbled

½ teaspoon thyme

2 teaspoons salt (omit if garlic salt is used)

¼ teaspoon black pepper

1⅔ cups chicken stock

10 oz. can whole green chilies, drained (reserve juice), and cut in long strips or fresh or frozen green chilies

reserved chili juice plus water to equal ¾ cup

1 to 2 jalepeno peppers, minced (1 pepper makes a mild posole, 3 makes a torridone)

1 can (5 or 15 oz. depending on taste) tomato sauce

Place posole and water in large heavy pot if using dry posole. Bring to a simmer, cover and cook slowly until kernels burst and are almost tender, about 3½ hours. Lightly brown onions and garlic in 2 tablespoons cooking oil. Drain. Add remaining 2 tablespoons cooking oil to skillet and brown pork cubes, a few at a time. Drain. Mix all remaining ingredients together in large heavy pot. Mix well and simmer, covered for 3 hours, stirring occasionally. Taste for salt and adjust if needed.

**Serves 8 to 10.**

*Serve with margaritas and red chili sauce.*

Much of the cuisine of the Midwest is flavored by the ethnic traditions of the immigrant populations who settled here. Pockets of immigrants settled together for a sense of unity and mutual support as they learned the ways of their new communities. Each large Midwestern city has ethnic areas well known for their native cuisine and customs. Rural areas, too, were frequently settled by those with similar ethnic backgrounds.

Handed down through families of Mediterranean immigrants comes our Chicken with Feta and Pine Nuts. Richly flavored with garlic, red onion, olives and sun-dried tomatoes, this elegant but easy entree will tempt you with the heady aroma of a Mediterranean kitchen. Some will experience a flood of memories of times when aunts and cousins gathered in the kitchen to prepare these cherished dishes for their extended families.

The rich flavors and colorful presentation of this dish require only a simple grilled vegetable as an accompaniment. We suggest them here subtly seasoned with garlic and olive oil. Crusty bread, a bottle of wine, and a kitchen full of friends will bring your memories back to life.

# Poultry & Game

## Chicken With Feta and Pine Nuts

1 cup red onion, finely chopped

2 Tablespoons olive oil, divided

1½ teaspoons garlic, minced

½ cup pitted olives, cut into thin strips

¼ cup pine nuts, toasted slightly

½ cup drained oil-packed sun dried tomatoes, drained, cut into thin strips

¼ lb. feta cheese, crumbled, about 1 cup

2 Tablespoons freshly grated Parmesan cheese

1 Tablespoon fresh marjoram or 1 teaspoon dried marjoram

2 whole boneless chicken breasts, with skin, halved

Preheat oven to 350°F.

Cook onion in 1 tablespoon oil in a large ovenproof skillet over medium heat, stirring until softened. Add garlic and cook, stirring, 1 minute. Transfer mixture to a bowl and let cool. Stir in olives, pine nuts, tomatoes, cheeses, marjoram, salt and pepper to taste. Stir to combine. Insert a sharp paring knife into thicker end of each chicken breast half and cut lengthwise to make a pocket. Fill each breast half with ¼ of the filling. In a clean skillet, heat remaining tablespoon of oil over moderate heat until hot, but not smoking, and brown chicken skin side down. Leaving chicken skin side down, transfer to oven and bake until just cooked through, about 12 minutes.

Serves 4.

## Smoky Hill Pheasant

¼ lb. bacon, chopped fine
2 pheasants, quartered
all purpose flour
1 clove garlic, pressed
8 oz. fresh mushrooms, sliced
6 pieces rosemary
2 Tablespoons fresh parsley
1 teaspoon salt
pepper to taste
2 oz. dry white wine (¼ cup)
1½ cups water

ry bacon, remove from pan leaving drippings. Dredge pheasant in flour and brown in bacon drippings. Add garlic, mushrooms, rosemary, parsley, salt and pepper. Cook 5 minutes. Add wine and cook 2 to 3 minutes. Add water. Cover, place in oven and cook at 300°F for 2½ to 3 hours.

Serves 6 to 8.

*Serve with wild rice, a gravy made with the pheasant juices, and Johannesburg Riesling.*

## Chicken and Sausage Jambalaya

3 Tablespoons butter
1 cup diced ham
1½ lbs. sausage (andouille)
1 lb. boneless chicken, cut into bite-sized pieces
⅓ teaspoon ground bay leaf
2 teaspoons dried thyme
¼ teaspoon ground sage
1½ teaspoons salt
1 teaspoon white pepper
1 teaspoon black pepper
2 teaspoon cayenne
2 teaspoons Tabasco
1 large onion, chopped
2 green peppers, chopped
4 cloves garlic, chopped
4 ribs of celery, chopped
6 green onions, chopped
28 oz. can whole tomatoes, coarsely chopped
3½ cups chicken stock
2 cups uncooked rice
3 Tablespoons parsley, chopped

elt butter over medium high heat in a Dutch oven. Add ham and sausage and increase heat to high. Cook, stirring constantly, until meat starts to brown, about 3 minutes. Add the chicken and continue to cook 3 to 5 minutes, stirring frequently, until the chicken is browned. Keep scraping the bits from the bottom of the pan. Reduce heat to medium. Mix together bay leaf, thyme, sage, salt and peppers and sprinkle over the meat mixture. Stir in onion, green pepper, garlic, celery and green onions. Cook until the vegetables are tender, about 5 minutes, stirring frequently to keep mixture from sticking. Stir in the tomatoes and blend well. Add the stock, rice and parsley and bring to a boil. Reduce heat to simmer, cover and cook until rice is tender, about 20 minutes.

Serves 8.

## Smoked Pheasant Enchiladas

*Sauce:*

16 fresh tomatoes
2 teaspoons salt
2 teaspoons pepper

*Filling:*

1 green pepper, diced
1 red pepper, diced
1 red onion, diced
6 smoked pheasant breasts
3 cups goat cheese
3 cups mozzarella cheese, grated
1 bunch fresh cilantro, chopped
1 Tablespoon salt
1 Tablespoon pepper
12 flour tortillas

Puree tomatoes. Pour pureed tomatoes into a pan, add the salt and pepper and cook until smooth. Prepare filling while sauce is cooking.

Saute pepper and onion until translucent. Shred pheasant by hand. Place peppers, onion, pheasant, goat cheese, mozzarella cheese, cilantro, salt and pepper in a mixing bowl, stir until well mixed. Divide filling into 12 equal parts and place in tortillas. Roll each tortilla and place in a casserole pan. Cover tortillas with sauce, then cover pan with foil. Cook in a 375°F oven until heated through.

Serves 12.

*Presented at Grand Street Cafe by Chef Mike Peterson.*

## Lemon Basil Chicken

½ cup oil
¼ cup lemon juice, freshly squeezed
2 Tablespoons white wine vinegar
1 Tablespoon lemon zest, grated
2 cloves garlic, minced
½ teaspoon salt
¼ teaspoon pepper, freshly ground
½ cup chopped fresh basil or 1 Tablespoon dried basil
4 chicken breasts

Combine all ingredients for marinade. Place chicken in dish, cover with marinade and refrigerate overnight. Grill over medium heat 3 to 4 minutes on each side until juices run clear.

Serves 4.

*Chicken can marinate 30 to 45 minutes, but best flavor comes from marinating overnight. Serve with snap peas and angel hair pasta.*

## Apple Glazed Turkey Thighs with Sweet Potatoes

½ cup apple cider or apple juice

2 Tablespoons apple jelly

1 teaspoon cornstarch

¼ teaspoon ground nutmeg

2 turkey thighs (2 lbs.)

Warm cider, apple jelly, cornstarch and nutmeg in a small saucepan. Cook and stir until thickened and bubbly. Remove from heat and set aside.

Remove skin from turkey. Grill on barbecue grill at medium heat and brush with glaze frequently. Turkey should grill 15 to 20 minutes on each side. Turkey is done when juices run clear.

## Sweet Potatoes

12 oz. sweet potatoes, peeled and cut into ½-inch slices

2 medium Granny Smith apples, peeled and cut in wedges

Toss the sweet potatoes and apples together. Tear a large sheet of extra heavy aluminum foil. Place sweet potato mixture in center of foil and drizzle with half of the glaze. Place another sheet of foil to cover and fold both sheets of foil at the edges to make a pillow with the sweet potato mixture inside. Poke a small hole in the middle of the foil for steam release. Grill the foil packet for 30 to 40 minutes along with the turkey.

Cut the turkey meat from the bones and serve with the sweet potatoes.

Serves 4.

## Southwestern Marinated Chicken Breasts

2 Tablespoons fresh orange juice, or frozen concentrate

1 Tablespoon orange or lemon zest, grated

1 Tablespoon white wine vinegar

1 clove garlic, minced

¾ teaspoon dried oregano

¼ teaspoon ground cinnamon

¼ teaspoon cayenne pepper, optional

½ teaspoon ground cumin

1 cup crushed pineapple

½ teaspoon salt, optional

pepper, freshly ground, to taste

8 boneless chicken breasts

To make marinade, mix all ingredients except chicken. Pour over chicken in a glass dish and refrigerate overnight or longer. Remove chicken from marinade and grill, or cover and bake in 325°F oven for 45 minutes or until tender.

Serves 8.

## Tarragon and Garlic Roasted Chicken

6 cloves garlic
6 oz. unsalted butter, softened
2 Tablespoons fresh tarragon or 2 teaspoons dried
finely grated rind of 1 lemon
salt and freshly ground pepper to taste
3½ lbs. roasting chicken, oven ready
fresh tarragon

Crush 4 garlic cloves, then mix with butter, tarragon, lemon rind, salt and pepper. Cut remaining 2 garlic cloves in half.

Put the 4 garlic halves into the cavity of the chicken. With your fingers, peel the breast skin of the chicken away from the meat, being careful not to tear the skin. Spread the butter mixture between the skin and flesh of the chicken. Spread any remaining butter mixture over the outside of the skin, especially the legs. Sprinkle liberally with salt and pepper.

Bake in a tightly covered casserole at 425°F for 1 hour until juices run clear. Serve chicken hot with fresh tarragon as a garnish.

**Variation:**

If desired, a roasting brick may be used. (A roasting brick is a porous casserole with 2 halves.) Soak the brick in cold water for 30 minutes. After soaking, drain the brick, and fill with the chicken. Put the lid on the brick. Set heat for 425°F and bake for 1½ hours. Do not open the oven door during this time.

Rub the inside of the brick with garlic before soaking. This will act as a seal for the brick. Serve directly from the brick for an unusual presentation.

## Chicken Enchiladas

2 lbs. cooked chicken, shredded
1 lb. Monterey Jack cheese, shredded
2 to 4 Tablespoons cumin, to taste
corn tortillas
1 can enchilada sauce
1 cup Monterey Jack cheese for topping
vegetable oil

Combine chicken, 1 pound cheese and cumin. Mix well. Lightly cook each tortilla in hot vegetable oil in a skillet. Cook tortilla approximately 10 seconds, no longer. Use paper towels to blot extra oil from tortilla shells. Make a small line of the chicken and cheese mixture down center of tortilla. Roll. Place seam side down in a baking dish. Continue until chicken mixture is gone. Cover enchiladas with the sauce and 1 cup shredded cheese. Bake at 350°F until cheese on top is melted and bubbly, approximately 30 minutes.

**Serves 4 to 8 depending on size of tortillas.**

*It is best to season to taste with cumin. It's spicy! Serve with Mexican rice, black beans, and a salad. May also be garnished with sour cream.*

## Turkey Grill with Salsa

¼ cup vinegar
2 Tablespoons dry sherry
2 Tablespoons soy sauce
1 teaspoon ground ginger
1 clove garlic, minced
1 teaspoon crushed red pepper
4 turkey breast tenderloin steaks (about 1 lb.)
1 medium tomato, peeled, seeded and chopped
1 small onion
¼ cup green pepper, chopped
1 Tablespoon cilantro, chopped
2 Tablespoons marinade

Combine vinegar, sherry, soy sauce, ginger, garlic, and red pepper in a small bowl for marinade. Reserve 4 tablespoons of the marinade. Set aside.

Place turkey in a rectangular baking dish and pour all but the reserved marinade over the turkey. Seal the dish and refrigerate 6 to 24 hours.

In a small mixing bowl, combine the salsa ingredients and 2 tablespoons of the reserved marinade (do not use the mixture in which the turkey was marinated). Cover and chill salsa until serving time.

Grill over medium heat, until turkey is tender and the juices run clear (6 to 8 minutes each side) basting occasionally with the reserved marinade. Remove from the grill and serve with the salsa.

**Serves 4.**

*Serve with warm tortillas.*

## Cornish Hens with Marinade

½ cup vegetable oil
⅓ cup wine vinegar
1 clove garlic, crushed
¼ teaspoon ginger
1 small onion, finely chopped
⅔ cup honey
⅔ cup soy sauce
4 to 6 Cornish hens

Mix all ingredients except hens. Set aside ¼ cup marinade; store in refrigerator for basting. Pour remaining marinade over hens and marinate in refrigerator for 24 hours. Place hens in baking pan and bake uncovered at 400°F for 15 minutes. Cover with foil and bake at 250°F for about 2 hours. Baste with reserved marinade occasionally. Can be served whole or halved for presentation.

Hens can marinate longer than 24 hours if desired and are delicious when butterflied and cooked on the grill.

**Serves 8 to 12.**

*This dish goes well with a fruity white wine. A long grain or wild grain rice makes a complementary side.*

## Turkey Stroganoff

1 cup turkey or chicken stock
1 green pepper, diced
½ lb. fresh mushrooms, sliced
8 Tablespoons butter, divided
½ cup flour
1 cup cream
1 cup milk
1½ teaspoons salt
3 to 4 cups turkey, diced
3 Tablespoons pimento
½ cup sherry

Cook diced green pepper in stock. Saute mushrooms in 2 tablespoons butter. Make cream sauce with 6 tablespoons butter, flour, cream and milk. Add salt, turkey, mushrooms, pimento, green pepper and stock and heat to blend flavors. Add sherry before serving, but do not boil after sherry is added. Serve over toast points, rice or noodles.

Serves 4.

## Tarragon Chicken Basting Sauce

½ cup unsalted butter, melted
½ cup grated Parmesan cheese
3 Tablespoons dried tarragon
salt and pepper to taste

Mix together butter, parmesan cheese and tarragon and baste chicken with mixture. Grill chicken on indoor or outdoor grill, basting often until done.

## Herbed Chicken

1 sweet red pepper
1 clove garlic
½ onion, chopped
handful of fresh basil
1 cup red burgundy wine
16 oz. can tomatoes, diced
2 Tablespoons fresh rosemary
1 Tablespoon fresh sage
1 Tablespoon fresh thyme
6 chicken breasts, skinless and boneless
1 cup sliced mushrooms

Blister red pepper by broiling for 5 minutes. Peel. Seal in plastic bag while preparing rest of recipe. Place garlic, onion, and basil in food processor and process. Add wine, tomatoes and herbs. Process again. Place chicken breasts in roasting pan. Pour sauce on top. Sprinkle on chopped red pepper and mushrooms. Bake at 350°F for 30 to 40 minutes or until chicken is done.

Serves 6.

## Breast of Chicken With Mustard Sauce

4 skinless, boneless chicken breast halves (about 1½ lbs.)
salt and pepper to taste
2 Tablespoons vegetable oil
12 baby carrots, trimmed and peeled
½ lb. small mushrooms
2 Tablespoons shallots, chopped
1 teaspoon garlic, finely chopped
1 Tablespoon flour
½ cup dry white wine
1 cup fresh or canned chicken broth
1 Tablespoon tomato paste
1 bay leaf
3 sprigs fresh thyme or 1 teaspoon dried thyme
2 Tablespoons Dijon mustard
2 Tablespoons finely chopped parsley

Sprinkle chicken breasts with salt and pepper. Heat oil in skillet over medium high heat and add chicken. Cook until golden brown, about 4 minutes, and turn. Cook and brown 4 more minutes. Pour off fat from skillet and add carrots, mushrooms, shallots and garlic. Continue cooking and stirring about 3 minutes. Sprinkle the flour over chicken and vegetables, stirring to distribute the flour evenly. Add wine and stir. Add the broth, tomato paste, bay leaf, thyme and mustard. Blend well. Cover and simmer for 10 minutes. Uncover for 5 minutes to reduce the sauce. Remove the bay leaf. Sprinkle with parsley and serve.

**Serves 4.**

## Sauteed Chicken Bonne Femme

2 egg yolks
2 Tablespoons dry white wine
1 Tablespoon lemon juice
½ cup butter
¼ teaspoon salt
¼ teaspoon tarragon
dash cayenne pepper
2 whole large chicken breasts, skinned, boned and split
2 Tablespoons butter
½ lb. medium mushrooms, thinly sliced
1 medium carrot, cut into thin coins

Beat egg yolks, white wine and lemon juice in small, heavy saucepan over low heat. Beat constantly with wire whisk until slightly thickened. Add ½ cup butter one tablespoon at a time, beating constantly with wire whisk until butter is melted and mixture is thickened. Stir in salt, tarragon and cayenne pepper. Keep sauce warm. Cook chicken breasts in 2 tablespoons hot butter in 12-inch skillet over medium-high heat until tender and browned on both sides, about 10 minutes. Remove chicken to warm platter with a spatula. Cook sliced mushrooms and carrot strips in drippings remaining in skillet, over medium heat until tender, stirring mixture frequently. Pour sauce over chicken. Top with vegetable mixture.

**Serves 4.**

*Vegetables contrast rich sauce for a perfect balance your guests will appreciate.*

## Crab Stuffed Chicken Breasts

4 chicken breasts, halved, skinned and boned
¼ cup margarine
½ cup green onions, thinly sliced
¼ lb. mushrooms, thinly sliced
¼ teaspoon dried thyme
3 Tablespoons flour
½ cup chicken broth
½ cup milk
½ cup dry white wine
¼ teaspoon salt
¼ teaspoon garlic salt
¼ teaspoon white pepper
8 oz. fresh crab or 6½ oz. can, drained
⅓ cup parsley, finely chopped
½ cup fine, dry bread crumbs
1 cup Swiss cheese, shredded

reheat oven to 400°F.

Pound chicken between waxed paper until ¼-inch thick. In margarine, saute onions and mushrooms. Stir in thyme and flour. Blend in broth, milk, and wine. Cook and stir until thickened. Season to taste with salt, garlic salt and white pepper. Stir together ¼ cup of sauce with crab, parsley, and bread crumbs. Spoon onto each chicken breast, dividing mixture evenly. Roll and place seam down in pan. (May use toothpick.) Pour remaining sauce over stuffed breasts. Sprinkle with cheese. Cover and bake 40 minutes.

**Serves 8.**

## Chicken Cordon Bleu

2 Tablespoons melted butter
4 chicken breasts, boneless and skinless
salt and pepper to taste
seasoned salt (optional)
4 long slices Swiss cheese
4 long slices ham
1 Tablespoons milk
seasoned bread crumbs
2½ Tablespoons water
¼ cup dry white wine

reheat oven to 350°F.

Lightly grease baking pan with butter. Lightly pat chicken breasts flat. Season with salt, pepper and a dash of seasoned salt, if desired. Place sliced cheese and ham on top of chicken. Roll up and secure with toothpicks. Brush chicken breasts with milk. Roll in seasoned bread crumbs. Place chicken breasts, not touching each other, in pan. Bake 40 minutes or until tender.

Stir water and wine together with pan drippings and boil in small saucepan. Spoon over chicken breast rolls before serving.

**Serves 4.**

*An easy recipe for an elegant dinner.*

## Black Tie Chicken

3 whole chicken breasts, cut into chunks
¾ lb. mushrooms, sliced thickly
4 green onions, chopped
¼ to ½ teaspoon garlic salt
¼ to ½ teaspoon seasoned salt
1½ teaspoon chervil
1 Tablespoon flour
¼ cup white wine
¼ cup fresh parsley, chopped
1 cup cream
4 Tablespoons Romano cheese
2 cups cooked pasta bows

Saute chicken breasts in a little olive oil until browned. Add mushrooms and green onions. Saute for one minute. Add garlic salt, seasoned salt, chervil and flour. Coat well. Add wine, parsley, cream and Romano cheese. Cook down until thickened. Add cooked bows after liquid.

**Serves 4.**

*Serve with French bread and green salad with vinaigrette dressing.*

## Orange Roast Pheasant

1 orange
2½ lbs. pheasant, dressed
salt and freshly ground pepper to taste
½ teaspoon dried tarragon
¼ teaspoon paprika
3 cloves garlic
3 sprigs fresh parsley
4 Tablespoons unsalted butter, room temperature
4 slices bacon
1 cup dry white wine
½ cup golden raisins

Preheat oven to 350°F.

Cut orange in half. Squeeze the juice from half of the orange into the cavity of the pheasant and over the skin. Rub the bird inside and out with salt, pepper, tarragon and paprika. Cut in half the remaining orange half and place, along with the garlic and parsley, in the cavity of the bird.

Spread the butter over the breast and place the bird breast side up, in a shallow roasting pan. Lay the bacon across the bird to cover. Cover the pheasant with aluminum foil and bake for 45 minutes.

Heat the wine in a small saucepan over high heat to the boiling point. Add the raisins, remove from the heat and let stand while the pheasant cooks.

Remove the foil and pour the wine and raisins over the pheasant. Bake uncovered, basting frequently, until the juices run clear when a thigh is pierced with a sharp skewer. This may take 35 to 45 minutes.

Remove the pheasant with the bacon to a small serving platter. Spoon some raisin sauce over the top and serve the remaining sauce as a side accompaniment.

**Serves 2.**

## Pollo Romano

4 boneless chicken breasts
4 Tablespoons olive oil
4 Tablespoons butter
4 Tablespoons proscuitto, finely chopped
pinch of fresh rosemary
2 cups mushrooms, sliced
4 baby artichokes, cut in half
4 cups Marsala wine
4 cups chicken stock
salt and pepper to taste
pinch of fresh basil
1 cup peas, frozen or fresh

Saute chicken breast in the oil until lightly browned. Remove chicken and drain oil.

In the same skillet, melt the butter, then add the prosciutto, rosemary, mushrooms, artichoke, Marsala and chicken stock. Season with salt, pepper and basil and bring to a rolling simmer for 15 minutes, until sauce is thick and reduced by half. Add peas and cook 2 minutes. Return chicken to pan to warm through in the sauce and serve.

**Serves 4.**

## Chicken Scarparella

½ lb. sweet Italian sausage
4 chicken breasts, boneless and skinless
flour for dusting
1 Tablespoon olive oil
2 teaspoons shallots, sliced
½ cup sherry
½ cup chablis
2 Tablespoons red wine vinegar
2 cups chicken stock
10 pepperoncinis
10 black olives
2 bay leaves
1 Tablespoon fresh Italian parsley, chopped
½ teaspoon salt
freshly ground black pepper to taste
6 to 8 fresh rosemary leaves
3 Tablespoons unsalted butter
6 red cherry peppers, cut in half, optional

Saute the sausage until cooked through. Cut into ¼-inch rounds. Dust chicken breasts with flour and saute in olive oil over medium-high heat until cooked through, about 10 minutes. Remove chicken from pan. Saute the shallots in pan drippings. Stir in the sherry, chablis and vinegar, scraping any bits from bottom of pan. Add the stock, pepperoncinis, olives, bay leaves, parsley, salt and pepper, and simmer for 10 minutes. When ready to serve, add the rosemary leaves. Whisk in butter. Add the cherry peppers, if desired. Warm the chicken in the sauce before serving.

**Serves 4.**

## Arroz Con Pollo

2 8 oz. chicken breasts
1 Tablespoon olive oil, divided
salt and pepper to taste
½ medium onion, diced
1 medium green pepper, diced
3 medium garlic cloves, crushed
½ cup long grain rice
1 cup chicken stock
½ teaspoon saffron strands
¼ cup sherry
4 plum tomatoes, diced
½ cup frozen tiny peas
8 pitted green olives, halved

Preheat oven to 350°F.

Heat ½ tablespoon oil in non-stick skillet. Cut chicken into small pieces and brown on both sides, about 2 minutes per side. Remove chicken and season with salt and pepper. Add remaining ½ tablespoon oil to pan and saute onions, without browning, about 5 minutes. Add green pepper and garlic and saute 5 minutes more. Place rice in a strainer and rinse under cold water. Drain well and add to skillet. Saute 1 minute. Add chicken stock and saffron. Bring to a simmer and add sherry and tomatoes. Cover and simmer 5 minutes. Return chicken to skillet and simmer, covered for 15 minutes. Add peas and olives and cook 2 minutes. Taste for seasoning and add more salt and pepper, if desired.

Serves 2.

## Pasta Primavera With Chicken

2 Tablespoons lemon juice
1 Tablespoon olive oil
1 clove garlic, finely chopped
1 teaspoon dried basil, crumbled
½ teaspoon oregano, crumbled
8 oz. skinless, boneless chicken breasts, cut into 1-inch pieces
12 oz. fresh asparagus, trimmed and cut into ½-inch pieces
1 sweet yellow pepper, cored, seeded and cut into strips
2 carrots, pared and cut into ½-inch pieces
¼ cup chicken broth, divided
14½ oz. can stewed tomatoes
2 cups hot cooked rotini pasta (4 oz. uncooked)
2 Tablespoons shredded Parmesan cheese, optional

Combine lemon juice, oil, garlic, basil and oregano in medium-sized bowl. Add chicken. Cover and marinate in refrigerator 10 minutes. Heat nonstick Dutch oven over medium-high heat until hot. Add chicken and marinade and cook, stirring occasionally until cooked through, about 5 minutes. Remove chicken with slotted spoon and set aside. Add asparagus, yellow pepper and carrot to Dutch oven. Add half the chicken broth. Cook, stirring occasionally, until vegetables are crisp-tender, about 8 minutes. Add remaining chicken broth as needed to prevent vegetables from sticking. Add stewed tomatoes and chicken. Gently heat through, about 2 minutes. Toss vegetable mixture with pasta. Sprinkle with Parmesan cheese, if desired.

Serves 4.

*Use tri-colored rotini for a festive look.*

## Chicken and Wild Rice Casserole

6 to 8 chicken breasts
1 cup water
1 cup dry sherry
1½ teaspoons salt
½ heaping teaspoon curry powder
1 medium onion, sliced
1 rib celery, sliced
1 lb. fresh mushrooms
¼ cup butter or margarine
2 6 oz. packages long grain and wild rice with seasonings
1 cup sour cream
2 Tablespoons flour
½ cup milk

Place chicken breasts in a deep kettle; add water, sherry, salt, curry powder, onion and celery. Cover and bring to a boil; reduce heat and simmer for 1 hour. Remove from heat; strain broth. Puree vegetables and add as much as desired to strained broth. This adds flavor to broth. Refrigerate chicken and broth mixture at once, without cooling first.

When chicken is cool, discard skin and bones. Cut meat into bite-sized pieces. Rinse mushrooms and pat dry; slice and saute in butter until golden, about 5 minutes, stirring constantly. (Reserve enough whole caps to garnish top of casserole; they may be sauteed along with the sliced mushrooms.)

Measure chicken broth; use as part of liquid for cooking rice, following directions for firm rice on the package. Combine chicken, mushrooms, and rice in a 3½ quart or 4 quart casserole. Blend sour cream and flour, then milk, and toss with chicken and rice mixture. Arrange reserved mushroom caps in a circle over top of casserole. Cover; refrigerate overnight if desired. To heat, bake covered at 350°F for 15 minutes. The casserole may be completely prepared and frozen ahead of time.

**Serves 8 to 10.**

## Lemon Basil Pasta With Smoked Chicken

1 teaspoon cornstarch
1 Tablespoon water
12 oz. can evaporated skim milk
⅛ teaspoon salt
¼ cup vodka, gin or vermouth
3 strips lemon peel, yellow part only
½ red pepper
1 lb. fettuccine or linguine
⅓ to ½ cup basil leaves, minced
1 Tablespoon grated Parmesan cheese
8 oz. smoked chicken breast, diced

Dissolve cornstarch in water in small bowl. Place milk, salt, vodka, lemon peel and cornstarch mixture in heavy bottomed skillet. Bring to boil. Reduce heat and simmer gently until volume is reduced by a third. Bring water to boil in large pot and blanch pepper for 1 to 2 minutes; remove and mince. Cook and drain pasta. Remove lemon peel from sauce and add pepper, basil, Parmesan cheese, chicken and pasta. Adjust seasoning to taste.

**Serves 4.**

*Serve with extra cheese and basil leaves. This dish doubles as a side dish or main course.*

4 slices bacon, cut into ½-inch pieces
4 rabbit quarters
4 celery stalks, chopped
1 bunch green onions, chopped
1 bay leaf
8 oz. carrots, sliced
2 Tablespoons flour
2 cups chicken stock
salt and freshly ground pepper

## Rabbit Casserole with Sage Dumplings

lace bacon pieces into an ovenproof casserole. Fry for 5 minutes until fat runs. Add rabbit and fry gently, then add celery, green onions, bay leaf and carrots. Sprinkle the flour over the mixture and stir well. Add the stock slowly and bring the dish to a boil, stirring occasionally. Season to taste.

Cover the casserole and cook at 325°F for 1½ hours until rabbit is tender. Make dumplings while rabbit is cooking.

**Serves 4.**

## Dumplings

3 oz. self rising flour (6 Tablespoons)
1½ oz. suet, shredded, or lard, finely chopped
1 teaspoon fresh sage, chopped, or ½ teaspoon dried
salt and freshly ground pepper to taste
2 to 3 Tablespoons water

ombine the flour, suet, sage, salt and pepper. To make a soft dough sprinkle flour mixture with 1 tablespoon cold water and toss lightly with a fork. Repeat, using only as much water as necessary. Start with 1 tablespoon and add more water as needed to form the dough. This dough will be soft, but not sticky. Divide dough into 4 portions and shape into balls.

After rabbit has cooked until tender (1½ hours), take from oven and remove lid. Place dumplings on top of casserole. Cover and return to oven for 20 to 25 minutes, until dumplings have risen and are cooked through.

*Call ahead to have the butcher set aside suet. Request the suet be put through the meat grinder to shred.*

¼ cup Dijon mustard
3 Tablespoons honey
2 teaspoons lemon juice
º cup unflavored bread crumbs
1 to 1½ lbs. boneless chicken
1 Tablespoon vegetable oil
Cajun spice to taste (optional)

## Honey Mustard Chicken

n shallow dish combine mustard, honey and lemon juice. Place bread crumbs in another dish. Roll chicken in honey mixture and then in bread crumbs; place on baking pan lined with aluminum foil. Drizzle evenly with oil and sprinkle with Cajun spice, if desired. Bake in a 375°F oven for 30 to 35 minutes or until fork tender.

**Serves 4.**

## Ginger Chicken with Fruit Salsa

½ cup creamy peanut butter
½ cup hot water
¼ cup chili sauce
¼ cup soy sauce
2 Tablespoons salad oil
2 Tablespoons vinegar
4 cloves garlic, minced
½ teaspoon ginger
¼ teaspoon red pepper
6 boneless chicken breasts (3 lbs.)

ix peanut butter slowly with the hot water in a small mixing bowl. Add chili sauce, soy sauce, salad oil, vinegar, garlic, ginger and red pepper to mixture. Set marinade aside.

Remove skin from chicken, rinse and pat dry. Place chicken in a large bowl and pour marinade into bowl. Cover and refrigerate for 6 to 24 hours, stirring mixture occasionally. Remove chicken from bowl and discard marinade.

## Salsa

1 cup fresh fruit, chopped (peaches, pears, nectarines)
1 cup cucumber, seeded and chopped
1 green onion, thinly sliced
2 Tablespoons parsley or cilantro, chopped
1 Tablespoon sugar
1 Tablespoon salad oil
1 Tablespoon vinegar

ombine all salsa ingredients. Cover and chill for 1 to 2 hours.

Place chicken on a barbecue grill at medium heat. Cover grill and cook chicken 6 to 8 minutes each side until done.

Serves 6.

*Serve chicken with salsa spooned over the top. Serve remaining salsa on the side. Salsa may also be used with other meat and game.*

Family mealtime in the Midwest has traditionally meant meat and potatoes, or some other hearty fare appropriate for feeding farmhands or a hungry suburban family at the end of a hectic day. Emphasis on family mealtime is a long-standing tradition in the Midwest which many families seek to reclaim today.

My mother worked at home raising a family, helping the PTA raise the funds to hire a kindergarten teacher (not supplied by the state) and later leading a Scout troop. Many of my clothes were made by my mother on the sewing machine which occupied our enclosed porch. This room served much like a family room does today. Each evening, a meal was served at 6:00 sharp, our family's regular mealtime. Hungry and ready to eat even before being called to the table, we were summoned by the aroma of the roasting meat taunting us as we tried to concentrate on the homework at hand.

Marinated Roast Pork with its tangy Currant Glaze accompanied by pungent Apple Horseradish Sauce was by far one of our favorite meals.

# Meats & Main Dishes

## Marinated Roast Pork

1 Tablespoon Dijon mustard
¼ teaspoon pepper
3 lb. boneless single pork tenderloin
½ teaspoon salt
¼ teaspoon crushed dry leaf thyme
½ cup plus 1 Tablespoon tawny port wine
¼ cup soy sauce
2 teaspoons ground ginger
3 cloves garlic, minced
10 oz. jar red currant jelly
1 Tablespoon soy sauce
2 Tablespoons lemon juice

emove any excess fat from the pork roast. Mix mustard, salt, pepper and thyme and rub over pork roast outer surface. Place pork roast in self sealing plastic bag.

Combine ½ cup wine, soy sauce, ground ginger and garlic. Pour marinade over the roast and seal the bag then refrigerate 8 hours or more; turning the bag occasionally.

Transfer roast to 13x9-inch roasting pan. Reserve marinade. Insert meat thermometer. Cover loosely with aluminum foil, roast at 325°F for 1 hour. Uncover and roast 1½ to 2 hours or until thermometer reads 155 degrees for medium or 165 degrees for well done. Baste frequently with reserved marinade.

Heat jelly, soy sauce, 1 tablespoon wine, and lemon juice in a small pan to boiling. Boil 5 minutes stirring constantly. Pour jelly mixture over roasted meat and let stand at room temperature for 30 minutes. Baste pork with jelly mixture several times. Remove pork to serving platter and slice into serving pieces. Strain jelly from pan and pour over sliced meat. Serve with Apple Horseradish Sauce.

Serves 8.

## Apple Horseradish Sauce

4 tart apples (MacIntosh or Granny Smith)
½ cup water
2 Tablespoons fresh lemon juice
1 3-inch long vanilla bean, split
1 cinnamon stick
½ cup sugar
3 Tablespoons horseradish sauce

eel, core and quarter apples. Cook apples, water, lemon juice, vanilla bean, cinnamon stick and sugar in a saucepan, over medium heat until apples turn to sauce, about 20 minutes.

Remove vanilla bean and cinnamon stick and discard. Add horseradish and stir. Cover and chill in refrigerator.

This page generously sponsored by Charlotte Morrow.

## Tenderloin with Red Wine

1 cup water
½ teaspoon minced onion
2 Tablespoons beef bouillon
¼ teaspoon thyme
½ teaspoon garlic salt
1 Tablespoon kitchen bouquet
4 to 5 lbs. beef tenderloin

ie tenderloin in 3 places with kitchen twine. Combine above ingredients, pour over meat that has been placed in a deep bowl. Marinate 2 to 4 hours or overnight. When ready to cook, remove from marinade (save marinade). Preheat skillet 5 minutes on high. Brown meat on both sides in 2 tablespoons oil. Cook 6 to 7 minutes per pound depending on desired doneness, meat thermometer will read 140 to 160°F for rare; 160 to 170°F for medium; 170 to 175°F for well done. Turn frequently while cooking.

**Serves 8 to 12.**

## Mushroom Sauce

½ lb. fresh mushrooms
reserved marinade
2 Tablespoons burgundy wine
3 Tablespoons cornstarch
¼ cup water

icrowave ½ pound fresh mushrooms 2 minutes covered, on high. Remove from microwave and add the reserved marinade, add burgundy wine, cook 2 minutes on high. Add cornstarch mixed with ¼ cup water. Stir well. Mix into marinade and return to microwave. Cook for 2 minutes or until thickened.

## Sauteed Pork and Apples With Mustard Sauce

½ cup plus 1 Tablespoon flour
salt and pepper to taste
4 lean boneless pork chops (approximately 3 oz. each)
3 Tablespoons butter, divided
2 Tablespoons vegetable oil
2 apples, pared, cored and sliced
2 Tablespoons onion, minced
1 cup apple juice
½ cup dry white wine
½ cup plain yogurt
2 Tablespoons Dijon mustard
¼ teaspoon dried thyme, crushed

ombine ½ cup flour with salt and pepper; mix well. Dredge pork chops in seasoned flour. In non-stick skillet, saute chops in 2 tablespoons butter and oil until browned on both sides and juices run clear. Remove to heated platter. Add remaining butter to skillet. Add apples and onions then saute until tender. Remove apples to a heated platter. Add apple juice and wine to skillet then simmer 5 minutes. In bowl combine yogurt, mustard, remaining tablespoon flour and thyme. Stir into apple juice mixture and simmer 5 minutes until smooth. Stir in salt and pepper. To serve, spoon sauce over chops and apples.

**Serves 4.**

## Magnificent Midwest Meat Loaf

¾ cup onion, minced
¾ cup green onion, minced
½ cup celery, minced
½ cup carrot, minced
¼ cup green pepper, minced
¼ cup sweet red pepper, minced
2 Tablespoons garlic, minced
3 Tablespoons butter or margarine
1 teaspoon salt
¼ teaspoon cayenne pepper
1 teaspoon black pepper
½ teaspoon white pepper
½ teaspoon ground cumin
½ teaspoon ground nutmeg
½ cup half and half
½ cup ketchup
1½ lbs. lean ground round
½ lb. ground pork
3 eggs, beaten
¾ cup dry bread crumbs

aute onion, green onion, celery, carrot, green pepper, red pepper and garlic in butter or margarine until vegetables are soft and liquid is absorbed. Cool and set aside.

Combine salt, cayenne pepper, black pepper, white pepper, cumin and nutmeg and add to vegetable mixture. Stir in half and half, ketchup, ground beef, ground pork, eggs and bread crumbs, mix well.

Form into loaf and place in a greased 13x9-inch pan or 9x5-inch loaf pan. Bake at 350°F 50 to 60 minutes or until meat thermometer registers 170°F . Let stand 10 minutes. Pour off excess fat. Slice and serve with sauce.

**Serves 6 to 8.**

## Sauce

4 shallots, minced
2 Tablespoons butter or margarine
1 sprig thyme
1 bay leaf
dash crushed black pepper
1 cup dry white wine
1 cup beef or veal stock
1 cup chicken stock
salt and pepper to taste

aute shallots in 1 tablespoon butter or margarine with thyme, bay leaf and black pepper. Add white wine and simmer over high heat until reduced to glaze. Add beef or veal stock and chicken stock and simmer over high heat until reduced by ⅓ to ½. Stir in remaining 1 tablespoon butter or margarine and season to taste with salt and pepper. Discard bay leaf and thyme sprig. Serve with meat loaf.

**Makes 1 cup.**

## Stuffed Pork Chops a L'Orange

2 medium oranges
2 Tablespoons honey
1 Tablespoon Dijon mustard
2 Tablespoons orange marmalade
2 Tablespoons vinegar
¾ cup chicken broth
½ cup acini de pepe
4 green onions, thinly sliced
¼ teaspoon ground ginger
½ cup celery, finely chopped
4 pork loin rib chops, 1¼ inches thick

Peel and section oranges, coarsely chop and reserve juices. In a small saucepan blend honey and mustard. Stir in orange marmalade and vinegar. Heat and stir mixture till the marmalade is completely melted. Remove from heat and set aside.

In a separate saucepan bring chicken broth to boiling; add acini de pepe, sliced green onion, and ground ginger. Reduce heat and simmer uncovered for 5 minutes or until acini de pepe is tender. Remove from heat and fold in orange sections, 2 tablespoons reserved juice, 2 tablespoons of the honey mixture and celery.

Spoon 2 to 3 tablespoons stuffing into a pocket made in each pork chop. Fasten pockets with a wooden pick. Spoon remaining stuffing onto a large sheet of foil and fold into a pouch. Set pouch aside.

Place stuffed pork chops on grill over a drip pan rather than directly over the coals. Grill for 15 minutes. Turn chops and brush with some of the honey mixture. Place foil of stuffing on grill next to chops and continue to grill 15 to 20 minutes more until the chops are done. Brush chops with remaining honey mixture before serving. Serve with extra stuffing.

**Serves 4.**

## Favorite Barbecued Beef Brisket

7 lbs. beef brisket, trimmed
1 teaspoon dry mustard
2 teaspoons onion salt
1 Tablespoon celery salt
1 teaspoon garlic salt
2 Tablespoons Worcestershire sauce
1½ Tablespoons liquid smoke

*Barbecue Sauce:*
1 cup ketchup
¼ cup Worcestershire sauce
1 teaspoon chili powder
½ cup water
¼ cup vinegar
¼ cup lemon juice
1 teaspoon celery seed
1 cup brown sugar

Rub brisket with onion, celery, dry mustard and garlic salts and let stand for about 30 minutes. Place in a roaster and pour Worcestershire sauce and liquid smoke over surface of roast. Cover and refrigerate several hours.

Drain off marinade, wrap brisket, fatty side up, in heavy duty aluminum foil and seal. Bake 5 hours at 300°F. Allow to cool. Slice thinly across the grain, place in a baking dish, cover with barbecue sauce and bake 20 minutes at 325°F.

**Serves 10 to 12.**

**Sauce:**

Combine all ingredients and simmer 20 minutes over medium heat. Yields 1 quart.

*This sauce is good to barbecue any kind of meat.*

## Country Style Eggplant Parmesan

2 to 3 Tablespoons olive oil
2 cups onion, chopped
1 bell pepper, diced
2 teaspoons basil
1 teaspoon oregano
1 teaspoon thyme
1½ teaspoons salt
16 oz. can tomatoes, diced
6 oz. can tomato paste
1 teaspoon sugar
pepper to taste
5 cloves garlic, minced
2 medium eggplants
2 cups bread crumbs
1 teaspoon basil
½ teaspoon thyme
½ teaspoon oregano
¾ cup milk
1 lb. mozzarella cheese, grated
½ cup Parmesan cheese, grated
2 teaspoons basil

Preheat oven to 375°F.

Saute onion, bell pepper, basil, oregano, thyme, and salt in olive oil until onion is tender. Add tomatoes, tomato paste, sugar, black pepper and garlic. Bring to a boil, then simmer for 30 to 40 minutes.

Cut eggplant into ½-inch thick slices. Combine bread crumbs with 1 teaspoon basil, ½ teaspoon thyme and ½ teaspoon oregano. Dip slices of eggplant into milk then into bread crumb mixture until each slice is well coated. Place slices on baking sheet and bake at 375°F for 25 minutes. Remove from the oven. Ladle ½ cup of sauce into a 9x13x2-inch pan. Arrange layers of eggplant and mozzarella cheese over sauce. Repeat process until all ingredients are used. Sprinkle top with Parmesan cheese and 2 teaspoons of basil. Bake uncovered for 40 minutes until it bubbles around the edges. Let set prior to serving.

**Serves 8.**

## Boned Leg of Lamb

8 lb. leg of lamb, boned and rolled
(save the bones for use as a rack)
1 to 1½ teaspoons salt
1 Tablespoon dry mustard
1 teaspoon rosemary
½ teaspoon pepper
2 Tablespoons butter
2 leeks, sliced
4 carrots, sliced
1 cup celery, chopped
2 cloves garlic, sliced
2 Tablespoons parsley, minced
2 cups dry white wine
2 cups water

ombine salt, dry mustard, rosemary and pepper. Rub into rolled leg after excess fat has been trimmed from the leg. Saute vegetables, garlic and parsley in butter. Put lamb bones in shallow pan, spread sauted vegetables over bones reserving parsley butter. Pour half of wine and water over vegetables and bones. Place roast on top of bone rack and vegetables. Pour parsley butter over lamb. Roast at 325°F until meat thermometer reads 175 degrees for rarer meat to 180 degrees for more well done meat. Adding remaining water and wine as needed while cooking. Remove to hot platter and cover with foil. Strain juices from pan, discarding vegetables, skim off fat and make gravy.

**Serves 6 to 8.**

## Beef Stroganoff

7 lbs. top sirloin, sliced in strips
4 lbs. mushrooms, sliced
4 large onions, thinly sliced
4 cloves garlic, crushed
2 Tablespoons prepared mustard
2 to 3 cans consomme
¾ cup madeira wine
12 oz. can tomato paste
4 cups sour cream
1 Tablespoon Worcestershire sauce
½ fresh lemon, juiced
8 to 12 Tablespoons butter
flour
seasoned salt and pepper to taste

Combine flour with salt and pepper. Roll meat in mixture. Preheat 4 tablespoons butter in pan. Add meat turning to brown all sides. Add 3 more tablespoons butter and saute onion and garlic until soft. Add mushrooms and saute until just tender. May use more butter if needed for sauteing. Combine tomato paste, mustard, madeira, Worcestershire sauce, 2 cans consomme and 1 cup sour cream. Mix with meat mixture. Heat over low temperature until heated through. A few hours prior to serving combine 3 cups sour cream and 2 cans consomme. Add to meat mixture as needed, should not be too thin.

Serves 15.

## Sweet and Sour Chops

4 boneless pork chops, ½- to ¾-inch thick, about 1½ lbs.
1 Tablespoon oil
1 clove garlic
2 teaspoons oil
4 Tablespoons dry sherry or broth
4 Tablespoons brown sugar
4 Tablespoons soy sauce
¼ teaspoon crushed red pepper
2 teaspoons cornstarch
2 Tablespoons water

Trim pork chops of excess fat. Heat oil in skillet. Brown chops on both sides. Remove and add a little more oil if needed. Saute garlic for a minute, being careful not to burn. In a separate bowl combine oil, sherry or broth, soy sauce, brown sugar and red pepper. Place chops in skillet. Pour sauce over them. Cover tightly. Simmer over low heat until chops are tender and cooked through, 30 to 35 minutes. Add a little water, 1 to 2 tablespoons, if needed to keep sauce from cooking down too much. Turn once. Remove chops to warmed platter. Stir in cornstarch dissolved in water. Cook until thickened. Pour over chops and serve.

Serves 4.

*Good served with thin spaghetti or noodles tossed with butter.*

# Vegetable Lasagna

*Vegetable Sauce:*

2 small zucchini, quartered

½ medium green pepper, quartered

1 small onion, quartered

16 oz. can pasta style stewed tomatoes, drained

2 cloves garlic, minced

8 oz. can tomato sauce

1 teaspoon dried basil

1 teaspoon dried oregano

¼ teaspoon white pepper

¼ teaspoon fennel seed

*Filling:*

1 large egg

1 Tablespoon fresh parsley, chopped

15 oz. carton ricotta cheese

¼ cup Romano cheese

1 Tablespoon Romano cheese

vegetable oil spray

3 uncooked lasagna noodles

½ cup mozzarella cheese, shredded

To prepare sauce:

Place the zucchini, pepper and onion in bowl of food processor; pulse for 10 seconds, just until coarsely chopped. Transfer to a 2 quart saucepan; add drained tomatoes, garlic and tomato sauce. Heat to boiling; reduce heat and simmer, uncovered, until vegetables are tender and most liquid has evaporated, 10 to 12 minutes. Blend in basil, oregano, white pepper and fennel seed; set aside.

Filling:

Whisk the egg until foamy in a medium mixing bowl; combine with parsley, ricotta and ¼ cup Romano cheese. Set aside.

Preheat oven to 350°F; position rack in center of oven. Coat a 10x6-inch baking dish with vegetable oil spray; wipe lightly with paper towel. Spread ⅓ of the vegetable sauce over bottom of dish. Break noodles in half and place crosswise in a single layer over sauce. Spread another ⅓ of the sauce over noodles and top with half of the cheese mixture. Layer with remaining sauce and cheese mixture.

Cover casserole tightly with foil and bake for 1 hour or until sauce is hot and bubbly. Remove foil.

Combine mozzarella and 1 tablespoon Romano; sprinkle over top of lasagna. Bake, uncovered, until cheese is bubbly and slightly browned, 10 to 15 minutes. Allow lasagna to rest 10 minutes before serving.

Serves 6.

*Great made with spinach lasagna noodles.*

## Margarita Beef with Orange Salsa

1½ lb. flank steak, cut 1-inch thick
⅔ cup frozen orange juice concentrate, thawed
½ cup tequila
⅓ cup fresh lime juice
2 Tablespoons extra virgin olive oil
2 Tablespoons fresh ginger, chopped
2 medium cloves garlic, crushed
1 teaspoon salt
1 teaspoon dried oregano
¼ teaspoon red pepper flakes
cilantro springs and lime wedges for garnish

Combine orange juice concentrate, tequila, lime juice, oil, ginger, garlic, salt, oregano and red pepper. Place steak in a self sealing plastic bag; add marinade, turning to coat. Close bag securely and marinate in refrigerator 4 hours to overnight.

Remove steak from bag and discard marinade. Grill steak over medium coals for 22 to 26 minutes for medium rare. Remove steak to carving board; let stand 10 minutes. Carve steak crosswise into thin slices; arrange on serving platter. Garnish with cilantro and lime. Serve with Orange Salsa.

Serves 4 to 6.

## Orange Salsa

2 small oranges, peeled and cut into ½-inch pieces
1 small red or white onion, chopped
1 jalapeno pepper, finely chopped
¼ cup fresh cilantro, chopped
2 to 3 Tablespoons fresh lime juice
2 Tablespoons olive oil
½ teaspoon salt
½ teaspoon oregano leaves

Combine all ingredients in a non-metallic bowl and refrigerate at least 1 hour to allow flavors to develop.

*Great for summertime entertaining!*

## Roast Ham with Apricot-Pecan Stuffing

10 to 12 lb. fully cooked whole ham, boned
½ lb. ham, ground
½ cup dried apricots, coarsely chopped
1½ cups pecans or walnuts, chopped
8½ oz. can crushed pineapple, undrained
1 teaspoon dried thyme leaves
½ cup fresh white bread crumbs
¼ cup light brown sugar
1 Tablespoon Dijon mustard
2 egg whites
1 cup apple juice
1 cup light brown sugar, packed
1 cup grated fresh white bread crumbs

Have butcher bone ham to make cavity for stuffing. Also ask to have about ½ pound lean ham removed from cavity and ground—you'll need 1 cup ground ham for stuffing.

Wipe ham with damp paper towels. Soak apricots in warm water to cover ½ hour, drain well.

Combine ground ham with apricots, nuts, pineapple, thyme, ½ cup bread crumbs, ¼ cup brown sugar, mustard and egg whites; mix well. Spoon into cavity in ham; draw opening together with poultry pins, and tie with twine. Place ham on foil-lined, shallow, open roasting pan.

Insert meat thermometer in thickest part of meat. Pour apple juice into bottom of pan; cover pan tightly with foil.

Bake 2 hours. Remove ham from oven; remove foil, then string. Remove rind from ham. Increase oven temperature to 375°F. Pat surface of ham with a mixture of brown sugar and bread crumbs; bake until surface is golden-brown and meat thermometer registers 130°F, about 40 minutes.

**Serves 20.**

## Spinach Mediterranean Pie

½ lb. ground beef
¼ lb. ground sausage
1 medium onion, chopped
15 oz. ricotta cheese
8 oz. mozzarella cheese, shredded
½ teaspoon salt
10 oz. package frozen chopped spinach, thawed and drained
6 to 8 phyllo pastry sheets
¼ cup butter, melted

Cook beef, sausage and onion over medium high heat until juices evaporate and meat is well browned. Drain any remaining fat. Spoon meat mixture into large bowl and stir in ricotta and mozzarella cheeses, salt and spinach; set aside. Place phyllo pastry sheet in a 9-inch pie plate and brush with melted butter. Place another sheet over the first, staggering the corners, and brush with butter. Continue in same manner using up the phyllo sheets. Spoon meat and cheese mixture in the pie plate and fold the edges over until the top is closed. Brush with remaining butter. Bake at 350°F for 1 hour.

**Serves 6.**

## Mexicalli Casserole

1 lb. extra lean hamburger
1 cup cooked red beans
1 small onion, chopped
2 cloves garlic, minced
½ teaspoon cumin
½ teaspoon red pepper flakes, divided
1 teaspoon chili powder
2 8 oz. cans tomato sauce
½ cup salsa
1 jalapeno pepper, chopped
1 cup lowfat plain yogurt
1 cup lowfat cottage cheese
4 oz. can chopped green chilies
8 small flour tortillas
2 cups shredded mozzarella cheese

Cook hamburger and onion until crumbly. Drain well. Add beans, garlic, cumin, red pepper, chili powder, tomato sauce, salsa and jalapeno pepper. In separate bowl mix yogurt, cottage cheese and chilies. Bake tortillas on cookie sheet at 400°F until crisp and golden, approximately 5 minutes on each side. Crush baked tortillas slightly. Put half the tortilla pieces in 2½ quart casserole which as been sprayed with vegetable cooking spray. Add half the meat mixture, half the yogurt mixture and sprinkle with half the cheese. Repeat, ending with the cheese. Bake casserole at 350°F for 30 to 35 minutes or until cheese is bubbling.

Serves 8.

*Simple to make—a real crowd pleaser. Combine with other Mexican favorites for a real fiesta.*

## Mediterranean Veal With Olives

2 Tablespoons flour
salt and pepper to taste
½ lb. veal stewing meat, cut into 1-inch cubes
½ medium onion, diced
2 medium cloves garlic, crushed
¼ teaspoon oregano
1 bay leaf
½ cup white wine
1 cup crushed canned tomatoes
8 black olives, pitted
1 Tablespoon pine nuts

Season flour with salt and pepper and dredge the veal. Spray a skillet with cooking spray and brown veal on all sides, about 3 minutes. Remove veal, add onion and garlic and cook 1 minute. Add the wine, oregano and bay leaf and cook another minute. Add tomatoes and return meat to the pan. Cover and simmer 15 minutes. Add olives and pine nuts. Cook 5 minutes. Remove bay leaf prior to serving.

Serves 2.

*Serve over brown rice, accompanied by a fresh spinach salad.*

## Flank Steak With Spinach

*Steak and Marinade:*

½ lb. flank steak

⅔ cup dry red wine

1 small onion, thinly sliced

2 medium garlic cloves, minced

1 teaspoon dried basil

1 teaspoon dried oregano

¼ teaspoon whole black peppercorns

*Stuffing:*

10oz. package frozen chopped spinach, defrosted, drained

2 cups fresh bread crumbs

1 egg

2 egg whites

¼ teaspoon salt

½ teaspoon dried basil

½ teaspoon dried oregano

4 paper thin slices prosciutto

1 tablespoon olive oil

14½ oz. can stewed tomatoes, pureed

**To prepare the steak and marinade:**

With a small sharp knife open the steak by cutting flaps in the meat that widen and lengthen the rectangle.

Combine the wine, onion, garlic, basil, oregano and peppercorns in a small bowl.

Place the steak in a glass 9x13-inch dish and pour the marinade over the meat. Cover and refrigerate overnight. Turn the meat once during this time.

**To prepare stuffing:**

Press the excess water out of the spinach with your hands and again in paper towels. Fluff the spinach with your fingers. Combine the spinach, bread crumbs, egg, egg whites, salt, basil and oregano in a bowl.

Drain the meat and onions from the marinade, reserving the marinade. Lay the meat out flat and top with the prosciutto. Spread the stuffing on top. Roll, tucking the sides in. Tie in several places with kitchen twine.

In large ovenproof Dutch oven heat the oil over medium-high heat. Brown the meat and onions. Add the pureed tomatoes and marinade. Bring to boil, cover and place in a preheated 325°F oven for 2 hours. Baste occasionally.

Remove the meat from the braising liquid and let rest 5 minutes. Remove the string and slice. Serve the braising liquid as gravy on the side.

**Serves 8.**

## Braised Lamb Shanks

4 lamb shanks

salt and pepper to taste

1½ cups flour

2 15 oz. cans tomato sauce

2 teaspoons prepared mustard

1 Tablespoon lemon juice

⅛ teaspoon Worcestershire sauce

1 teaspoon garlic, crushed

¼ cup red wine, medium dry

3 carrots, cut into 1-inch chunks

2 stalks celery, chopped

1 onion, cut into ¼-inch slices

4 oz. fresh mushrooms

redge lamb shanks with seasoned flour. Broil in oven till brown on both sides. Place in ovenproof large casserole dish. Mix all other ingredients except vegetables. Pour over lamb. Cover and braise at 325°F for 1 hour. Baste ounce or twice during cooking. Remove lamb to separate casserole. Place in refrigerator. When cold, skim off all fat. Place lamb back in casserole with sauce and add carrots, celery, onions. Bake at 325°F for 30 minutes. Last 15 minutes add mushrooms.

**Serves 4.**

## Savory Liver and Onions

3 Tablespoons olive oil, divided
1 large onion, sliced
2 Tablespoons golden raisins
2 Tablespoons balsamic vinegar
¼ teaspoon crushed rosemary
1 Tablespoon sugar
salt and freshly ground black pepper to taste
10 oz. calf's liver
2 Tablespoons pine nuts

eat 2 tablespoons oil in large skillet. Add onions and saute over medium heat until tender and golden brown, about 15 minutes. Stir in raisins, vinegar, rosemary and sugar. Cook over low heat until syrupy, about 1 minute. Season to taste with salt and pepper. Spoon mixture into bowl and keep warm.

Heat remaining 1 tablespoon oil in skillet. Season liver with salt and pepper. Place liver in skillet and saute on both sides until no longer pink, but still tender, 1 to 2 minutes per side.

Place liver slices on dinner plates. Top each portion with half of the onions. Sprinkle with pine nuts.

**Serves 2.**

## Vegetable Enchiladas with Almonds

2 teaspoons olive oil
1 cup onion, minced
½ teaspoon salt
1½ teaspoon cumin
2 teaspoons chili powder
3 cups tomato, chopped
1 cup tomato juice
black pepper to taste
5 cloves garlic, minced
1 Tablespoon olive oil
1 cup onion, minced
6 cups eggplant, peeled and diced
1 teaspoon salt
black pepper to taste
4 cloves garlic, minced
1 red bell pepper, minced
4 oz. can green chilies, chopped
1 cup lightly toasted almonds, minced
¾ cup Monterey Jack cheese, grated
¼ cup cheddar cheese, grated
12 corn tortillas

aute 1 cup onion in 2 tablespoons olive oil over medium heat until tender. Add salt, cumin and chili powder and saute 5 more minutes. Add tomatoes and tomato juice and bring to a boil. Simmer for 30 minutes. Add black pepper and garlic last 10 minutes of simmering. Set aside.

Saute 1 cup onion in 1 tablespoon olive oil until tender, add eggplant, salt, and pepper and mix well. Simmer for 10 minutes over medium heat until eggplant is soft. Add garlic, red bell pepper and green chilies. Cook 5 to 8 more minutes. Remove from heat and stir in almonds and cheeses.

Preheat oven to 350°F. Moisten each tortilla in water. Place approximately ¼ cup of filling in tortilla and roll up. Place in baking dish with flap facing down. Pour tomato sauce mixture over tortillas and bake uncovered for about 30 minutes.

**Serves 7.**

## Cincinnati 5-Way Chili

2 onions, chopped
2 cloves garlic, minced
1 Tablespoon oil
1 lb. lean ground beef
2 teaspoons chili powder
2 teaspoons paprika
1 teaspoon black pepper
½ teaspoon cumin
½ teaspoon allspice
½ teaspoon marjoram
½ teaspoon turmeric
¼ teaspoon nutmeg
¼ teaspoon cinnamon
¼ teaspoon ground cloves
¼ teaspoon ground coriander
¼ teaspoon cardamom
1 cup tomato sauce
1 Tablespoon cocoa powder
1 teaspoon molasses or honey
1 cup canned beef or chicken broth
1 Tablespoon red wine vinegar
salt and pepper to taste
1 lb. cooked spaghetti
15 oz. can kidney beans, heated
onions, chopped
cheddar cheese, grated

Cook the onions and garlic in oil until soft. Add meat and brown. Add all the spices and stir. Add tomato sauce, cocoa, molasses or honey, beef or chicken broth, vinegar, salt and pepper. Cover and simmer over low heat for 1 hour. Add more broth if needed. Serve over cooked spaghetti topped with the kidney beans. Add onions and cheddar cheese for garnish.

**Serves 4 to 6.**

## Lasagna Roma

1 lb. ground beef
½ lb. pork sausage
1 clove garlic, minced
¾ cup onions, chopped
15 oz. can tomato sauce
16 oz. can tomatoes
2 Tablespoons parsley, chopped
2 teaspoons sugar
1 teaspoon salt
¼ teaspoon marjoram
¼ teaspoon thyme
¼ teaspoon oregano
¼ teaspoon basil
8 oz. package lasagna noodles, cooked
1½ lbs. ricotta cheese
1 cup Parmesan, grated
1½ cups mozzarella cheese, cubed

Brown ground beef, pork sausage, garlic and onion in a large saucepan. Drain off all fat. Add tomato sauce, tomatoes, parsley, sugar, salt and herbs. Simmer uncovered 1 hour or until sauce is the consistency of spaghetti sauce.

Heat oven to 350°F. Pour ½ cup sauce into 9x13x2-inch baking pan and alternate with layers of noodles, grated cheese, mozzarella, spoonfuls of ricotta cheese and tomato sauce until all ingredients are used. Top layer should be sauce and grated cheese. Bake for 1 hour.

**Serves 8 to 10.**

*Use fresh herbs for an even more flavorful meat sauce.*

## Szechuan Beef & Vegetables

1 lb. trimmed boneless steak
2 teaspoons sesame oil
1 Tablespoon soy sauce
1 Tablespoon sherry
1½ teaspoon sugar
2 teaspoons cornstarch
2 teaspoons minced ginger, divided
2 cloves garlic, finely chopped, divided
¼ cup chicken stock, divided
3 scallions, cut into 1 inch pieces
¼ lb. fresh mushrooms, sliced
½ lb. snow peas
1 small red pepper, cut into strips
1 medium yellow squash, cut in half, then sliced into ¼-inch slices
½ teaspoon crushed red pepper flakes

Cut steak into thin, ¼-inch strips. In a bowl, combine sesame oil, soy sauce, sherry, sugar, cornstarch, half the ginger and half the garlic. Add steak, toss to combine and set aside.

Heat half the chicken stock in a nonstick skillet over medium-high heat. Add remaining garlic, ginger, scallions and mushrooms. Stir-fry for 1 to 2 minutes. Transfer to a bowl. Add the remaining chicken stock and heat. Add remaining vegetables; stir-fry until crisp-tender, about 3 to 4 minutes. Add to the scallions and mushrooms. Heat the skillet again. Add the steak and pepper flakes. Stir-fry until brown and tender, about 3 to 4 minutes. Return vegetables to the skillet and heat through. Serve with rice.

**Serves 4.**

## Herbed Zucchini and Cheese Casserole

¾ cup bulgur
¾ cup boiling water
2½ Tablespoons vegetable oil
2 cups onions, sliced
4 cloves garlic, minced
6 cups zucchini, thinly sliced
½ teaspoon dried oregano
½ teaspoon dried basil
½ teaspoon dried marjoram
⅛ teaspoon freshly ground black pepper
2 eggs
1 cup feta cheese, grated
1 cup ricotta cheese
¾ cup fresh parsley, chopped
2 Tablespoons tomato paste
1 Tablespoon tamari soy sauce
1 cup Monterey Jack cheese, grated

Pour boiling water over bulgur in a bowl, cover and let sit until all the water has been absorbed and bulgur is soft. Saute onions and garlic in olive oil until onions are tender. Add zucchini, dried herbs and black pepper and continue to saute until zucchini is tender.

In a bowl, lightly beat eggs. Mix in the feta and ricotta cheeses. In a separate bowl combine chopped parsley, tomato paste, and soy sauce. Add to bulgur and mix well.

Oil a 9x9-inch casserole dish. Layer ingredients in casserole dish. Start with bulgur mixture, top with sauted vegetables then feta cheese mixture. Top the casserole with grated Monterey jack cheese and bake at 350°F for 45 minutes. Uncover casserole for the last 15 minutes of baking. Let sit for 5 to 10 minutes prior to serving.

**Serves 6.**

## Stuffed Sirloin with Mushroom Saute

1 medium onion, halved, sliced, and separated into rings
1 clove garlic, minced
1 Tablespoon margarine or butter
¼ teaspoon lemon pepper seasoning
2 lb. boneless beef top sirloin steak, cut 1½ inches thick
1½ cups fresh shiitake mushrooms, sliced
1 tablespoon margarine or butter
¾ cup beef broth
2 teaspoons Worcestershire sauce
2 teaspoons cornstarch
2 Tablespoons dry red wine
1 Tablespoon parsley, snipped

Cook onion and garlic in margarine or butter in a large skillet until onion is tender but not brown. Stir in lemon-pepper seasoning.

Prepare steak by making a horizontal pocket. Spoon onion stuffing into the pocket made in steak. Close pocket by securing with wooden picks.

In same skillet cook mushrooms in margarine or butter till tender. Combine beef broth, Worcestershire sauce, and cornstarch. Carefully add to skillet. Cook and stir till thickened and bubbly then cook and stir 2 more minutes. Add wine and parsley. Keep warm while grilling steak.

Grill steak directly over medium hot coals to desired doneness, turning once. Allow 14 to 18 minutes for rare, 18 to 22 minutes for medium, or 24 to 28 minutes for well done. Serve with mushroom sauce.

**Serves 6 to 8.**

Although the Midwest rivers, lakes, and streams provide opportunities for fishermen to catch a wide variety of fish, a trip up north to fish for salmon was an annual ritual for my father and his fishing buddies. They brought back the usual fish tales, stories of not just the process of catching the fish, but also various methods of preparing them. Salmon grilled over a campfire with olive oil and a little juice from the oranges they brought along for lunches started as a way to make do with the seasonings readily available, and was transformed into the recipe of choice for the salmon brought home to be grilled for friends and family.

Marinated in a blend of orange juice, olive oil, garlic and tarragon, the aroma of salmon on the grill extends an invitation to all the neighbors to enjoy our catch. When prepared on the indoor grill, the fragrant aroma of garlic and orange fill the house, never the odor of fish! Now that salmon is readily available at the seafood counter of local supermarkets, you can enjoy this dish any time of the year.

# Fish & Seafood

## Orange and Herb Salmon

½ Tablespoon olive oil
zest of 1 orange, finely grated
¼ cup orange juice, freshly squeezed
2 teaspoons garlic, minced
2 teaspoons dried tarragon
salt to taste
coarsely ground black pepper to taste
4 salmon steaks
2 teaspoons freshly snipped chives

Combine olive oil, orange zest, orange juice, garlic, tarragon, salt and pepper in medium mixing bowl to make marinade. Place salmon steaks in ovenproof dish. Pour marinade over steaks. Marinate for at least 1 hour at room temperature (or let marinate in refrigerator overnight).

Preheat grill or oven to 450°F. Place steaks directly on the grill; spoon some of the marinade over steaks. If preparing in the oven, fish may be baked in marinade. Bake for 7 to 8 minutes, turning after four minutes or until salmon is just cooked through. Fish should flake easily when tested with a fork. Place on serving platter and sprinkle with chives.

**Serves 4.**

*Halibut steaks, sea bass or snapper may be substituted for salmon.*

This page generously sponsored by Ashner Construction Company.

## Salmon with Wine Sauce

9 oz. Pinot Noir
¼ cup tarragon vinegar
1¼ teaspoons shallots, minced
½ cup unsalted butter, softened and cut into 8 pieces
salt to taste
freshly ground black pepper to taste
olive oil
4 salmon fillets (6 to 7 ounces each)

To prepare sauce, put wine, vinegar and shallots in a small, non-reactive saucepan. Boil until it is reduced to 6 tablespoons. Strain out shallots and return reduced wine mixture to pan. Over low heat, whisk in the butter one piece at a time, waiting until each is fully incorporated before adding another. Add salt and pepper to taste; keep warm. Heat oven to 450°F. Heat a film of oil in a heavy, ovenproof skillet over high heat; add the fish, skin side up, and sear quickly. Turn with a heat resistant spatula and transfer to oven. Bake until fish is no longer pink in the center, 8 to 10 minutes. Salmon can be grilled over a charcoal fire, if desired. To serve, spoon sauce on plates and top with a salmon fillet.

Serves 4.

*A very impressive entree, simple to prepare, elegant to serve. Tossed salad with light dressing, angel hair pasta with Parmesan cheese and lemon water make perfect accompaniments. A light enough meal to be served with dessert.*

## Tuna Nicoise

¼ cup olive oil
1 cup red onion, thinly sliced
2 Tablespoons grated lemon zest
1 to 2 teaspoons lemon juice
4 teaspoons garlic, minced
2 teaspoons capers, rinsed well
6 Calamata olives, pitted and quartered
¾ lb. fresh tuna, grilled and broken into 1-inch chunks
salt to taste
freshly ground black pepper to taste
½ lb. spaghetti, cooked
2 teaspoons fresh parsley, chopped

Heat the olive oil in a saute pan over high heat. Add the onions and cook, stirring frequently, until tender but not soft. Stir in the lemon zest, lemon juice, garlic, capers, olives and tuna. Heat through and season with salt and pepper to taste. Toss the tuna sauce with the cooked spaghetti and sprinkle with parsley.

Serves 2 to 4.

## Red Snapper Veracruz

1 small red bell pepper, diced
1 small yellow bell pepper, diced
1 red onion, diced
1 hot chili pepper, cut into thin rings
1 large tomato, seeded and diced
3 fresh tomatillos, husked and diced
8 green olives, halved
¼ cup fresh cilantro, chopped
3 Tablespoons olive oil
2 to 3 Tablespoons fresh lime juice
1 Tablespoon fresh orange juice
salt to taste
freshly ground black pepper to taste
1 large whole red snapper, dressed (about 4 lbs.)
additional oil to brush fish
cilantro sprigs for garnish

Combine peppers, onion, chili pepper, tomato, tomatillos, olives and cilantro in a medium bowl. Add oil, juices, salt and pepper and mix well. Brush fish lightly with oil. Grill over an indirect fire, turning once, until fish is cooked through, 25 to 30 minutes. Warm vegetable mixture over low heat. To serve, spoon some of the vegetable mixture onto a large platter; top with fish and spoon more vegetables over fish. Garnish with springs of cilantro.

**Serves 4.**

*Can substitute fillets of sole for a lighter meal.*

## Grilling Fish Steaks or Fillets

Clean, oil and preheat grill to prevent fish from sticking. Use a hot fire. Most problems come from too little heat rather than too much. A fire that is too cold will not sear the surface of the fish, so much of the moisture will be lost before the fish is cooked.

Hotter and cooler spots can be arranged on the fire by concentrating or spreading out the coals. This gives flexibility to move each piece around by how it is cooking.

When choosing fish, keep in mind that fillets with the skin on are much easier to cook on the grill. Place fish skin side down first, then turn carefully with a wide metal spatula. Because of its delicacy and tendency to break apart, turn fish only once.

All fish, shrimp, and scallops should be opaque through to the center, but still moist and tender. Be sure to take fish off the grill as soon as it is done. Like meat, fish will continue cooking for a minute or two after it is removed from the grill.

## Crunchy Salmon Loaf

15 oz. can of salmon with juice
1 cup bread crumbs
½ cup celery, chopped
¼ cup green pepper, chopped
½ cup onion, chopped
1 Tablespoon mayonnaise or salad dressing
1 teaspoon dried dill, chopped
2 eggs
paprika for garnish

Mix together all ingredients, except paprika. Spray microwave-safe dish with vegetable cooking spray. Sprinkle with paprika; add salmon mixture. Cook in microwave on high for 6 to 8 minutes, until firm. To serve, turn out onto plate and slice. Serve with dill sauce.

**Serves 6 to 8.**

## Dill Sauce

½ cup sour cream
⅛ cup mayonnaise
½ Tablespoon chives, chopped
½ teaspoon vinegar
⅛ teaspoon salt
¼ teaspoon dried dill
¼ teaspoon grated onion (optional)

Combine all ingredients, mix thoroughly and chill for at least 30 minutes. Store refrigerated in a covered container.

*Light, appealing meal. Serve with flavorful rice dish and a green salad for a healthy brunch or dinner.*

## Oriental Grilled Tuna Steaks

2 inch piece of fresh ginger, peeled and grated
2 large cloves garlic, minced
1 teaspoon honey
½ cup dry white wine
2 Tablespoons soy sauce
¼ teaspoon hot chili oil
¼ cup cooking oil
6 tuna steaks (6 ozs. each and ½ inch to 1 inch thick)

Combine ginger, garlic, honey, wine, soy sauce and oils in a shallow glass dish. Blend well using a whisk. Lay the tuna steaks side by side in the dish and cover with marinade. Cover dish and refrigerate 3 to 4 hours.

Grill steaks on medium-high heat. Do not crowd steaks on the grill. Cook 3 to 5 minutes on each side or until desired doneness. When done, flesh will be pink in center.

**Serves 6.**

## Swordfish in Mango and Black Bean Salsa

1 cup olive oil
½ cup annatto seeds or 1 Tablespoon turmeric
8 swordfish steaks (6 oz. each)
freshly ground black pepper to taste

Heat oil with annatto seeds or turmeric in a heavy saucepan. Bring to a simmer and turn off heat. Allow to steep 30 minutes. If using annatto seeds, strain and reserve seeds for another use. If using turmeric, it will have settled to the bottom; do not disturb it. Arrange fish in a shallow pan. Pour oil mixture over fish and turn to coat. Refrigerate at least one hour, turning the fish from time to time; for best color, refrigerate overnight. Drain fish and grill over moderate heat a total of 10 minutes for each inch of thickness. Serve with Mango and Black Bean Salsa (recipe follows).

Serves 8.

*Flavored oil can be made one day ahead and stored (covered) in refrigerator.*

## Mango and Black Bean Salsa

6 cups mango, diced
2 cups red onion, finely diced
2 cups black beans, cooked
3 to 4 small Scotch bonnet, jalapeno or serrano peppers, seeded
4 Tablespoons cilantro, chopped
4 teaspoons fresh garlic, minced
2 Tablespoons olive oil
4 Tablespoons freshly squeezed lime juice
4 teaspoons cumin
salt to taste
freshly ground black pepper to taste

Gently mix all ingredients together; avoid stirring which mashes the salsa. Refrigerate until serving time. Serve at room temperature, using some salsa on top of the swordfish, the rest on the side.

*Spicy and sweet, Mango and Black Bean Salsa is a sensational twist to top off the swordfish. This salsa may also be used on chicken or pork for a tangy change.*

## Salmon Steaks in Marinade

4 fresh salmon steaks (about 1 inch-thick)

*Fresh oregano-basil marinade:*
⅓ cup fresh oregano, finely minced
⅓ cup fresh basil, finely minced
½ cup olive oil
4 Tablespoons balsamic vinegar
6 Tablespoons fresh lime juice
1 garlic clove, finely minced
pimento, diced (for color)
freshly ground black pepper to taste

Combine marinade ingredients in a bowl. Place the salmon steaks in a shallow baking dish and pour on the marinade to coat both sides of the steaks. Cover dish with plastic wrap and place in the refrigerator for 1 hour.

Grill for 10 to 12 minutes, turning once and basting 2 or 3 times; fish flesh will become a light opaque pink.

**Serves 4.**

*Great for grilling indoors or out.*

## Marinating Fish

Always use a china or glass dish to marinate fish, never metal. Marinate for at least 30 minutes. Basic marinades consist of oil, lemon juice or wine vinegar, pepper and other selected herbs and spices.

**Suggestions for Marinades:**

- Olive oil, chopped chili, thyme, crushed fennel and lemon juice.
- Peanut oil, parsley, chopped green onion, lemon juice, pepper and ginger.
- Olive oil, lemon juice, lemon pepper and onion.
- Olive oil, onion, wine vinegar, garlic and crushed red pepper.
- Olive oil, lemon juice, garlic, cumin, marjoram, thyme and ginger.

## Swordfish Pepper Steak

2 to 3 Tablespoons green peppercorns
2 swordfish steaks
3 Tablespoons butter, divided
½ cup mushrooms, sliced
½ cup tomato, peeled, seeded and diced
3 Tablespoons brandy
4 Tablespoons cream
pinch of fresh rosemary

Preheat oven to 400°F. Press the peppercorns into only one side of the steaks. Melt 2 tablespoons butter in a skillet over medium-high heat. Sear fish, pepper side down in the pan for 2 minutes. (This will make the peppercorns stick to the fish.) If a few peppercorns fall off, leave them in the pan for the sauce. Remove the swordfish to a baking dish, pepper side up, and finish in the oven for 5 to 6 minutes.

While fish is baking, add 1 tablespoon butter to the skillet and saute mushrooms for 1 minute. Add diced tomato and cook for 30 seconds over medium heat. Add brandy and cook for another 30 seconds. Then add cream and rosemary and simmer for 2 to 3 minutes. Remove swordfish to dinner plates and top with sauce.

Serves 2.

## Honey Bar-B-Q Swordfish

¼ cup honey
2 Tablespoons lime juice
2 Tablespoons soy sauce
2 Tablespoons hoisin sauce
¼ cup onion, chopped
2 cloves garlic, minced
1 medium sized jalapeno pepper, seeded and minced
1 teaspoon fresh ginger, minced
1½ lbs. swordfish (about 1 inch thick)
additional lime juice and honey or hoisin sauce

Combine all ingredients, except fish. Marinate fish in the mixture for at least one hour at room temperature or longer in the refrigerator. Oil the grilling surface and cook over hot coals, basting with the marinade several times. Cook about 4 to 5 minutes per side or until fish flakes when tested with a fork. Serve with a mixture of honey and lime juice or extra hoisin sauce.

Serves 4.

*Can substitute tuna steaks for a tasty, light meal.*

## Green Chili Fish

¼ cup mayonnaise
¾ cup non-fat yogurt
1 teaspoon Dijon mustard
1 Tablespoon unbleached flour
2 Tablespoons green chilies, coarsely chopped
2 green onions, sliced
2 Tablespoons red bell pepper, chopped
salt to taste
freshly ground black pepper to taste
1 lb. firm white fish fillets
1 small tomato, sliced

Mix together mayonnaise, yogurt, mustard, flour, chilies, onions and bell pepper. Let stand 30 minutes. Transfer to small baking dish that will hold the fish. Season the fish with salt and pepper and lay in baking dish, spooning sauce over fish. Cover the fish with tomato slices. Bake in a preheated 400°F oven 8 to 10 minutes.

**Serves 4.**

*Serve with Mexican rice and avocado slices or Caesar salad and fresh, crunchy vegetables.*

## Tarragon Shrimp Sauce over Vermicelli

2 Tablespoons unsalted butter
¾ lb. medium shrimp, shelled and deveined
¼ cup shallots, finely chopped
2 cups heavy cream
1 teaspoon dried tarragon
8 sundried tomatoes packed in oil, drained and julienned
salt to taste
freshly ground black pepper to taste
1 lb. vermicelli
2 Tablespoons salt
fresh tarragon, basil or parsley for garnish

Melt butter in large skillet over moderate heat. Add shrimp and stir rapidly until firm and pink, about 3 minutes; do not overcook. Remove shrimp from pan and set aside; lower the heat; add the shallots to the pan. Cover and cook gently until softened but not brown, about 15 minutes. Add the cream, tarragon, sundried tomatoes, salt and pepper. Stir to combine; simmer uncovered for 15 minutes until the sauce is slightly reduced. Return shrimp to the pan and cook only long enough to heat shrimp through. Prepare pasta in boiling, salted water. Scoop pasta on warmed serving plates and spoon the sauce over pasta, dividing the shrimp evenly. Garnish with fresh tarragon, basil or parsley. Serve immediately.

**Serves 4 to 5.**

*This is an easy recipe to prepare in a short time. Have the store steam the shrimp and buy sundried tomatoes already cut julienne for a fast gourmet meal.*

## Mussels Provencal

2 teaspoons olive oil
2 onions, finely chopped
1 red bell pepper, finely chopped
1 yellow bell pepper, finely chopped
¼ teaspoon fennel
1 clove garlic, finely chopped
1 to 2 zucchini, finely chopped
28 oz. can tomatoes, chopped
1 cup dry white wine
2 lbs. mussels

eat oil in large saucepan. Saute onion over medium heat. Add peppers, fennel and garlic to the onions, continue to saute. Add zucchini, tomatoes, wine and mussels. Mix well and cover. Cook about 4 minutes, until mussels open. Serve with crusty bread.

**Serves 2 to 3.**

*Very good for a winter meal; warm, flavorful and comforting.*

## Linguine Postiluppo

¼ cup olive oil
½ small onion, diced
4 cloves garlic, minced
4 anchovies in oil, drained
½ cup white wine
16 clams in shell, washed
24 mussels in shell, washed
2 quarts (64 oz.) whole canned plum tomatoes, crushed
½ teaspoon crushed red pepper
12 basil leaves, crushed
(may substitute 3 Tablespoons basil, chopped)
2 Tablespoons Italian parsley, chopped
¼ teaspoon oregano
12 oz. calamari, cleaned and sliced
20 medium shrimp, shelled
salt to taste
freshly ground black pepper to taste
1 lb. linguine, cooked

eat olive oil in a covered heavy skillet over medium heat. Add onions; cook until translucent. Add garlic, stir and allow to cook 2 minutes, but do not brown. Add anchovies and stir briefly, then mash with back of spoon. Stir again. Add white wine.

Add clams, mussels and tomatoes, crushed red pepper, basil, parsley and oregano. Cover. Allow to steam until clams are open, 3 to 4 minutes.

Add calamari and shrimp; season with salt and pepper. Simmer all until done (about 3 to 5 minutes). Serve over cooked linguine.

**Sauce and one pound linguine serves 4.**

## Mint Shrimp Saute

¼ cup lemon juice, divided

1 medium red bell pepper, cut into thin strips

16 pitted ripe olives

⅓ cup fresh parsley, chopped

1 Tablespoon olive oil

2 Tablespoons margarine, melted

¼ cup fresh mint leaves, chopped
(may substitute 1 Tablespoon dried)

1 Tablespoon lemon zest

½ teaspoon freshly ground black pepper

1 lb. 2 oz. medium shrimp, peeled and deveined

Combine 2 tablespoons lemon juice with remaining ingredients in a nonmetallic bowl. Let stand 20 minutes. Cook mixture, over medium heat in large skillet stirring frequently, for about 4 minutes, or until shrimp are just tender. Stir in remaining lemon juice.

**Serves 3 to 4.**

*Combine ingredients, except for shrimp, early in day if desired. Garlic may be added to enhance mint flavoring.*

## Spicy Party Shrimp

5 lbs. large shrimp

1 cup butter or margarine, melted

juice of 2 lemons

4 Tablespoons freshly ground black pepper

24 oz. bottle of Italian salad dressing

Wash shrimp (but do not peel). Place shrimp in a large baking dish. Mix remaining ingredients and pour over shrimp. Bake covered at 350°F just until shrimp curl (about 20 to 30 minutes). Stir occasionally to coat shrimp.

**Serves 8.**

*Serve with salad or colorful vegetable, French bread and lots of napkins. Great for casual dinner or party. Excellent with white wine.*

## Scallop Rice Medley

2 Tablespoons butter, divided
2 Tablespoons onion, finely chopped
1 zucchini, diced
¼ teaspoon salt
¼ teaspoon freshly ground black pepper
1 cup long grain rice, rinsed and drained
1½ cups chicken stock, heated
1 teaspoon fennel seed
½ lb. fresh mushrooms, sliced ¼-inch thick
1 Tablespoon chives, chopped
¾ lb. small scallops (bay scallops)
1 to 2 Tablespoons soy sauce

reheat oven to 350°F. Heat 1 tablespoon butter in ovenproof saucepan. Add onion and mix well; cook 2 to 3 minutes over medium heat. Add zucchini, salt and pepper; continue cooking 2 minutes. Mix in rice and cook 2 minutes. Add chicken stock and fennel seed; stir well and bring to a boil. Cover and bake 18 minutes in oven.

While rice is cooking, heat 1 tablespoon butter in frying pan. Add mushrooms and chives; cook 3 minutes. Stir in scallops; cook 2 minutes over high heat. Add soy sauce and mix ingredients well. Stir scallops into rice mixture 4 minutes before rice is finished cooking. Finish cooking process and adjust seasoning, if desired.

**Serves 4.**

## Savory Seafood Pizza

1 Boboli crust (large size)
1 garlic clove, minced
5 green onions, chopped
4 roma tomatoes, chopped
1 Tablespoon olive oil
1 lb. shrimp, cooked and peeled
splash of white wine, optional
¼ teaspoon dried crushed red pepper or more to taste
1 cup Mozzarella cheese, shredded

reheat oven to 400°F.

Spray pizza pan with cooking spray and put crust on pan. Lightly saute garlic, onion, and tomatoes in olive oil. Add shrimp, wine and red pepper flakes and heat through; cover and turn off burner. Sprinkle crust with half of the cheese. Heat crust until cheese melts. Put shrimp mixture on top of cheese with slotted spoon, arranging shrimp around Boboli crust. Top with remaining cheese and bake until cheese is melted.

**Slice pizza into 6 to 8 slices.**

*A new twist for pizza. Shelled popcorn shrimp can be substituted if desired.*

## Shrimp and Artichoke Brochettes

8 to 12 baby artichokes
½ cup olive oil
¼ cup fresh lemon juice
1 clove garlic, minced
1 teaspoon dried oregano
1 teaspoon rosemary
1 Tablespoon Dijon mustard
¼ to ½ teaspoon crushed red pepper flakes to taste
salt to taste
freshly ground black pepper to taste
16 jumbo shrimp, peeled with tail left intact

Cook artichokes in boiling water until just tender, about 8 to 12 minutes. Drain well and hold under cold water until cool. Artichokes can be cooked a day in advance and refrigerated.

Combine oil, lemon juice, garlic, oregano, rosemary, mustard, pepper flakes, salt and pepper in a large plastic food bag. Add shrimp, seal tightly and refrigerate at least 30 minutes.

Leave very small artichokes whole and cut larger ones in half, lengthwise. Trim leaf tips. Thread artichokes and shrimp onto 4 skewers. Brush with remaining marinade. Grill over a medium hot fire, turning once, until shrimp is cooked, about 7 to 9 minutes.

**Serves 4.**

*Button mushrooms and chunks of red onion or salad tomatoes can be added to offer variety the whole family will enjoy.*

## Red Curry Shrimp

1 pound raw shrimp, shelled and deveined
2 cups coconut milk (canned)
2 Tablespoons red curry paste
1 to 2 Tablespoons fish sauce
1 fresh red chili, seeded, optional
3 Tablespoons fresh cilantro, chopped

Clean shrimp prior to cooking sauce because sauce cooks quickly. Pour coconut milk in a medium sized skillet with the curry paste, fish sauce and the chili. Bring slowly to the simmering point, stirring frequently. Add the shrimp and cook uncovered, stirring frequently, on low heat until the shrimp are cooked and the flavors mellow (the cooking time in this step depends on the size of shrimp that you have selected). Serve with basmati or texmati rice. Sprinkle with cilantro before serving.

Coconut milk, red curry paste, fish sauce and basmati rice can be purchased at Indian or Asian markets. Curry sauce can be prepared ahead and reheated.

**Serves 4.**

## Crab Cakes Supreme

6½ oz. can lump crab meat

1 slice bread, torn with crust removed

2 Tablespoons skim milk

1 Tablespoon mayonnaise

½ teaspoon Old Bay seasoning

½ Tablespoon Worcestershire sauce

½ small green pepper, diced

2 scallions, chopped

1 teaspoon Dijon mustard

⅛ teaspoon salt

dash cayenne pepper (optional)

1 egg white

½ loaf sourdough bread or saltine crackers

Preheat broiler. Line baking tray with foil and spray with cooking spray. Drain crab meat and place in a mixing bowl. Flake with a fork and pick out any pieces of shell or cartilage. Mix in bread, milk, mayonnaise, Old Bay, Worcestershire sauce, bell pepper, scallions, mustard, salt, cayenne pepper and egg white.

Shape into two cakes about 4 inches in diameter and place on baking tray. Broil about 4 inches from heat for 5 minutes. Turn and broil another 5 minutes. Serve crab cakes with warm bread or cut into fourths and sandwich between 2 crackers spread with mustard.

**Serves 2.**

*May also be browned in butter instead of broiling.*

## Shrimp and Clam Sauce for Shell Pasta

1 Tablespoon olive oil

3 large garlic cloves, chopped

½ teaspoon dried, crushed red pepper

28 oz. can Italian plum tomatoes, drained and chopped (juices reserved)

10 oz. can baby clams, drained (juices reserved)

4 Tablespoons fresh parsley, chopped and divided

1 teaspoon dried basil, crumbled

1 teaspoon anchovy paste

¾ lb. large shrimp, peeled and deveined

salt to taste

freshly ground black pepper to taste

8 to 12 oz. pasta, cooked (large shell pasta preferred)

Heat oil in large heavy skillet over medium heat. Add garlic and red pepper; saute until fragrant, about one minute. Mix in tomatoes with reserved tomato juices, clam juices, 2 tablespoons parsley, basil and anchovy paste. Cover skillet and cook 15 minutes. Uncover and simmer until sauce thickens stirring occasionally, about 15 minutes. Add clams and shrimp. Simmer until shrimp are just cooked through, about 3 minutes. Season to taste with salt and pepper. Add pasta to sauce. Toss to combine. Transfer to large serving bowl. Garnish with remaining 2 tablespoons of parsley.

**Serves 4.**

*Very colorful, spicy and easy to make. A low-fat recipe with a lot of flavor for lunch or dinner.*

# Lobster and Shrimp Enchiladas

12 to 16 corn tortillas
2 medium white onions, coarsely chopped
7 oz. can green chilies, coarsely chopped (skin discarded)
1½ lbs. frozen lobster tails, thawed and coarsely chopped
1 lb. large raw shrimp, peeled, deveined and coarsely chopped
1 cup walnut halves or sliced almonds, toasted (optional)
12 oz. can pitted ripe olives, well drained and halved
1 lb. Monterey Jack cheese, shredded
1 lb. longhorn cheddar cheese, shredded
2 cups half and half
1 cup sour cream
½ cup butter, melted
1½ teaspoons oregano leaves
1 teaspoon garlic salt

*Optional Garnish:*
additional longhorn cheddar cheese, shredded
sliced red pimentos
avocado slices
additional black or green olives

reheat oven to 300°F. Generously butter large Mexican casserole dish or 4 quart baking dish.

Cover bottom with about ⅓ of tortillas. Sprinkle with half of onion and top with half of chilies. Add half of lobster and shrimp. Sprinkle with half of the nuts and half of the olives. Combine Jack and cheddar cheeses; remove about 1½ cups and set aside. Sprinkle half of remaining cheese over olives.

Combine half and half, sour cream, butter, oregano and garlic salt in medium saucepan. Place over medium-low heat and stir frequently until lukewarm and well blended. Remove 1 cup and set aside. Pour half of remaining sauce over casserole. Repeat layering, as above, covering top with remaining half of sauce. Add remaining tortillas, 1 cup reserved sauce and ¾ cup of the reserved cheese.

Bake 60 to 70 minutes, until casserole is bubbling hot. Remove from oven and increase temperature to 450°F. Sprinkle casserole with remaining cheese and return to oven for 5 to 7 minutes, until top is golden brown and cheese is bubbly. If using optional garnish, add more cheddar and return to oven just until cheese is melted. Alternate pimentos, avocado slices and olives in wagon-wheel design and heat briefly until toppings begin to sink into cheese.

Serves 12.

*Other shellfish or cooked chicken may be substituted for lobster and shrimp. Enchiladas can be prepared several hours in advance and held in warm (180°F) oven. Freezes well. Defrost in refrigerator overnight before reheating.*

## Tangy Seasoned Shrimp

1 cup butter
1 cup margarine
1 Tablespoon all purpose flour
½ cup fresh lemon juice
¼ teaspoon salt
1 Tablespoon Worcestershire sauce
1 Tablespoon freshly ground black pepper
⅛ teaspoon white pepper
1 Tablespoon garlic, crushed
2 Tablespoons white wine
3 lbs. shrimp, peeled and deveined
pasta of your choice, cooked (linguine works well)

Melt butter and margarine together; blend in flour. Add all other ingredients, except shrimp and pasta and mix well. Stir in shrimp to coat. Bake in casserole dish at 350°F oven for 20 minutes or until shrimp is cooked. Be careful not to over bake shrimp. Serve over pasta.

**Serves 8 to 10.**

## Seafood Benedict on French Rafts

2 8 oz. loaves French bread, halved horizontally
4 12 oz. packages frozen spinach souffle, thawed
2 teaspoons dried dill
12 oz. crabmeat
2 lbs. fresh medium shrimp, shelled (reserve some for garnish)
1½ cups butter or margarine
6 egg yolks
¼ teaspoon salt
⅛ teaspoon white pepper
3 Tablespoons lemon juice
3 Tablespoons hot water

Preheat oven to 375°F. Scoop out small amount of bread from each half, leaving a thick shell. Place bread shells on cookie sheets. In large bowl mix spinach souffle, dill, crabmeat and shrimp just until blended. Spoon equal amount on each bread half. Bake for 25 minutes. Garnish with reserved shrimp. Bake 10 to 15 minutes longer until filling is set and lightly browned. With serrated knife cut each half crosswise in thirds.

For Hollandaise sauce, heat butter in heavy saucepan until foaming but not browned. In blender container rinsed with hot water, whirl remaining ingredients 3 seconds, just until blended. With blender running, add hot butter, clear part only, in slow steady stream. (Do not add milky residue in bottom of pan.) Whirl just until smooth and slightly thickened. Keep warm over warm water up to 30 minutes, or in thermos several hours. Serve bread hot with Hollandaise Sauce. Garnish with lemon wedges if desired.

**Serves 10 to 12.**

*Excellent! Lemon in Hollandaise sauce enhances the seafood flavor. Can substitute canned crabmeat and shrimp with fine results.*

The Midwest is a land of four seasons, each with its own beauty and variation of lifestyle. In the fall we savor our harvest, enjoy the vibrant colors of nature, and cherish the contrasting Indian summer and crisp fall days. In winter, we curl up at the fireside and watch the snowflakes swirl around us while we feast on meat and potatoes. The spring brings tender greens, strawberries, and a time for planting between spring rains. We look forward to sunny summer days and dining *al fresco*. Entertaining on a porch, deck, or patio, cooking on a grill exemplifies the lifestyle of Midwestern summers.

A neighbor who took advantage of every opportunity to use his grill would welcome his guests with Grilled Fruit with Honey-Lemon Yogurt Sauce. The fresh, firm fruit maintains its shape as the flavor intensifies on the grill. The sauce adds a tang to the warm, sweet fruit for a treat your guests will relish whether served alone or as part of a meal served with warm hospitality on your patio or veranda.

# Fruits & Vegetables

## Grilled Fruit with Honey-Lemon Yogurt

8 oz. carton vanilla yogurt
2 to 3 teaspoons lemon juice
1 teaspoon lemon zest
2 Tablespoons honey
1 fresh pineapple
4 bananas
4 peaches, halved and pitted
4 pears, halved and cored
2 yellow apples, halved and cored
2 red apples, halved and cored

ombine vanilla yogurt, lemon juice, lemon zest and honey. Refrigerate. Peel, core and cut pineapple into rings. Peel bananas; cut each in half. Grill peaches, pears and apples covered with grill lid, over medium hot coals for about 10 minutes. Add bananas and pineapple to grill in a grill basket. Grill 10 additional minutes or until fruit reaches desired degree of doneness. Serve grilled fruit with yogurt mixture.

Serves 8.

This page generously sponsored by 1994 JLWJC Sustainers.

## A Terrine of Summer Fruits

15 oz. sparkling rose wine
(use only 15 oz. of wine, not the entire bottle)

½ cup confectioners' sugar

1 envelope unflavored gelatin

1 Tablespoon fresh lime juice

12 oz. small strawberries

8 oz. red raspberries

4 oz. black raspberries

4 oz. blueberries

4 oz. blackberries

or any combination of berries that total 32 oz.

2 loaf pans that equal at least 125 cubic inches
such as: 7½x4¾x3½-inch or 9½x5½x2¾-inch

Heat 7 ounces of rose wine in a small saucepan until it is simmering. Whisk in the sugar and gelatin making sure everything is completely dissolved. Add 8 ounces of wine and the lime juice. Cool in the refrigerator.

To prepare fruit remove stems and halve strawberries if too large. Spray one loaf pan with cooking spray (if not non-stick). Using the prettiest shaped fruits make a single, solid layer on the bottom of the pan. This will be the top of the terrine. Gently mix together the rest of the fruit and spoon into the pan. Pour 10 ounces of the liquid over the fruit. Cover with a sheet of plastic wrap. Place the other loaf pan directly on top of it to rest as if to stack loaf pans, and put in two unopened cans of vegetables to act as weights, to keep fruit from floating. Place in refrigerator for about 1 hour to let set.

When first layer is set remove weights, pan and plastic wrap. Warm up the remaining wine mixture and pour over the terrine. Cover with wrap, loaf pan, and weights. Return to refrigerator overnight to set until firm.

When ready to serve, turn out terrine by dipping loaf pan very briefly in hot water and inverting it onto a plate. Use a very sharp knife that can be dipped in hot water to cut into slices. May be topped with whipped cream, creme fraiche, or plain yogurt.

Serves 8.

## Curried Fruit

2 lbs. fresh pears, halved

2 lbs. fresh pineapples, chunked

2 lbs. fresh peaches, halved

2 lbs. fresh apricots, halved

½ cup butter

1 cup brown sugar

1 Tablespoon cornstarch

1 to 1½ teaspoons curry powder

maraschino cherries, as desired

Preheat oven to 325°F. Place all fruit in 9x13x2-inch casserole dish, making sure to mix well. In a small bowl, combine butter, brown sugar, cornstarch and curry powder to make a paste. Spoon the paste over the fruits. Bake for 1 hour, basting several times with the juices.

Serves 8 to 10.

*This can be made ahead of time, refrigerated, and reheated. Serve hot while the inviting aroma lures guests to the kitchen.*

## Cinnamon Spiced Apples

3 cups water
2 cups sugar
6 thin lemon slices
1 Tablespoon orange rind, grated
2 teaspoons whole cloves
1 cinnamon stick, broken into pieces
6 apples
10 maraschino cherries
2 Tablespoons cornstarch
¼ cup cold water
1 to 3 drops red food coloring

Bring water and sugar to a boil. Add lemon, orange rind, spices, and apples. Simmer uncovered until tender. Remove apples and lemons. Bring syrup to rolling boil. Boil about 5 minutes. Combine cornstarch and cold water. Add to syrup. Cook 2 minutes. Add red food coloring. Mix in maraschino cherries. Cool slightly and pour over apples. Serve warm.

**Serves 6.**

## Pineapple au Gratin

4 14 oz. cans pineapple (or 3 20 oz. cans)
¾ cup sugar
¾ cup flour
½ cup pineapple juice
1 lb. sharp cheddar cheese, grated

Drain pineapple and reserve juice. Mix the sugar, flour and gradually stir in pineapple juice to make a sauce. Place pineapple in bottom of a 2½ quart casserole. Sprinkle with cheese then top with sauce. Bake at 325°F for 45 minutes or until the cheese is melted.

**Serves 6 to 8.**

## Berry-Citrus Twist

2 quarts fresh strawberries, halved
2 fresh pineapples, peeled, cored and chunked
½ cup orange marmalade
¼ cup orange juice
2 Tablespoons lemon juice
½ cup fresh or frozen blueberries

Combine strawberries and pineapple in a bowl. Set aside. Combine orange marmalade, orange juice and lemon juice. Pour over fruit and toss gently. Add blueberries just before serving.

**Serves 8 to 10.**

## Judy's Rhubarb

½ cup butter
red food coloring, few drops
3 cups day old bread, dried and cubed
1 cup sugar
2 cups frozen rhubarb, cut into 1-inch pieces

elt butter and add red food coloring. Coat bread in butter mixture. Add sugar. Mix well. Fold in rhubarb. Pour into a lightly greased 8x8-inch or 9x9-inch square pan. Put 1 teaspoon water in each corner. Bake at 325°F for 45 minutes.

**Serves 4.**

## Gingered Fruit

8 oz. package cream cheese, softened
⅓ cup orange juice
2 Tablespoons sugar
½ teaspoon ground ginger
3 cups green grapes, halved
3 cups strawberries, hulled and halved
3 Granny Smith apples, cored and chopped
11 oz. can mandarin oranges, drained

ombine cream cheese, orange juice, sugar and ginger. Mix well. Combine grapes, strawberries, apples and mandarin oranges in a large bowl. Toss with dressing and serve immediately.

**Serves 6 to 8.**

## Citrus Fondue

1 cup sugar
3 Tablespoons cornstarch
¼ teaspoon salt
¼ teaspoon cinnamon or nutmeg
1 cup orange juice
¼ cup lemon juice
¼ cup hot water
1 teaspoon orange zest
1 teaspoon lemon zest
apples, peaches, pears, oranges, melons, grapes, shelled nuts, bananas, kiwi

Mix sugar, cornstarch, salt and spice in a medium saucepan. Slowly stir in orange and lemon juices. Mix well. Add hot water and heat to boiling, stirring constantly. Boil and stir one minute. Stir in orange and lemon zest. Pour into fondue pot and keep warm.

Cube fruit and dip into fondue.

**Serves 10 to12.**

## Swiss Spinach

2 10 oz. packages frozen spinach, chopped
¾ cup milk
¾ cup shredded Swiss cheese, divided
3 eggs, beaten
3 Tablespoons onion, chopped
⅛ teaspoon salt or ¼ teaspoon Beau Monde seasoning
dash pepper
1 cup soft bread crumbs
1 Tablespoon margarine

Preheat oven to 350°F. Cook spinach according to package directions, drain well. Pat spinach dry with paper towels. Mix spinach with milk, ½ cup cheese, eggs, onion, salt or Beau Monde seasoning, and pepper. Turn into greased 8x8x2-inch baking pan. Bake for 25 minutes. Combine crumbs, remaining cheese, and margarine; sprinkle on top spinach. Bake 10 to 15 minutes more or until knife inserted just off-center comes out clean. Let stand 5 minutes before serving.

Serves 6.

## Marinated Asparagus with Proscuitto

2 lbs. fresh asparagus
¾ cup vegetable oil
¼ cup white wine vinegar
2 Tablespoons Dijon mustard
2 Tablespoons honey
2 teaspoons dried tarragon
¼ lb. proscuitto or thinly sliced ham, cut into strips

rim ends of asparagus and remove scales from stalks. Steam asparagus in steamer, about 4 minutes or until crisp-tender. Drain. Plunge into ice water to stop cooking process. Drain well. Set aside. Combine oil, vinegar, mustard, honey and tarragon. Cover tightly and shake well to combine. Pour over asparagus and chill, covered, for abut 2 hours. Remove asparagus, reserving dressing. Arrange asparagus on serving platter in a single layer. Top with prosciutto and drizzle with remaining marinade.

Serves 6 to 8.

## Mushrooms Au Gratin

1 lb. fresh mushrooms
4 Tablespoons butter
⅓ cup sour cream
½ teaspoon salt
pepper to taste
1 Tablespoon flour
¼ cup fresh parsley, chopped
½ cup shredded Swiss cheese

Wash mushrooms well. Dry. Slice mushrooms lengthwise. Melt butter in skillet over medium heat and saute mushrooms until light brown. Cover pan for 2 minutes, until mushrooms exude juice. Blend sour cream, salt, pepper and flour until smooth. Stir into mushroom mixture until blended and very smooth. Bring to boil and remove from heat. Pour into 1 quart baking dish. Sprinkle with parsley and Swiss cheese. Bake at 425°F for 10 to 12 minutes.

**Serves 4 to 6.**

## Broiled Tomatoes

4 fresh tomatoes, peeled, cut in half and at room temperature
½ cup Italian salad dressing
2 cups French bread crumbs
1 cup extra sharp cheddar cheese, grated
1 Tablespoon fresh parsley, chopped
Parmesan cheese to taste

Marinate peeled, halved tomatoes in salad dressing for several hours. Mix bread crumbs, cheese and parsley together and moisten with marinade. Pile mixture on top of tomatoes and sprinkle with Parmesan cheese. Broil until cheese is melted and top is bubbly and hot.

**Serves 4.**

## Kansas Blackeyed Peas

salted water
1 lb. frozen blackeyed peas
½ cup celery, chopped
1 teaspoon freshly ground black pepper
6 Tablespoons butter
3¼ teaspoons seasoned salt
¼ teaspoon cayenne pepper
½ green bell pepper, diced
1 teaspoon salt
¾ teaspoon ground cumin
¾ teaspoon garlic powder

Place blackeyed peas in boiling salted water. Cook over low heat for 40 to 45 minutes or until tender. Drain. Add all remaining ingredients and mix well. Add enough water to cover. Simmer covered for 2 hours to allow flavors to blend.

**Serves 12.**

## Herbed Harvest Vegetable Casserole

4 new potatoes, thinly sliced
¼ cup butter
1 teaspoon dried sage
1 teaspoon dried tarragon
2 sweet red peppers, seeded and diced
1 onion, thinly sliced
½ cup uncooked long grain rice
2 medium zucchini, thinly sliced
3 medium tomatoes, sliced
1 cup shredded Swiss cheese

Grease 2½ quart baking dish and arrange half of the potato slices in overlapping rows. Dot with half the butter. Sprinkle with half the sage and tarragon. Sprinkle with half the peppers, onion, rice and zucchini. Repeat layers, beginning again with the potatoes. Cover tightly and bake for 1½ hours at 350°F. Remove cover and top with tomato slices and cheese. Bake uncovered for 10 more minutes. Allow to stand 10 minutes before serving.

Serves 6 to 8.

*Looks very old world!*

## Gratin of Cauliflower with Gingered Crumbs

1½ lbs. cauliflower, leaves trimmed, core removed
3 Tablespoons unsalted butter, divided
2 Tablespoons all purpose flour
1 cup light cream or half and half
1 teaspoon lemon juice
¼ teaspoon grated fresh nutmeg
¼ teaspoon salt
dash of hot pepper sauce
¼ cup grated Swiss cheese
¼ cup fresh bread crumbs
⅛ teaspoon ground ginger
2 Tablespoons freshly grated Parmesan cheese

Preheat oven to 350°F. Cook the cauliflower in at least 3 quarts of salted boiling water until just tender (10–12 minutes). Rinse under cold running water. Drain. Cut or break the cauliflower into florets (if using out of season cauliflower, soak in cold water for 30 minutes prior to cooking and add 1½ teaspoons white wine vinegar to the cooking water). Set aside. Melt 2 tablespoons of butter in a medium saucepan over medium low heat. Stir in flour. Cook, stirring constantly for 2 minutes. Whisk in the cream. Raise the heat slightly and cook until thick. Add the lemon juice, nutmeg, salt, hot pepper sauce and Swiss cheese. Remove from the heat and set aside. Place the cauliflower in a well buttered 1½ to 2 quart souffle dish or casserole. Spoon the cheese sauce over the top.

Melt the remaining 1 tablespoon butter in a small skillet over medium heat. Stir in the bread crumbs and ginger. Cook, stirring constantly, until golden brown. Spoon the crumb mixture over the cauliflower and sprinkle with the Parmesan cheese. Bake until bubbly, 15 to 20 minutes. Let stand 5 minutes before serving.

Serves 4 to 6.

## Sweet and Sour Cabbage

1 medium head cabbage, shredded
2 onions, chopped
2 Tablespoons salt
boiling water
2 Granny Smith apples, cored, peeled and chopped
1 Tablespoon sugar
4 Tablespoons cider vinegar
¼ cup raisins
¼ teaspoon salt
⅛ teaspoon freshly ground black pepper
4 slices bacon
1 Tablespoon flour

ombine cabbage with onion. Cover with 2 tablespoons salt and let stand for 1 hour. Squeeze out liquid and cover with boiling water. Let stand 10 minutes and drain. Reserve liquid. Cover again with boiling water and add apples, sugar, vinegar, raisins, salt and pepper and cook until tender. Fry bacon and remove. Reserve drippings. Blend flour into drippings. Add 1 cup cabbage liquid and cook until thickened. Add to drained cabbage mixture. Garnish with chopped bacon.

**Serves 4.**

## Asparagus with Creamy Mushroom Dressing

3 lbs. (about 3 bunches) fresh asparagus, bottoms trimmed
½ lb. mushrooms, very thinly sliced
3 Tablespoons fresh lemon juice
½ cup whipping cream
2 Tablespoons Dijon mustard
⅓ cup olive oil
1 teaspoon packed fresh tarragon, chopped or ½ teaspoon dried
salt and pepper to taste

ook asparagus in large pot of boiling salted water until just crisp-tender, about 4 minutes. Drain. Rinse under cold water. Drain. Pat asparagus dry.

Toss mushrooms with lemon juice in medium bowl; season with salt and pepper, set aside. Whisk cream and mustard in small bowl to blend; gradually whisk in oil. Let mushroom mixture and dressing stand 30 minutes or cover and refrigerate up to 2 hours.

Arrange asparagus on platter. Whisk tarragon into dressing. Drain mushrooms well and return to bowl. Mix in dressing. Season to taste with salt and pepper. Spoon mushroom dressing over asparagus and serve. The asparagus can be prepared up to 1 day ahead. Wrap in paper towels and plastic bags, then refrigerate.

**Serves 10.**

## Herbed Sweet Potato Bake

4 cups sweet potato, peeled and thinly sliced
4 cups red potato, peeled and thinly sliced
2 Tablespoons fresh onion, minced
3 Tablespoons margarine, melted and divided
½ teaspoon salt, divided
¼ teaspoon pepper, divided
¼ teaspoon nutmeg
¾ cup skim milk
2 Tablespoons fresh parsley, minced
2 Tablespoons fresh Parmesan cheese, grated

Coat an 11x7x2-inch baking dish with cooking spray.

Layer 2 cups sweet potato in half of the dish and 2 cups red potato in the other half. Sprinkle with onion. Drizzle with 1½ tablespoons margarine. Sprinkle with half the salt, pepper and nutmeg. Repeat procedure. Bring milk to a boil and pour over potato mixture. Cover with aluminum foil, cut slits in foil. Bake at 425°F for 30 minutes. Bake uncovered for an additional 10 minutes. Remove from oven and sprinkle with parsley and Parmesan cheese.

**Serves 8.**

## Melange of Vegetables

¼ cup olive oil
2 whole cloves garlic
4 medium red potatoes, chopped
1 cup fresh snow peas
2 cups zucchini, sliced
2 ripe tomatoes, diced or chopped
1 large pinch basil, crushed
½ teaspoon black pepper
1 teaspoon Tabasco sauce
¼ teaspoon salt

Brown garlic cloves in oil in large skillet. Remove and discard garlic. Add potatoes. Cook for 4 minutes. Add snow peas, zucchini, tomatoes, basil, black pepper, Tabasco sauce and salt. Cook until vegetables are tender.

**Serves 4.**

## Twice Baked Potatoes with Garlic

1 bulb garlic
4 large red potatoes
3 Tablespoons olive oil or garlic oil, divided
½ cup blue cheese, crumbled
¾ teaspoon salt
¼ teaspoon freshly ground black pepper

ut about ½-inch from top of garlic. Wrap the garlic in foil and roast in a 275°F oven about 1 hour. Set aside. Rub potatoes with 1½ tablespoons olive oil. Wrap in foil and bake at 350°F for 1 hour and 10 minutes. Remove from oven. Cut in half and cool slightly. Press the roasted garlic pulp from the skins and mash with a fork. Scoop the pulp from the potatoes with a spoon. Combine potatoes, garlic, blue cheese, salt and pepper. Place potato shells on a baking sheet. Stuff with potato mixture. Bake at 350°F for 20 minutes if preparing fresh, or 30 minutes if potatoes have been refrigerated.

**Serves 4.**

## Scalloped Corn

14½ oz. can whole corn, drained
14¼ oz. can creamed corn
2 Tablespoons flour
2 Tablespoons sugar
2 Tablespoons butter, melted
8 slices American cheese, broken into pieces
1 small green pepper, chopped
1 small jar pimento, drained
2 eggs, beaten

rain whole kernel corn and put into bowl. Add creamed corn, along with liquid. Stir in flour, sugar and melted butter. Add cheese, green pepper, pimento and eggs. Mix well. Turn into a 1 quart greased baking dish. Bake 45 minutes at 350°F.

**Serves 6 to 8.**

## Roasted Vegetables

4 cups carrots, sliced ½ inch thick
4 cups parsnips, sliced ½ inch thick
4 cups turnips, cubed
2 Tablespoons olive oil
2 Tablespoons dried tarragon
½ teaspoon salt
¼ teaspoon pepper
vegetable cooking spray

ombine carrots, parsnips and turnips in a large bowl. Add olive oil, tarragon and pepper, mix well. Place in a 13x9x2-inch casserole coated with cooking spray. Bake uncovered at 450°F for 45 minutes or until tender and browned; stirring frequently.

**Serves 8.**

## Midwestern Spuds

4 medium large baking potatoes scrubbed but unpeeled
2 Tablespoons oil
2 cups leeks or green onions, well cleaned and chopped
2 cups shredded Monterey Jack cheese with jalapeno peppers
½ cup plus 2 Tablespoons sour cream
8 strips bacon, cooked and crumbled
1 teaspoon salt or to taste

Wrap potatoes in foil and bake at 350°F for 1¼ hours. Heat oil in heavy skillet over medium heat. When hot, add leeks, saute and stir until softened, 3 to 4 minutes. Set aside. When potatoes are cool, cut them in half lengthwise. Scoop out all pulp but a thin layer from each half. Place pulp in mixing bowl and mash with potato masher or wood spoon until smooth. Stir in sauteed leeks, cheese, sour cream, bacon and salt. Taste and add more salt if needed. Mound potato mixture in reserved halves. If not using immediately, cool, then cover. Can be refrigerated up to one day.

Serves 8.

## Stuffed Zucchini

4 medium zucchini
4 Tablespoons butter
2 cups fresh mushrooms, chopped
4 Tablespoons all purpose flour
½ teaspoon dried oregano, crushed
1½ cups Monterey Jack cheese, shredded
2 Tablespoons pimento, chopped
½ cup grated Parmesan cheese

Cook whole zucchini in boiling salted water for 10 minutes or until tender. Slice a thin slice off bottom of each zucchini, so they will sit flat on baking sheet. With sharp knife, hollow out each zucchini, reserving pulp, and leaving a ¼-inch shell. Chop center pulp portion of zucchini and set aside. Melt butter in large skillet. Saute mushrooms about 3 minutes or until tender. Stir in flour and oregano. Remove from heat. Stir in Monterey Jack cheese and pimento; add the reserved chopped zucchini. Heat mixture through. Preheat broiler. Fill zucchini shells using ¼ mixture in each zucchini. Sprinkle with Parmesan cheese. Broil 3 to 5 minutes or until hot and bubbly.

Serves 8.

*Great with steak and a salad. Makes a nice presentation.*

## Old Settler Baked Beans

½ lb. bacon, diced
½ lb. ground beef, crumbled
1 large onion, chopped
½ cup sugar
½ cup brown sugar
¼ cup ketchup
¼ cup barbecue sauce
2 Tablespoons molasses
½ teaspoon chili powder
1 teaspoon salt
½ teaspoon pepper
16 oz. can kidney beans
16 oz. can butter beans
31 oz. can pork and beans

In a skillet brown bacon, ground beef and onion over medium heat. Remove and drain. Mix with remaining ingredients in a large greased casserole. Bake at 350°F for 1 hour.

**Serves 10 to 12.**

*For variety, serve on a bun as a sandwich.*

## Broccoli Blue

2 lbs. broccoli (fresh or frozen), cut into bite size pieces
2 Tablespoons butter
2 Tablespoons flour
3 oz. package cream cheese, softened
½ to ¾ cup blue cheese, crumbled
1 cup sour cream
⅓ cup butter crackers, crushed

Steam broccoli until tender. While broccoli is cooking, melt butter in small saucepan over low heat. When melted, stir in flour. Blend. Add cream cheese and blue cheese to saucepan and stir until very smooth. Add sour cream and bring to a boil. Remove from heat. Pour over broccoli and mix well. Place in a one quart baking dish. Top with cracker crumbs. Bake for 30 minutes at 350°F.

**Serves 8.**

## Dilled Green Beans and Onions

1 lb. fresh green beans (leave whole)

2 sweet onions, thinly sliced

¼ cup butter

dill to taste

vinegar to taste

ead and tail green beans. Saute onions in butter. Boil beans in salted water 8 to 12 minutes, but keep them crisp. This part can be done early in the day. To serve: Combine onions and beans and reheat. Add dill and vinegar to taste.

**Serves 4.**

## Grilled Herbed Potatoes

4 medium potatoes, thinly sliced

½ lb. mushrooms, sliced

1 large onion, thinly sliced

¼ cup margarine, melted

2 Tablespoons fresh parsley, finely chopped

2 Tablespoons fresh dill, finely chopped

1 large clove garlic, minced

salt and pepper to taste

reheat grill or broiler to medium. Place potatoes, mushrooms and onions on 24 x18-inch double thickness of heavy duty aluminum foil.

Combine margarine and seasonings; spoon over potato mixture. Fold foil edge over and wrap securely.

Place on grill or broiler pan 6 inches from heat source. Grill or broil 15 to 20 minutes or until potatoes are tender, turning packet over once.

**Serves 4 to 6.**

## Fried Stuffed Tomatoes

2 cloves garlic, minced
1 Tablespoon parsley
¼ teaspoon celery salt
8 oz. package cream cheese, softened
12 thick slices tomato
2 Tablespoons milk
1 egg
1 cup bread crumbs
1 teaspoon basil
½ cup flour
6 Tablespoons oil

Blend garlic, parsley, celery salt and cream cheese with electric mixer until smooth. Spread mixture on 6 tomato slices and top with remaining 6 slices. Set aside. Beat milk and egg together. Set aside.

Combine bread crumbs and basil. Coat tomatoes with flour. Dip each tomato in egg/milk mixture and then coat with bread crumb mixture. Heat oil in large skillet and fry tomatoes over medium high heat for 10 to 15 minutes on each side. Serve hot.

**Serves 6.**

## Carrot Souffle

1 teaspoon baking powder
2 Tablespoons flour
½ teaspoon salt
1 teaspoon cinnamon
½ cup sugar
2 cups carrots, cooked and mashed
¼ cup butter, melted
3 eggs, slightly beaten
1 cup evaporated milk
1 cup brown sugar
⅓ cup flour
⅓ cup butter
1 cup pecans

Mix together baking powder, flour, salt, cinnamon and sugar. Set aside. Place mashed cooked carrots into a mixing bowl. Add melted butter. Mix thoroughly. Add slightly beaten eggs and mix again. Add evaporated milk and mix well. Add dry mixture to liquid mixture. Pour into 2 quart baking dish. Bake at 350°F for 30 minutes.

While carrot mixture is baking combine brown sugar, flour, butter and pecans in a small mixing bowl. Mixture will be crumbly. Remove souffle from oven and top with crumb mixture. Return to oven and bake an additional 30 minutes.

**Serves 6 to 8.**

## Marinated Tomatoes

2 cloves garlic, thinly sliced
1½ cups olive oil
6 Tablespoons vinegar
2 teaspoons oregano
1 teaspoon salt
1 teaspoon pepper
10 tomatoes, sliced about ⅛-inch thick (horizontally)
1 to 2 red onions, thinly sliced
2 ozs. feta cheese, crumbled, optional

Peel garlic and place in olive oil for several hours. Discard garlic cloves. Mix olive oil, vinegar, oregano, salt and pepper. Shake. This will be the dressing.

Place a layer of tomatoes in a shallow dish, topped with a layer of onions and feta cheese. Drizzle ⅓ of the dressing mixture on top. Place another layer of tomatoes, onions, and dressing mixture. Repeat. Cover tightly and refrigerate. Before serving, gently stir together. Be careful when stirring as the tomatoes will break apart.

**Serves 10.**

*Eye appealing when served on a bed of greens or as a summer side dish with steak or chicken.*

## Brussels Sprouts with Chestnuts

1 quart Brussels sprouts
2 large chestnuts
2 Tablespoons butter, divided
1 Tablespoon flour
1 teaspoon savory (start with ½ teaspoon), divided
salt and pepper to taste
1 cup milk
1 teaspoon salt
½ cup soft buttered bread crumbs

Parbroil Brussels sprouts until they still retain some crispness. Set aside. Simmer chestnuts in a small saucepan of water for 15 minutes. While chestnuts cook prepare white sauce. Melt 1 tablespoon butter, blend in flour. Season with savory, salt and pepper. Whisk in milk all at once. Stir until thickened. Keep warm.

Remove shells and skins from chestnuts while still warm. Chop or slice and add to Brussels sprouts with 1 tablespoon butter, 1 teaspoon salt, pepper, savory and white sauce.

Preheat oven to 350°F. Place Brussels sprout mixture in buttered casserole, cover with bread crumbs and bake for 30 minutes.

**Serves 8.**

These moist, rich bar cookies of the 1950's are now time honored traditional treats 50's moms serve to their 90's grandchildren. Some were torn from pages of women's magazines, others were traded by neighbors or friends. Military wives who moved frequently, found that giving gifts of food and sharing recipes helped them to make a supportive community in the absence of their own extended families.

The bar cookies pictured are appropriate for any occasion from a formal tea to a tailgate party or Scout meeting treat. These easy to prepare, take anywhere goodies are especially compatible with our desire for an attractive, rich dessert which can be prepared quickly and served anywhere. Whether you indulge in chocolaty rich Peppermint Brownies, savor the varied textures and flavors of Brazil Nut Orange Bars, enjoy the chewy richness of Luscious Apricot Bars, or reach for the familiarity of Mom's Lemon Bars you're sure to please everyone you serve.

If cakes are your choice, our deliciously different Cinnamon Carrot Cake from a military wives' cookbook combines the flavor of spice cake and the moistness of traditional carrot cake recipes. The Italian Cream Cake, a favorite of an entire farm community, is a treasure graciously shared with you in the tradition of women everywhere.

# Desserts

## Brazil Nut Orange Bars

¼ cup soft butter or margarine
¼ cup sugar
1 cup sifted all purpose flour
¼ teaspoon salt
2 eggs, well beaten
¾ cup brown sugar, packed
1 cup finely chopped Brazil nuts
1 teaspoon vanilla extract
¼ teaspoon salt
2 Tablespoons all purpose flour
¼ cup butter
2 cups sifted confectioners' sugar
2 Tablespoons orange juice
2 teaspoons grated orange zest
slivered Brazil nuts

reheat oven to 375°F.

Thoroughly mix crust ingredients of butter, sugar, flour and salt. Spread evenly in a 9x9x2-inch pan; press down with spatula. Bake 15 minutes. In a separate bowl, mix eggs and sugar, beat well. Add Brazil nuts, vanilla, salt and flour, mix well. Spread evenly over baked layer. Bake 15 minutes. Cool in pan.

Cream butter with confectioners' sugar in a separate bowl adding orange juice a little at a time as needed to maintain a creamy consistency. Blend in orange zest. Frost cooled bars in pan and top with slivered Brazil nuts. Cut into bars. Store in a cool place, serve at room temperature.

**Makes 16 bars.**

## Mom's Lemon Bars

1 cup butter
2 cups all purpose flour
½ cup confectioners' sugar
4 eggs
4 Tablespoons lemon juice
½ teaspoon lemon extract
2 cups sugar
4 tablespoons all purpose flour
1 teaspoon baking powder
½ teaspoon salt
confectioners' sugar

Preheat oven to 350°F. Grease bottom and sides of 9x13x2-inch pan.

Cut butter into 2 cups flour and confectioners' sugar with a pastry blender or two knives. Set aside. Sprinkle flour mixture into pan; do not pat down. Bake in preheated oven for 20 minutes.

Beat eggs, lemon juice and lemon extract in a large bowl. Add sugar, 4 tablespoons flour, baking powder and salt. Pour on hot crust. Bake 10 minutes or until firm but not brown. Sprinkle immediately with confectioners' sugar. May be made one day in advance of serving.

**Makes 2 dozen bars.**

*An old fashioned favorite which continues to be a popular treat today.*

This page generously sponsored by Mrs. Leland Speer and Family.

## Peppermint Brownies

2 squares unsweetened chocolate
½ cup margarine
2 eggs
1 cup sugar
½ teaspoon vanilla
⅛ teaspoon peppermint extract
½ cup all purpose flour
⅛ teaspoon salt
½ cup chocolate chips
½ cup chopped walnuts
crushed peppermint candy, optional

Preheat oven to 350°F.

Melt margarine and chocolate, set aside. Beat eggs until thick. Gradually add sugar beating constantly. Mix in margarine and chocolate mixture. Add vanilla and peppermint. Combine flour and salt then add to moist ingredients. Stir in chocolate chips and nuts. Bake in a greased 8x8-inch pan for 20 to 30 minutes. Do not overbake. Completely cool then frost with Peppermint Brownie Frosting.

**Makes 16 bars.**

## Peppermint Brownie Frosting

2½ Tablespoons margarine, softened
1⅓ cups confectioners' sugar, sifted
1½ Tablespoons milk
½ teaspoon peppermint extract
1 Tablespoon margarine
1 square unsweetened chocolate

Cream margarine and sugar. Add milk and peppermint. Spread over brownies and let set.

In a small saucepan melt margarine and chocolate together and drip over frosting. Chill to set chocolate. Garnish with crushed peppermint hard candy if desired.

*These keep best in a sealed container in the refrigerator, especially in hot weather. Allow brownies to return to room temperature before serving.*

## Luscious Apricot Bars

⅔ cup dried apricots
½ cup butter or margarine, softened
¼ cup granulated sugar
1 cup sifted all purpose flour
⅓ cup sifted all purpose flour
½ teaspoon baking powder
¼ teaspoon salt
1 cup brown sugar
2 eggs, well beaten
½ teaspoon vanilla extract
½ cup nuts, chopped
confectioners' sugar

Rinse apricots; cover with water; boil for 10 minutes. Drain, cool, chop.

Preheat oven to 350°F. Grease an 8x8x2-inch pan. In a separate bowl mix butter, granulated sugar, and 1 cup flour with pastry blender until crumbly. Press into bottom of pan. Bake until lightly browned, about 25 minutes. Sift together ⅓ cup flour, baking powder, and salt. Gradually beat brown sugar into eggs. Add sifted flour mixture; mix well. Mix in vanilla, nuts, and apricots. Spread over baked layer. Bake 30 minutes. Cool in pan; cut into bars, roll in confectioners' sugar.

**Makes 16 bars.**

## Italian Cream Cake

½ cup margarine
½ cup shortening
2 cups sugar
5 egg yolks, added one at a time
2 cups all purpose flour
½ teaspoon salt
1 teaspoon baking soda
1 cup buttermilk
2 teaspoons vanilla
1 cup coconut
1 cup pecans, chopped
5 egg whites, beaten
½ cup margarine
8 oz. cream cheese
1 lb. confectioners' sugar
coconut
pecans

Preheat oven to 350°F.

Cream ½ cup margarine, shortening and sugar well. Add egg yolks, one at a time, beating well after each addition. Sift together dry ingredients and add to sugar mixture, alternating with buttermilk. Mix in vanilla, coconut and pecans. Set aside. Beat egg whites until stiff. Fold into batter by hand. Divide batter evenly between three greased and floured 8-inch round cake pans. Bake 30 to 35 minutes or until cake bounces back when touched lightly in center. Cool completely on racks.

Cream margarine, cream cheese, and sugar until fluffy. Frost cooled cake and garnish with coconut and pecans.

**Serves 12 to 16.**

## Cinnamon Carrot Cake

1½ cups oil
2 cups sugar
4 eggs
2 cups all purpose flour
2 teaspoons baking soda
3 teaspoons cinnamon
1 teaspoon salt
3 cups grated carrot
2 Tablespoons vanilla
½ cup margarine or butter
8 oz. cream cheese
1 lb. confectioners' sugar
1 teaspoon vanilla
1 cup pecans, chopped

Preheat oven to 350°F.

Blend oil and sugar, beat in eggs one at a time. Sift in dry ingredients; mix in carrots and vanilla. Pour into a greased and floured 9x13x2-inch pan or two 9-inch layer pans. Bake for 1 hour and 15 minutes for 9x13-inch pan or 18 to 25 minutes for layer pans. Cool.

Cream margarine then cream with cream cheese and sugar. Add vanilla and nuts. Spread on cake.

**Serves 12 to 16.**

*A very different blend of spice and carrots which appeals to those who love traditional carrot cake and those who prefer a lighter cake.*

## Ricotta Nut Cookies

1 lb. butter (2 cups)
2 cups sugar
3 eggs
1 lb. ricotta cheese
2 teaspoons vanilla
1 teaspoon salt
4 cups all purpose flour
1 teaspoon baking soda
2 Tablespoons butter
2 cups sifted confectioners' sugar
2 Tablespoons milk
½ teaspoon vanilla or ¼ teaspoon almond extract
1 cup walnuts, coarsely ground or finely chopped

Preheat oven to 350°F.

Combine butter, sugar, eggs, cheese, vanilla and salt. Sift flour and baking soda and gradually add to creamed mixture, mixing well. Spoon by scant teaspoon onto parchment covered cookie sheet. Bake for 10 to 12 minutes. Cool.

Mix butter, confectioners' sugar, milk and extract until spreading consistency. Ice cookies then immediately dip them into chopped nuts while frosting is still wet.

**Makes 8 dozen.**

*These cookies taste very rich and are good any time of the day. They freeze well.*

# Caramel Espresso Cake

½ cup light brown sugar, firmly packed
¼ cup sugar
⅓ cup heavy whipping cream
2 Tablespoons unsalted butter
2 Tablespoons light corn syrup
1 Tablespoon instant espresso powder
1 cup walnuts, coarsely chopped
½ cup ground vanilla wafer or cookie crumbs
¼ teaspoon cinnamon
3 cups all purpose flour
1½ teaspoons baking powder
½ teaspoon baking soda
¼ teaspoon salt
1 cup sour cream
1 Tablespoon instant espresso coffee powder dissolved in 1 teaspoon hot water
2 teaspoons vanilla
1 cup unsalted butter, softened
1½ cups light brown sugar, firmly packed
3 extra large eggs
2 extra large egg yolks
confectioners' sugar, optional
2 oz. semisweet chocolate, melted, optional

ombine brown and white sugars, cream, butter, corn syrup and instant espresso powder in a small heavy saucepan. Bring to a boil over medium heat, stirring occasionally. Reduce heat and simmer, stirring occasionally, for 3 minutes. Remove from heat and stir in nuts, cookie crumbs and cinnamon. Cool. (This step can be done a day or two in advance if necessary; cover and refrigerate after mixture cools.)

Preheat oven to 350°F. Butter 12-inch fluted Bundt pan and dust with flour, tapping out excess. Combine flour, baking powder, soda and salt in a medium bowl. Set aside. Mix sour cream, dissolved espresso and vanilla in a small bowl. Set aside. Cream butter in the large bowl of an electric mixer on high speed until light. Gradually add the brown sugar in 2 additions and beat until light and fluffy. With mixer speed on medium, add the eggs and egg yolks, one at a time, beating well after each addition. With mixer on low speed, alternately beat in the dry ingredients and the sour cream mixture, beginning and ending with the dry ingredients and beating just until dry ingredients are moistened.

Spoon half the batter into prepared pan, smoothing the top. Top with half the caramel mixture, spooning it in a ring 1 inch from the center and edges of the pan. Spoon remaining batter into pan. Bake for 30 minutes. Remove from oven and spoon dollops of the remaining caramel mixture over the cake avoiding the edge and tube of the pan. Gently press dollops of mixture down into wet batter on top of cake until it's just covered by batter. Return to oven and bake another 30 minutes until cake is golden. If the cake begins to darken before it's finished, cover the top of the pan loosely with foil.

Cool the cake in the pan on wire rack for 30 minutes. Invert onto wire rack to cool completely. If desired, sift confectioners' sugar over cooled cake or pipe melted semisweet chocolate up and down fluted areas and top of cake.

## Angel Food Cake

2 cups sugar

1½ cups egg whites (about 6 to 8 egg whites)

½ teaspoon salt

1¼ cups cake flour

1 teaspoon cream of tartar

1 teaspoon vanilla

¼ to ½ teaspoon almond extract

reheat oven to 300°F.

Beat egg whites and cream of tartar together until stiff. Sift cake flour, sugar and salt together three times. Fold into egg whites and add vanilla and almond extracts. Pour into tube angel food cake pan. Bake at 300°F for 15 minutes, then at 325°F for 45 minutes. Invert pan with the center of the tube pan balanced on a shot glass to cool. When cool, remove from pan and frost with whipped cream garnished with crushed peppermint candy or with Seven-Minute Icing.

## Seven-Minute Icing

1½ cup sugar

2 egg whites

½ teaspoon vanilla

⅓ cup water

2 Tablespoons white corn syrup or pure maple syrup

dash of salt

ombine all ingredients in double boiler and beat for seven minutes over low heat. Stir in vanilla. Frosts one cake.

## All American Apple Pie

¾ cup sugar

½ teaspoon nutmeg

dash of salt

¼ cup all purpose flour

½ teaspoon cinnamon

6 cups tart apples, pared and thinly sliced (about 7 medium)

8- or 9-inch pastry crust (see recipe this chapter)

1 cup flour

½ cup butter, softened

½ cup brown sugar, packed

reheat oven to 425°F.

Mix dry ingredients. Stir in apples. Line pie pan with crust. Pour apple mixture into pie pan. Mix flour, butter and brown sugar in a small bowl. Blend until crumbly. Press on top of pie. Bake 40 minutes, cover with foil and bake 10 minutes more.

Best served warm with vanilla ice cream.

## Strawberry Shortcake

6 cups fresh strawberries, sliced
4 Tablespoons sugar, divided
1¾ cups all purpose flour
¼ cup cornstarch
2 Tablespoons sugar
4 teaspoons baking powder
1 teaspoon salt
6 Tablespoons butter
¾ cup milk

ombine strawberries and sugar in a medium bowl. Cover and let stand for at least one hour.

Preheat oven to 375°F. Spray an 8-inch round pan with non-stick cooking spray.

Combine flour, cornstarch, sugar, baking powder and salt in a large mixing bowl and stir to mix. Cut in butter until mixture resembles coarse crumbs. Add the milk to flour mixture all at once, stirring until combined but do not overmix. Pour into prepared pan. Bake 20 to 25 minutes or until golden. Cool in pan 10 minutes. May be served warm or cold.

Split shortcake into 2 layers. Place the bottom layer on a serving plate. Top with some of the berries, then add the second layer of shortcake. Spoon the remaining berries on top of the cake. Top with Sweetened Whipped Cream. Cut into wedges to serve.

Serves 8 to 10.

*May also be served by cutting into wedges, placing each wedge into a bowl, and passing cream to pour over individual servings of shortcake. Garnish with nutmeg, if desired.*

## Sweetened Whipped Cream

2 cups whipping cream
1½ teaspoons vanilla
½ cup confectioners' sugar

hill a large bowl and mixer beaters. Combine all ingredients in chilled bowl and beat until cream holds a shape. Use to top your favorite dessert.

## Brownie Cupcakes

1 cup margarine
4 1 oz. squares semi-sweet chocolate
1½ cups pecans, chopped
1 cup all purpose flour
1¾ cups sugar
4 eggs, beaten
1 teaspoon butter flavoring
1 teaspoon vanilla
¼ teaspoon salt

Preheat oven to 350°F.

Melt margarine and chocolate in microwave on medium power for 2 minutes, stirring every 30 seconds to blend. (Chocolate and margarine can also be melted in ovenproof bowl in oven.) Add pecans. In a separate bowl combine flour, sugar, beaten eggs, butter flavoring, vanilla and salt. Stir lightly, do not beat. Gently fold chocolate mixture into flour mixture; do not beat. Fill greased or paper lined muffin tins º full. Bake for 30 minutes.

**Makes 1½ dozen regular or 3 dozen mini cupcakes.**

## Apple-Apricot Crumb Tart

12 oz. dried apricots, coarsely chopped
8 oz. dried apples, coarsely chopped
3 cups water
¼ cup sugar
1 Tablespoon all purpose flour
1 pie crust
1 teaspoon all purpose flour
½ cup all purpose flour
½ cup sugar
¼ cup butter
ice cream or sweetened whipped cream to garnish

Combine fruit and water in a large saucepan and bring to a boil. Reduce heat and simmer 30 minutes. Drain well. Combine ¼ cup sugar and 1 tablespoon flour; stir into fruit mixture. Set aside. Fit pie crust into bottom and along sides of a 9-inch tart pan; sprinkle with 1 teaspoon flour. Spoon fruit mixture into prepared shell.

Preheat oven to 425°F. Combine ½ cup flour and sugar in a medium bowl. Cut in butter with a pastry blender or two knives. Sprinkle over tart. Bake at 425°F for 10 minutes then reduce temperature to 350°F and bake an additional 35 minutes or until lightly browned. Serve within 12 hours with vanilla ice cream or sweetened whipped cream.

Serves 8.

*An additional 6 oz. apricots may be substituted for apples for a tart dessert.*

## Cherry Pie

⅓ cup less 2 teaspoons cornstarch
2¼ cups sugar
¼ teaspoon salt
½ to ¾ teaspoon cinnamon, to taste
6 cups red sour cherries, pitted
¾ teaspoon almond extract
2 Tablespoons butter cut in pieces
pastry for 10-inch 2-crust pie

Mix dry ingredients together in a large bowl. Add cherries and almond extract and let stand 20 minutes, stirring occasionally.

Preheat oven to 425°F. Fit pastry into 10-inch pie pan. Pour cherry filling into pie shell and dot the top with the butter. Cover with top crust and crimp edges together. Cover pie loosely with foil for the first half of the baking to prevent top crust from becoming too brown. Bake at 425°F for 10 minutes then reduce oven temperature to 350°F and bake 35 minutes. Remove foil. Return pie to oven and bake an additional 20 to 25 minutes or until top crust is lightly browned and bubbly in the center.

## Peanut Blossoms

1¾ cup all purpose flour
1 teaspoon baking soda
½ teaspoon salt
½ cup butter or margarine
½ cup peanut butter
½ cup granulated sugar
½ cup brown sugar, packed
1 egg
2 Tablespoons milk
1 teaspoon vanilla
granulated sugar
12 oz. package chocolate kisses, unwrap each kiss

Preheat oven to 375°F.

Sift together flour, soda, and salt. Cream butter or margarine and peanut butter. Gradually add ½ cup each granulated sugar and brown sugar, creaming well. Blend in egg, milk and vanilla. Beat well. Add dry ingredients and mix thoroughly. Shape into balls (rounded teaspoonful each). Roll balls in sugar. Place on greased cookie sheet. Bake for 10 minutes. Remove from oven; top each with a chocolate kiss, pressing down firmly so cookie cracks around edge. Return to oven for 2 to 5 minutes. Cool on racks.

**Makes 2 to 2½ dozen.**

*These familiar, favorite cookies can be stored in a tightly sealed container for 3 to 4 weeks, if they are not eaten before then!*

## Richest Cheesecake Squares

1¾ cup graham cracker crumbs
⅓ cup margarine, melted
⅓ cup sugar
3 8 oz. packages cream cheese, softened
5 eggs
1 cup sugar
1½ teaspoons fresh lemon juice
1 pint sour cream
1½ teaspoons pure vanilla extract
½ cup sugar

ombine graham cracker crumbs, melted margarine and sugar in a medium bowl. Press into a 10x15x1½-inch jelly roll pan. Chill.

Preheat oven to 350°F. Beat cream cheese with mixer until well creamed. Add eggs one at a time mixing continuously. Mix in 1 cup sugar and lemon juice. Pour into chilled graham cracker crust. Bake on lowest rack of oven for 10 minutes. Decrease oven temperature to 300°F and continue baking until top has a dull finish (about 40 minutes). Remove from oven and cool 5 minutes.

While cake is cooling, mix sour cream, vanilla, and ½ cup sugar. Pour topping over cake and let rest 5 minutes. (Sprinkle with graham cracker crumbs to garnish if desired.) Return cake to oven for 5 more minutes. Remove from oven, cool, store chilled.

**Serves 24.**

*This very rich dessert is perfect for large gatherings and special occasions such as showers, graduation and receptions.*

## Rice Pudding Supreme

½ cup rice
1 cup water
4 cups milk
½ cup sugar
2 large eggs, beaten
1 teaspoon vanilla
cinnamon, optional

Cook rice in water in 1½ quart pan for 5 minutes. Add milk and simmer 30 minutes, stirring often. Add sugar and stir until dissolved. Take some of the hot liquid and whisk it into the beaten eggs. Then pour the egg mixture back into the pan until it reaches a custard-like consistency. Stir in vanilla. Transfer to serving dish. Mixture will thicken while cooling. Serve at room temperature or chilled. Top with fruit or whipped cream if desired. Garnish with a sprinkle of cinnamon.

Serves 8.

*Brown sugar may be substituted for white or maple flavoring may be added instead of vanilla.*

## Pumpkin Pie

½ teaspoon salt
1¼ teaspoons cinnamon
⅛ teaspoon cloves
1 teaspoon ginger
1¼ teaspoons nutmeg
⅛ teaspoon cardamom
⅓ cup boiling water
2 eggs
¾ cup brown sugar, packed
2 Tablespoons sorghum
16 oz. can pumpkin
12 oz. can evaporated milk
pastry for one crust pie, whole wheat crust preferred (recipe in this chapter)

Preheat oven to 425°F.

Mix salt and spices in a small bowl, add boiling water and blend. Set aside. Beat eggs; add sugar, sorghum, spice mixture, pumpkin and milk. Beat well. Pour into unbaked pie shell in 10-inch pan. Bake at 425°F for 15 minutes, reduce to 350°F and bake until set, about 45 minutes more. Pie is done when top no longer appears wet or when knife inserted into center comes out clean.

## Apple Brownies

½ cup margarine
1 cup sugar
1 egg
½ teaspoon baking soda
½ teaspoon baking powder
1 teaspoon cinnamon
1 cup all purpose flour
2 cups apple, coarsely chopped
½ cup nuts, chopped
2 Tablespoons sugar
½ teaspoon cinnamon

Preheat oven to 350°F.

Cream margarine and 1 cup sugar, add egg, beat well. Sift in baking soda, baking powder, cinnamon and flour. Mix well. Fold in apples and nuts. Pour into lightly greased 9x9-inch pan. Mix 2 tablespoons sugar and ½ teaspoon cinnamon. Sprinkle over batter. Bake for 35 to 40 minutes. Cool in pan before cutting.

**Serves 12.**

## Blueberry Cake and Sauce

1 cup blueberries
2 cups all purpose flour, divided
1 cup sugar
½ cup butter
1 egg
dash of salt
½ teaspoon baking soda
1 cup sour milk or buttermilk
sugar, to taste, to sprinkle on cake
½ cup sugar
4 Tablespoons all purpose flour
2 cups water
1 cup blueberries
3 Tablespoons rum, or to taste

Preheat oven to 350°F.

Mix berries with 1 cup flour. Set aside. Cream sugar and butter in a separate bowl. Add egg and salt, mix well. Add 1 cup flour and soda alternately with buttermilk. Beat. Stir in blueberry mixture. Pour into greased 8x8-inch pan. Sprinkle sugar on top. Bake 35 to 45 minutes until tester comes out clean.

Mix ½ cup sugar and 4 tablespoons flour in a medium saucepan. Add water. Bring to a boil, stirring until thick. Add blueberries. Cook 5 minutes. Remove from heat. Stir in rum. Serve warm over pieces of cake.

**Serves 8.**

*Excellent for a summer luncheon or coffee.*

## Peppermint Ice Cream

7 oz. red and white starlight peppermint candies
4 eggs, beaten
2 cups sugar
2 quarts half and half

Soak the peppermints in 2¾ cups of the half and half overnight. Warm the remaining half and half and beaten eggs in a medium saucepan, stirring constantly, until temperature of mixture reaches 160 to 165°F. Remove from heat and add the sugar, stirring well. Chill.

When ready to freeze, combine the two mixtures, stirring well. Freeze according to manufacturer's directions.

A drop or two of red food coloring can be added to make ice cream pink in color. If 1 cup pasteurized egg product is substituted for eggs, the milk and egg mixture will not need to be heated and cooled.

**Makes 2 quarts.**

*This family recipe was popular in the 1930s. Serve with chocolate sauce or garnished with whole or crushed peppermint candies.*

## Strawberry Granita

3 pints strawberries, fresh or frozen
2 cups sugar
1½ cups orange juice
½ cup lemon juice
¼ cup Grand Marnier

Put all ingredients into blender and liquefy. Freeze partially then turn into a bowl and beat with mixer until very smooth. Refreeze.

*Serve in stemmed glasses with a cookie for a light dessert after an elegant meal.*

## Genoise

6 eggs
1 cup sugar, divided
1 teaspoon vanilla extract
1 cup sifted cake flour
¼ cup butter, melted and held at 80°F or above

Preheat oven to 350°F.

Break eggs into top of double boiler. Cook over hot water until eggs are lukewarm. Add ⅔ cup sugar and beat with electric mixer at medium speed for 7 minutes. Add remaining ⅓ cup of sugar and beat on high speed for 2 more minutes or until mixture is lemon colored and stands in soft peaks. Gently add vanilla then fold in cake flour. Fold in melted butter. Pour batter into two 9-inch layer pans. Bake 40 minutes then immediately turn cakes out onto metal racks to cool.

## Tiramisu Supreme

6 egg yolks
1¼ cups sugar
1¼ cups mascarpone cheese*
1¾ cups whipping cream, whipped and lightly sweetened
6 oz. ladyfingers
⅓ cup coffee liqueur or brandy espresso (recipe follows)
½ pint sweetened whipped cream (recipe in this chapter)
unsweetened cocoa powder or grated semisweet chocolate

eat egg yolks and sugar until thick and lemon colored, about 1 minute. Place in top of double boiler; cook over simmering water 8 to 10 minutes, stirring constantly until candy thermometer placed in mixture reads 160°F. Remove from heat. Add mascarpone cheese; beat well. Beat cream in a separate bowl until stiff peaks form. Fold into yolk mixture; set aside.

Line the bottom and side of a 2½ to 3 quart glass bowl with ladyfinger halves, split sides up. Brush with coffee liqueur or brandy espresso. Spoon half of egg yolk mixture over ladyfingers. Repeat layers. Garnish with sweetened whipped cream and cocoa or chocolate. Cover and refrigerate for several hours or overnight.

**Serves 10.**

Serve in the large glass bowl or, just before serving, spoon into individual stemmed goblets, dust with cocoa powder, then garnish with a dollop of whipped cream and a chocolate curl or leaf. Genoise may be cut into strips and used in place of lady fingers. Recipe is on page 184.

*If unable to obtain mascarpone cheese a substitute can be made using the following:
8 oz. cream cheese
¼ cup sour cream
2 tablespoons whipping cream
Combine all ingredients then beat until fluffy.

## Brandy Espresso

⅓ cup hot water
2 teaspoons instant coffee crystals
1 teaspoon brandy

ombine all ingredients and stir until coffee is dissolved.

## Batons L'Orange

1 cup butter
1 egg
1 cup sugar
1½ teaspoons orange zest
1 teaspoon baking powder
2¼ cups all purpose flour
4 oz. semi-sweet chocolate, melted
colored sprinkles or ground nuts

Preheat oven to 350°F.

Beat butter, egg and sugar. Add orange zest and baking powder, mix. Stir in flour. Pack dough into cookie press. Use any disk that makes a long or bar cookie. Bake for 12 minutes. Melt chocolate. Dip ends of cooled cookies into melted chocolate and roll in sprinkles or ground nuts while chocolate is still wet.

**Makes 3 dozen.**

## Kansas Whole-Grain Apple Cake

1½ cups whole wheat flour
1 cup quick oats, uncooked
1 Tablespoon baking powder
¼ teaspoon salt
½ teaspoon ground cinnamon
½ cup sugar
2 eggs
½ cup oil
½ cup apple juice
1 large apple, cored and finely chopped (do not peel apple, should be about 1½ cups)
½ cup wheat germ
1 cups confectioners' sugar
2 Tablespoons butter or margarine, melted
1 Tablespoon apple juice

Preheat oven to 350°F. Grease a 6 cup oven-safe ring mold.

Combine flour, oats, baking powder, salt, cinnamon and sugar in a large bowl. Stir to mix well. Set aside.

Beat eggs in a small bowl. Stir in oil and apple juice. Add to dry ingredients and stir just until moistened. Stir in chopped apple.

Sprinkle ¼ cup of the wheat germ into prepared pan. Spread half the batter into the pan, then sprinkle with remaining wheat germ. Spread remaining batter over wheat germ. Bake 40 minutes, or until a wooden pick comes out clean. Invert onto a wire rack to cool.

Combine confectioners' sugar, butter and apple juice to make a glaze. Drizzle over cooled cake.

**Serves 8 to 10.**

## Elderberry Pie

1 quart elderberries, stems removed
1 cup granulated sugar
¾ cup brown sugar
2 Tablespoons lemon juice or vinegar
2 Tablespoons minute tapioca
½ teaspoon grated nutmeg
¼ teaspoon salt
pastry for a 9-inch 2-crust pie (recipe follows)
2 Tablespoons butter, cut into 6 pieces

ombine the elderberries, sugars, lemon juice, tapioca, nutmeg, and salt. Stir gently and allow mixture to stand for 10 minutes.

Preheat oven to 425°F. Roll out the crusts and line a 9-inch pie pan with the bottom crust. Pour the fruit mixture into the pie shell, dot with butter, and top with the second crust. Slash the top crust to allow steam to escape. Bake for 15 minutes, reduce heat to 350°F, and bake for an additional 25 to 30 minutes or until crust is golden and juices bubble up through the crust. Serve warm with vanilla ice cream.

**Serves 8.**

*Elderberries are tiny purple berries, rich in flavor, which grow wild along country roadsides and are in season mid to late summer. Some people are sensitive to the raw berries, but cooked berries can be enjoyed by all.*

## Whole Wheat Pie Crust

1½ cups whole wheat flour
½ cup all purpose flour
1 teaspoon salt
⅓ cup solid shortening
5 to 8 Tablespoons ice water

ombine flours and salt in a large bowl. Cut in shortening until the shortening pieces are the size of small peas. Sprinkle 2 tablespoons of water over the flour mixture then gently toss with a fork. Push the ball of dough that forms to the side then sprinkle another tablespoon of water over flour mixture, toss, then repeat the process until all the flour is moistened and dough can be formed into a ball. Divide dough into 2 balls and chill at least one hour.

Place dough on a lightly floured surface, press down to flatten, then roll first ball to make bottom crust. Use remaining ball to form another singe crust, a solid top crust, or roll out and cut in ½-inch strips to make a lattice-top crust.

For a double-crust pie, fit lower crust into pie pan and trim lower crust ½ inch beyond the edge of the pie pan. Place filling in bottom crust then place top crust over filling. Trim top crust to ½ to 1 inch beyond pie pan, fold under and flute edge by pressing dough from both crusts together against a wedge made with the finger and thumb of the opposite hand. Slit top crust to allow steam to escape. Bake as directed.

For a lattice-top pie, trim lower crust to ½ inch beyond pie pan, arrange strips of pastry at 1-inch intervals along top edge of crust. Fold back alternate strips to weave cross strips. Trim lattice strips even with edge of pie pan, fold over lower crust, then flute as directed above.

**Makes pastry for 2 single-crust pies or 1 double-crust pie.**

## Feathery Fudge Cake

⅔ cup butter

1¾ cups sugar

2 eggs

1 teaspoon vanilla

2½ oz. unsweetened baking chocolate, melted and cooled

2½ cups sifted cake flour

1¼ teaspoons baking soda

½ teaspoon salt

1¼ cups ice water

Preheat oven to 350°F. Grease, flour, and line two 9-inch round pans with wax paper .

Cream butter, sugar, eggs and vanilla; beat on high speed of mixer for 5 minutes. Blend in chocolate. Sift flour, soda and salt. Starting with flour mixture add flour alternately with ice water, beating well after each addition. Bake for 30 to 35 minutes. Cool on racks then frost with Feathery Fudge Frosting.

## Feathery Fudge Frosting

3½ oz. unsweetened baking chocolate

3 cups confectioners' sugar

4½ Tablespoons hot water

¼ cup pasteurized egg substitute

½ cup butter

1½ teaspoons vanilla

Melt chocolate. Blend in confectioners' sugar and water. Beat in egg, then butter and vanilla. Place bowl in a larger bowl filled with ice water; beat until frosting is of spreading consistency.

## Traditional Vanilla Ice Cream

5 eggs, beaten

2 quarts half and half

1¾ cups sugar

1 teaspoon salt

2 Tablespoons vanilla

milk to fill cylinder of ice cream maker to appropriate level

Mix beaten eggs with half and half and heat the mixture, stirring constantly, until temperature reaches 160 to 165°F, then remove from heat. Stir in sugar and salt. Chill. When ready to freeze, stir in vanilla and mix well. Pour into freezer container and add enough milk to bring level to the fill line of freezer container. Freeze according to manufacturer's directions.

Pasteurized egg product (1¼ cups) may be substituted for the eggs and the heating and cooling steps can be eliminated.

**Makes 1 gallon.**

## Whole Wheat Gingerbread Men

1 cup butter or margarine
1 cup brown sugar, packed
1 egg
⅓ cup light molasses
1 Tablespoon orange zest, finely chopped
2 Tablespoons orange juice
3 cups all purpose flour
1 cup whole wheat flour
2 teaspoons cinnamon
1 teaspoon ginger
½ teaspoon cloves
½ teaspoon baking soda
½ teaspoon salt

Cream together butter and brown sugar. Add egg, beat until light and fluffy. Add molasses, orange zest and orange juice; mix well. Stir flours, cinnamon, ginger, cloves, soda and salt together. Stir into creamed mixture, mix well. Chill dough.

Preheat oven to 375°F. Roll dough out on lightly floured surface and cut in desired shapes. Bake for 8 to 10 minutes on an ungreased cookie sheet. Cool 1 minute on pan then remove to rack to cool.

## Blueberry Cobbler

¾ cup sugar
¾ cup hot water
1 teaspoon lemon juice
1 quart blueberries, or more, if desired
½ cup butter or margarine
1½ cups self-rising flour
1 cup sugar

Preheat oven to 350°F. Lightly grease a 7x11-inch baking dish.

Dissolve sugar in water and combine with lemon juice and berries. Pour mixture into prepared baking dish.

Combine topping ingredients and cut with a pastry blender until mixture resembles cornmeal. Spoon over blueberry mixture. Bake for 25 to 30 minutes.

**Serves 6 to 8.**

*Serve with ice cream or sweetened whipped cream.*

## Supremes

2½ cups all purpose flour
1 teaspoon baking soda
½ teaspoon salt
1 cup butter
1 teaspoon instant coffee crystals
1 teaspoon vanilla
2 cups brown sugar, packed
2 eggs
3 cups oatmeal, dry, quick cooking type
2 cups walnuts or pecans, chopped, divided
14 oz. sweetened condensed milk
6 oz. chocolate chips
2 Tablespoons butter
pinch of salt
1 teaspoon vanilla

Preheat oven to 350°F. Grease a 9x13x2-inch baking pan.

Sift flour, baking soda and salt together then set aside. Cream butter with coffee, vanilla and sugar in a large bowl. Beat well, add eggs one at a time, beating well after each addition. Gradually beat in dry ingredients then the oatmeal. Mix in 1 cup of the nuts. Remove 2 cups of dough and set aside. Place the remaining dough in the pan.

Warm condensed milk, chocolate chips, salt and butter over low heat until all ingredients are melted. Remove from heat and stir in vanilla. Pour mixture over dough in pan. Spread reserved dough over filling. Sprinkle remaining nuts on top. Bake for 35 minutes. Cool before cutting.

**Makes 2 dozen bars.**

## Creamy Chocolate Ice Cream

1 quart half and half
6 eggs
2 cups sugar, divided
3 Tablespoons pure vanilla extract
1 pint whipping cream
15 oz. can chocolate syrup
1 quart milk (4 cups)

Heat half and half to almost scalding. Beat eggs until frothy. Add sugar ½ cup at a time, beating well after each addition. Beat until thick. Gradually add hot half and half to egg mixture, stirring constantly. Return mixture to pan and heat until at least 165°F. Remove pan from heat and add remaining ingredients except milk. Pour into cylinder of ice cream maker and add enough milk to fill ⅔ full. Chill in cylinder overnight or until cool. Stir well before freezing. Follow manufacturer's directions to operate ice cream maker to freeze ice cream.

## Bread Pudding with Whiskey Sauce

10 to 16 oz. loaf stale French bread, crumbled (or 6 to10 cups other bread)
4 cups milk
8 Tablespoons butter, melted
2 Tablespoons vanilla
1 cup coconut
1 Tablespoon cinnamon
2 cups sugar
3 eggs
1 cup raisins
1 cup chopped pecans
1 Tablespoon nutmeg

Combine all ingredients; mixture should be very moist but not soupy. Pour into buttered 9x12-inch or larger baking dish. Place into non-preheated oven. Bake at 350°F for approximately 1 hour 15 minutes, until top is golden brown.

**Serves 12.**

*Serve warm with Whiskey Sauce.*

## Whiskey Sauce

½ cup butter
2 egg yolks
1½ cups confectioners' sugar
½ cup bourbon or to taste

Cream butter and sugar in saucepan over medium heat until all butter is absorbed. Remove from heat and blend in egg yolks. Pour in bourbon gradually to your own taste, stirring constantly. Sauce will thicken as it cools.

**Makes 1 cup sauce.**

*Serve warm over bread pudding. May be kept warm in a thermos for tailgate parties.*

## Pineapple Sherbet

½ cup unsweetened pineapple juice
1 Tablespoon lemon juice (more if desired)
⅔ cup sugar
1 pint half and half or whipping cream

Combine juices and sugar and mix well. Chill. Pour cream into a medium bowl then add juice mixture stirring constantly. Freeze until hard. Turn sherbet into a large mixing bowl and beat until very light. Refreeze.

**Makes 1 quart.**

## Pineapple Upside Down Cake

20 oz. pineapple, crushed
¼ cup butter
1 cup brown sugar
1¼ cups all purpose flour
⅔ cup sugar
2 teaspoons baking powder
½ teaspoon salt
¼ teaspoon ground mace
⅓ cup butter, softened
½ cup milk
1½ teaspoons vanilla
1 egg

Preheat oven to 350°F. Grease the sides of a 9-inch square pan. Drain pineapple and discard liquid. Set aside. Melt ¼ cup butter in 9-inch pan in oven while preheating. Add brown sugar to butter and stir to blend. Spread the pineapple over the butter mixture; do not stir. Set aside. Sift flour, sugar, baking powder, salt and mace together. Add the softened butter, milk and vanilla. Stir to mix. Batter will be quite thick. Add egg and beat for 3 minutes. Spread the batter over the pineapple. Bake 35 to 40 minutes, or until a toothpick inserted into the middle of the cake comes out clean. Cut around edges of pan with a knife then immediately turn cake out onto a serving plate. Cool before serving.

## Cheesecake

1 cup all purpose flour
¼ cup sugar
1 teaspoon grated lemon zest
½ teaspoon grated orange zest
¼ teaspoon vanilla
½ cup butter
1 egg yolk
2½ lbs. cream cheese (5 8 oz. packages)
1¾ cups sugar
3 Tablespoons all purpose flour
¼ teaspoon salt
5 eggs plus 2 egg yolks
¾ teaspoon vanilla
¼ cup whipping cream
½ teaspoon grated lemon zest
½ teaspoon grated orange zest

Combine flour, sugar, lemon and orange zest and vanilla. Cut in butter; add egg yolk. Mix together, then form dough into a ball.

Preheat oven to 400°F. Remove bottom of a 9- or 10-inch springform pan from the sides of the pan. Press ¼ of dough into bottom of pan using a sheet of waxed paper over the dough to keep dough from sticking to your hands. The dough will be fairly thin. Bake 8 to 10 minutes, watching closely so dough does not burn. Cool. Increase oven temperature to 500°F. Carefully place the bottom (crust and pan bottom) into the side form of the springform pan. Pat the rest of the dough onto the sides of the pan as evenly as possible and lightly press the dough to seal with the bottom crust. Set aside or refrigerate while preparing the filling.

Beat cream cheese until fluffy. Mix sugar, flour and salt together and add to the cream cheese a few tablespoons at a time, stirring after each addition. Beat until smooth. Add 5 eggs, one at a time, beating after each addition, then add 2 egg yolks. Beat until very smooth. Add vanilla and whipping cream and stir. Stir in lemon and orange zest. Bake at 500°F for 12 minutes, then reduce oven temperature to 200°F and bake 1 hour. Do not open oven door. Cool in pan, then refrigerate several hours or overnight. Remove from springform pan before serving.

Cake may be served directly on bottom of cake pan placed on a serving plate, if desired.

*Excellent with berry sauces, chocolate sauce or liqueurs. Light cream cheese may be substituted for regular, if desired.*

## Raspberry Coconut Cake

2¼ cups cake flour or 2 cups all purpose flour
1½ cups sugar
3½ teaspoons baking powder
1 teaspoon salt
½ cup shortening
1 cup milk, divided
1 teaspoon vanilla
4 egg whites
3 cups flaked coconut, divided
1½ cups raspberry jam
fresh raspberries for garnish

Preheat oven to 350°F. Grease and flour three 9-inch round cake pans.

Measure flour, sugar, baking powder, salt, shortening, ⅔ cup milk and vanilla into a large mixing bowl. Blend on low speed for 30 seconds, scraping bowl constantly. Beat 2 minutes on high speed, scraping bowl occasionally. Add remaining milk and egg whites. Beat 2 minutes on high speed, scraping bowl occasionally. Fold in ⅔ cup coconut. Pour into prepared pans. Bake 20 to 30 minutes.

Mix jam and 1 cup coconut in a small bowl. When cake is cool, spread jam mixture between layers and frost with White Chocolate Frosting. Garnish cake with remaining coconut flakes and fresh raspberries.

6 oz. white chocolate
¼ cup whipping cream
1 cup cold unsalted butter, cut into pieces
1 cup confectioners' sugar

## White Chocolate Frosting

Warm white chocolate and cream in a microwave oven until chocolate is almost melted, about 2 to 2½ minutes on highest setting. Stir until chocolate is completely melted. Cool to room temperature. Beat butter and sugar slowly into cooled chocolate mixture with mixer until light and fluffy.

## Gingersnap Cookies

¾ cup unsalted butter
1 cup sugar
¼ cup molasses
1 egg, lightly beaten
1¾ cups all purpose flour
1 teaspoon cinnamon
½ teaspoon ground cloves
½ teaspoon ground ginger
¼ teaspoon salt
¼ teaspoon baking soda

Preheat oven to 350°F. Line a cookie sheet with foil.

Melt butter, add sugar and molasses, mix well. Stir in egg. Sift flour with spices, salt, and soda. Add to molasses mixture; batter will be wet. Drop tablespoons of batter onto foil lined cookie sheets, leaving 3 inches between cookies. Bake 8 to 10 minutes until cookies start to darken. Let cookies cool on foil; they will be soft.

**Makes 2 dozen large cookies.**

## Dutch Sugar Cookies

½ cup butter
½ cup margarine
½ cup solid shortening
1½ cups sugar
½ teaspoon baking soda
1 Tablespoon white vinegar
3 cups all purpose flour

Preheat oven to 325°F.

Cream butter, margarine, shortening and sugar. Dissolve baking soda in vinegar. Stir into butter mixture. Add flour, stirring to combine.

Make dough into 1-inch balls, place on ungreased cookie sheets and press down with a drinking glass which has been dipped in sugar. Bake 20 to 25 minutes.

## Bachelor Button Cookies

¾ cup margarine
1 cup brown sugar
¼ teaspoon salt
1 egg
2 cups all purpose flour, sifted
1 teaspoon baking soda
¼ teaspoon ginger
¼ teaspoon cinnamon
1 teaspoon vanilla
1 cup pecans, chopped
sugar

Preheat oven to 375°F. Lightly grease cookie sheets.

Cream margarine; add brown sugar and salt and beat well. Add unbeaten egg and beat until fluffy. Sift in dry ingredients. Add vanilla and chopped nuts. Chill dough several hours. Shape slightly rounded teaspoons of dough into balls. Roll balls in granulated sugar. Place 2 inches apart on cookie sheets and press down once with tines of fork. Bake 8 to 10 minutes or until nicely browned.

**Makes 5 to 6 dozen small cookies.**

## Pumpkin Cupcakes

2 cups sugar

1½ cups oil

4 eggs

2 cups pumpkin

2 cups flour (best with 1 cup all purpose, 1 cup whole wheat flour)

2 teaspoons cinnamon

2 teaspoons baking soda

2 teaspoons baking powder

½ cup nuts, chopped

reheat oven to 350°F.

Beat together sugar, oil, eggs and pumpkin. Set aside. Combine dry ingredients in a separate bowl. Gradually add dry ingredients to pumpkin mixture, mixing constantly. Stir in chopped nuts. Pour into greased or paper lined cupcake pans. Bake 20 to 30 minutes or until toothpick inserted in center comes out clean. Remove from pans and cool on racks.

**Makes 30 to 36 cupcakes.**

*Good plain or with Fluffy Frosting. Top with a candy corn for a Halloween treat.*

## Fluffy Frosting

1 lb. confectioners' sugar

9 Tablespoons butter

pinch of salt

2 Tablespoons pasteurized egg product

¼ cup milk

1½ teaspoons vanilla

eat all ingredients until smooth and of spreading consistency.

Orange or lemon juice (¼ cup) may be substituted for milk and vanilla.

## Russian Tea Cakes

1 cup butter, softened

½ cup confectioners' sugar

1 teaspoon vanilla

2¼ cups sifted all purpose flour

¼ teaspoon salt

¾ cup nuts, finely chopped

reheat oven to 400°F.

Mix butter, confectioners' sugar and vanilla until blended. Set aside. Sift flour and salt together; stir into butter mixture. Mix in nuts. Chill dough. Roll into 1-inch balls. Place on ungreased baking sheet (cookies do not spread). Bake for 10 to 12 minutes, until set but not brown. Roll in confectioners' sugar while still warm. Roll in sugar again when cooled.

**Makes about 4 dozen 1½-inch cookies.**

## Chocolate Truffle Loaf with Raspberry Sauce

2 cups heavy cream, divided
3 egg yolks, slightly beaten
16 oz. semi-sweet chocolate
½ cup light or dark corn syrup
½ cup butter or margarine
¼ cup confectioners' sugar
1 teaspoon vanilla
12 oz. raspberries, fresh or frozen
½ cup light corn syrup

ine a 9½x5½x2¾-inch loaf pan with plastic wrap.

Mix ½ cup cream with egg yolks in a small bowl. Warm chocolate, corn syrup and margarine in a 3 quart saucepan over medium heat until melted. Add egg mixture. Cook 3 minutes stirring constantly. Cool to room temperature.

Beat remaining cream, sugar and vanilla until soft peaks from. Fold into chocolate until no streaks remain. Pour into pan. Refrigerate overnight or chill in freezer for 3 hours.

Puree raspberries, then strain. Stir in corn syrup. Serve over Truffle Loaf.

Alternate microwave directions: Mix chocolate, corn syrup and butter in a 3 quart microwave safe bowl. Microwave on high for 2 to 2½ minutes, stirring twice. Stir in egg mixture. Microwave 3 minutes, stirring twice. Continue as above.

## Banana Pie

9-inch pie shell, baked
bananas
1 cup milk
½ cup sugar
2 egg yolks (reserve whites for meringue)
2 Tablespoons flour
meringue (recipe follows)

lice bananas into bottom of crust. Set aside. Combine milk, sugar, flour, and egg yolks in a small saucepan and bring to a boil. Let cool then pour over bananas. Top with Never Fail Meringue. Bake at 350°F for 10 minutes or until lightly browned.

**Makes a 9-inch pie.**

## Never Fail Meringue

1 Tablespoon cornstarch
2 Tablespoons cold water
½ cup boiling water
3 egg whites
6 Tablespoons sugar
1 teaspoon vanilla
pinch of salt

lend cornstarch and cold water in a small saucepan. Add boiling water and cook, stirring until clear and thickened. Let stand until completely cold. Beat egg whites with an electric mixer at high speed until foamy. Gradually add sugar and beat until stiff but not dry. Turn mixer to low speed; add vanilla and salt. Gradually beat in cold cornstarch mixture. Turn mixer again to high and beat well.

Preheat oven to 350°F. Spread meringue over cooled pie filling. Bake for 10 minutes or until top is lightly browned.

## Cream Pie Filling

3 cups milk, divided
4 Tablespoons cornstarch
½ cup sugar
½ teaspoon salt
4 egg yolks, save whites for meringue
2 Tablespoons butter
1 teaspoon vanilla
1 cup coconut
optional ingredients listed below
9-inch pie shell, baked

ix 1 cup milk, cornstarch, sugar, salt and egg yolks with wire whisk or rotary beater. Set aside. Scald remaining 2 cups milk in a medium saucepan. Gradually add milk and cornstarch mixture stirring constantly with a wire whisk. Bring to a boil and cook until thick. Remove from heat. Add butter and vanilla, stirring well. Add one of the ingredients below, stir to mix, then pour into baked pie shell. Top with Never Fail Meringue or sweetened whipped cream as desired.

**Makes a 9-inch pie.**

Coconut pie: ½ to 1 cup coconut
Raisin cream pie: steam ½ cup raisins then pat dry and stir in
Chocolate pie: add ¼ cup cocoa to dry ingredients

## Raspberry Creme Brulee

1 pint fresh raspberries
2½ cups heavy whipping cream
8 egg yolks
⅓ cup sugar
2 teaspoons vanilla
pinch of salt
12 teaspoons sugar, divided

lace 7 to 8 raspberries into each of six ramekins, set aside. Bring cream to simmer in a small sauce pan. Blend egg yolks, sugar and salt in a mixing bowl. Slowly whisk in hot cream, stir in vanilla. Pour mixture evenly into the ramekins. Set ramekins in a baking dish and pour boiling water into baking dish to come halfway up the ramekins. Bake at 300°F for 35 to 40 minutes or until set (do not overbake). Remove from water bath, cool, and chill thoroughly. Before serving sprinkle 2 teaspoons sugar over each custard. Heat salemander or a hot iron over stove burner until very hot, then hold over sugar for several seconds barely touching it until sugar melts and carmelizes. (Sugar may be carmelized under broiler, if desired.) Garnish with additional raspberries.

**Serves 6.**

## Lemon Pie Filling

9-inch pie shell, baked
⅓ cup flour
1¼ cups sugar
⅓ cup cold water
⅛ teaspoon salt
1 cup boiling water
1½ Tablespoons butter
3 egg yolks, well beaten (reserve whites for meringue)
1 large lemon, juiced

Mix flour, sugar, cold water and salt. Add boiling water and butter and cook in top part of double boiler (over water bath) for 10 minutes. Add egg yolks and cook 5 more minutes. Stir in lemon juice and pour into shell. Top with Never Fail Meringue (see page 196) and bake at 350°F for 10 minutes.

**Makes a 9-inch pie.**

## Black Raspberry Cobbler

4 to 5 cups black raspberries
½ cup granulated sugar
½ cup brown sugar
2 Tablespoons all purpose flour
¼ cup butter, in small pieces
2 Tablespoons lemon juice
½ teaspoon grated nutmeg
granulated sugar
grated nutmeg

*Dough:*

1½ cups all purpose flour
3 Tablespoons granulated sugar
1½ teaspoons baking powder
1 teaspoon salt
½ cup butter, cold
½ cup milk
½ teaspoon vanilla

Preheat oven to 350°F. Place raspberries in a 1½ quart oiled casserole with medium-high sides. Add sugars and flour; toss. Dot with butter; sprinkle with lemon juice and nutmeg. Bake for 15 minutes.

Meanwhile, make the dough. Place flour, sugar, baking powder and salt in a medium sized bowl. Cut in the chilled butter with a pastry blender. Combine milk and vanilla. Add to the flour mixture. Stir with a fork until a stiff ball forms, then turn out onto a well floured board. Roll out until approximately 1 inch thick. Shape the dough to fit the casserole. Roll dough onto a rolling pin, and unroll on top of the warm fruit. Slit the dough in 2 or 3 places. Sprinkle a mixture of sugar and nutmeg on top. Continue baking 30 to 40 minutes, or until the juices bubble through the slit and the crust is lightly browned. Serve warm, preferably with cream.

**Serves 6.**

## Fudge Bars

2 cups all purpose flour
2 cups sugar
¼ teaspoon salt
1 cup butter or margarine
¼ cup cocoa
1 cup water
½ cup buttermilk
1 teaspoon baking soda
2 eggs
1 teaspoon vanilla

*Frosting:*
½ cup butter or margarine
¼ cup cocoa powder
⅓ cup buttermilk
1 lb. confectioners' sugar
½ cup nuts, chopped
½ cup coconut
1 teaspoon vanilla
pinch of salt

reheat oven to 375°F. Grease 12x18x¾-inch jelly roll pan.

Sift flour, sugar and salt together into a large bowl. Set aside. Bring butter, cocoa and water to a boil in a small saucepan. Pour butter mixture over flour mixture, then add buttermilk, baking soda, eggs and vanilla and beat well. Pour into prepared pan and bake for 20 minutes.

Start to prepare frosting when cake has baked for 10 minutes. Bring butter, cocoa and buttermilk to a boil. Stir in confectioners' sugar, nuts, coconut, vanilla and salt. Spread frosting over hot cake. Cool cake in pan on a metal rack.

**Serves 18 to 24.**

## Cheesecake Cookies

½ cup brown sugar, packed
½ cup pecans, chopped
1 cup all purpose flour
⅓ cup butter, melted
8 oz. cream cheese, softened
¼ cup sugar
1 egg
2 Tablespoons milk
1 Tablespoon lemon juice
1 teaspoon vanilla

reheat oven to 350°F.

Blend together brown sugar, pecans and flour; add butter and mix until crumbly. Reserve 1 cup mixture. Press remaining mixture into an 8-inch square pan. Bake 12 to 15 minutes. Beat cream cheese with sugar until fluffy. Beat in egg. Add milk, lemon juice and vanilla, blend well. Pour onto baked crust, top with reserved crumbs and bake for 15 minutes. Cool and chill. Cut into squares.

**Makes 16 squares.**

## Pumpkin Bars

Beat eggs in a large bowl. Add sugar, oil and pumpkin, mix until smooth. Sift together flour, baking soda, baking powder, cinnamon and nutmeg and add to the pumpkin mixture. Pour into a greased jelly roll pan. Bake at 350°F for 25 minutes. Mix frosting ingredients and spread on cooled pumpkin bars.

Serves 16.

4 eggs
2 cups sugar
1 cup oil
2 cups pumpkin
2 cups flour
1 teaspoon baking soda
2 teaspoons baking powder
1 teaspoon cinnamon
½ teaspoon nutmeg

*Frosting:*

½ cup butter
3 oz. cream cheese
3 cups confectioners' sugar

## Traditional Carrot Cake

2 cups all purpose flour
2 cups sugar
½ teaspoon salt
1 teaspoon baking soda
2 teaspoons cinnamon
3 eggs
1½ cups vegetable oil
2 cups carrot, finely grated
1 teaspoon vanilla
20 oz. can crushed pineapple
1 cup shredded coconut
½ cup walnuts, chopped
8 oz. cream cheese
3 cups confectioners' sugar
½ cup butter or margarine, softened
1 teaspoon vanilla
½ cup walnuts

Preheat oven to 350°F. Grease and flour a 9x13x2-inch baking pan.

Combine dry ingredients in a mixing bowl. Add eggs, oil, carrots and vanilla; beat until combined. Stir in pineapple, coconut and walnuts. Pour into prepared baking pan. Bake for 50 to 60 minutes or until cake tests done. Cool.

Combine cream cheese, confectioners' sugar, butter and vanilla. Mix well until blended. Frost cooled cake. Sprinkle with walnuts. (Shredded carrots can be substituted for nuts on top of the cake.)

Serves 12 to 16.

## Chocolate Silk Pie

¾ cup butter, chilled
¾ cup sugar
1½ oz. unsweetened chocolate, melted, cooled slightly
1 teaspoon vanilla
½ cup pasteurized egg product, divided
8-inch pie shell, baked
whipped cream, sweetened

Cream butter; gradually beat in sugar. Beat well. Blend in cooled chocolate and vanilla. Beat well. Add ¼ cup egg product then beat for 5 minutes. Add remaining egg product and beat 5 more minutes. Filling should be stiff and satiny. Should keep peaks easily. If not stiff enough, may put in freezer for 10 minutes. Fill shell. Top with Sweetened Whipped Cream (recipe in this chapter). Garnish with chocolate curls or leaves.

## Melting Moments

1 cup butter
1⅓ cup confectioners' sugar, divided
¾ cup cornstarch
1 cup flour
3 oz. cream cheese
1 teaspoon vanilla
few drops food coloring, optional

Preheat oven to 350°F.

Cream butter and ⅓ cup confectioners' sugar. Add cornstarch and flour. Drop by scant teaspoons onto ungreased cookie sheets. Bake 12 to 15 minutes. Cool completely.

Blend cream cheese, confectioners' sugar, vanilla and food coloring. Frost cooled cookies.

**Makes 3 dozen.**

## Fresh Strawberry Pie

9-inch pie shell, baked
2 quarts fresh strawberries, washed, hulled and sliced
1 cup sugar
1 Tablespoon cornstarch
sweetened whipped cream (recipe in this chapter)

Crush 1 cup berries. Combine crushed berries, sugar and cornstarch and cook over low heat until slightly thickened. Set aside. Place remaining strawberries into baked pie shell, then pour cooked mixture over them. Top with whipped cream. Chill.

**Makes a 9-inch pie.**

## Oatmeal Chocolate Chip Cookies

1 cup all purpose flour
1 cup whole wheat flour
1 teaspoon baking soda
½ teaspoon baking powder
¾ cup margarine
¾ cup sugar
¾ cup brown sugar, packed
1 teaspoon vanilla
2 eggs
¼ cup water
2 cups chocolate chips
2 cups oatmeal, quick cooking
1 cup raisins or peanuts

Preheat oven to 350°F.

Combine dry ingredients in a large bowl. Set aside. Cream margarine, sugar, brown sugar and vanilla. Beat until creamy. Beat in eggs and water. Gradually add dry ingredients. Stir in chocolate chips, oatmeal and nuts. Drop by teaspoons onto ungreased cookie sheet. Bake 8 to 10 minutes. Allow to stand 2 minutes before removing from cookie sheet. Cool on racks.

**Makes 5 dozen.**

## Strawberry Sublime

1 cup all purpose flour
¼ cup brown sugar
½ cup margarine
½ cup chopped walnuts
1 cup sugar
2 Tablespoons lemon juice
½ cup pasteurized egg whites
10 oz. package of strawberries
1 cup heavy cream, whipped
½ teaspoon vanilla

Mix flour, brown sugar, margarine and nuts together. Spread out on a jelly roll pan and bake at 375°F for 10 minutes or until brown.

Combine and beat the sugar, lemon juice, egg whites and strawberries at high speed for 15 minutes. Fold in whipped cream and vanilla.

Place half of crumbs on bottom of 9x13-inch pan. Pour filling in pan and sprinkle top with remaining crumbs. Freeze until hard, at least 6 hours.

**Serves 12.**

## Fiesta Banana Cake

½ cup butter, softened
2 cups sifted cake flour
1 teaspoon baking powder
1 teaspoon baking soda
¾ teaspoon salt
1⅓ cups sugar
½ cup buttermilk, divided
1 teaspoon vanilla
1 cup bananas, mashed
2 eggs
½ cup walnuts, coarsely chopped

Preheat oven to 350°F.

Cream butter in a large bowl. Set aside. Measure sifted flour into a sifter; add baking powder, soda, salt and sugar. Sift dry ingredients into butter and stir. Add ¼ cup of buttermilk, vanilla and mashed bananas then mix until flour is moistened. Beat with electric mixer at low speed for 2 minutes. Add eggs, nuts and remaining buttermilk. Beat with mixer 1 minute longer. Pour batter into two 8- or 9-inch layer pans which have been greased and floured. Bake 25 to 30 minutes for 9-inch layer or 9x13-inch sheet pan and 35 to 40 minutes for 8-inch layers.

When cool, frost with Sophie's Ice Frosting.

## Sophie's Ice Frosting

½ cup granulated sugar
½ cup butter, softened
½ cup hot milk
1 Tablespoon all purpose flour
pinch of salt
vanilla to taste

Cream butter and sugar. Let milk cool slightly. Mix 2 tablespoons of the milk with flour to make a paste. Add to creamed butter and sugar. Beat creamed mixture with an electric mixer. While beating add remainder of milk 1 teaspoon at a time. Mix in salt and vanilla.

**Makes enough to frost 1 cake or 24 cupcakes.**

Melange seems a fitting title for this superb collection of some of our finest recipes for Midwestern hospitality. Melange is defined by Webster as a mixture, especially of incongruous elements. We have collected an array of recipes of various flavors and textures which can be used as an accompaniment to a special meal, an offering for a tea or holiday party, or as a special gift of love and appreciation. Our melange has been cultivated in the Midwest tradition of beautiful homemade gifts.

Basil Pesto and Spicy Pineapple Salsa make piquant gifts sure to be treasured by any hostess. Aromatic Cinnamon Apple Ornaments are simple enough for children to make as a family holiday tradition.

Sweets, always a favorite, include rich Candied Pecans and Chocolate Truffles coated with toasted coconut, cocoa, confectioners' sugar, or toasted hazelnuts.

In the tradition of our grandmothers' herb gardens and the current trend toward herbed specialty products we present herbed oil and blueberry vinegar.

As beautiful as they are delectable, these festive treats will add to any meal or occasion.

# Melange

## Basil Pesto

2 cups fresh basil leaves
4 medium size garlic cloves, chopped
1 cup walnuts
1 cup olive oil
1 cup freshly grated Parmesan cheese
¼ cup freshly grated Romano cheese
salt and freshly ground black pepper to taste

Process basil, garlic, walnuts and approximately ¼ cup of the olive oil in a food processor fitted with a steel blade, or in two batches in a blender, until finely chopped.

With the machine running, pour remaining olive oil in a thin, steady stream.

Add the cheeses, a pinch of salt, and a liberal grinding of pepper. Process briefly to combine. Remove to a bowl and cover until ready to use.

Any pesto not used immediately can be refrigerated. Bring to room temperature before using. When freezing for later use, combine all ingredients but cheeses. Add cheese after thawing just before use.

Makes two cups.

## Spicy Pineapple Salsa

1½ cups fresh pineapple, diced
¾ cup red pepper, diced
½ cup red onion, diced
¼ cup cilantro, chopped
2 teaspoons jalapeno pepper, diced
1 Tablespoon fresh lime juice
1 teaspoon olive oil

Mix all ingredients together. Refrigerate overnight, allowing flavors to blend. Serve at room temperature.

Serves 6.

*A healthy refreshing alternative to basic salsa.*

This page generously sponsored by Connie and Michael Grimes.

## Herbed Oil

6 large springs fresh rosemary
4 cups extra virgin olive oil

To release the full flavor of rosemary, place on a chopping block and lay a large steel spatula on top. With palm, press down firmly on spatula blade releasing the rosemary essence. Divide the rosemary sprigs equally between two sterilized pint (16 oz.) vinegar bottles. Pour in olive oil making sure the rosemary is completely covered. Seal each bottle and shake well. Label and set in a cool dark place for two weeks, shaking bottles occasionally. After two weeks flavors will be fully developed.

Other herbs can be used in place of the rosemary; try tarragon, mint, thyme or lemon balm.

## Candied Pecans

1 cup sugar
1 teaspoon cinnamon
1 teaspoon salt
1 egg white
1 Tablespoon cold water
1 lb. pecan halves

Mix sugar, cinnamon and salt until well blended. Beat egg white and water with a fork until frothy. Pour over pecans and stir until all the pecans are well coated. Pour sugar mixture over pecans and stir until all of the sugar has coated the pecans. Spread on a cookie sheet and bake at 225°F for one hour, stirring occasionally.

**Makes one pound.**

*Can be doubled and made in advance. These pecans make great holiday gifts.*

## Chocolate Truffles

⅓ cup butter
½ cup powdered cocoa
2½ cups confectioners' sugar
¼ to ⅓ cup cream
1½ teaspoons vanilla
1 teaspoon brandy or amaretto
powdered cocoa, coconut, confectioners' sugar, or hazelnuts

Melt butter, stir in cocoa. With mixer, combine cocoa mixture and sugar. Gradually add cream, vanilla, and extract. Chill until firm. Form into 1 inch balls. Roll in any of the coatings listed then cover and chill.

*These are great as a gift for party hosts!*

## Home Canned Spiced Peaches

4 lbs. fresh peaches
2⅓ cups white wine vinegar
12 black peppercorns
1 teaspoon whole cloves
4 cardamom pods
2 cinnamon sticks
2 star anise
5 cups sugar

Bring a saucepan of water to a boil and place each peach in it for 35 seconds. Remove the peaches with a slotted spoon and transfer to a bowl of ice water to cool, then drain and dry well. Cut each peach in half and then remove the skin and pit.

Bring the wine vinegar, peppercorns, cloves, cardamom, cinnamon and star anise to a boil in a large pot. Add the sugar and stir over low heat until it has completely dissolved. Boil the mixture for 2 minutes. Reduce heat, add the peach halves and simmer for 4 to 5 minutes or until the peaches are tender when pierced with a knife.

Place peaches in a warmed sterilized canning jar, to within ½ inch of the top. Boil the syrup for 2 to 3 minutes longer until it has slightly reduced.

Pour syrup over the peaches. Seal the jar and label. Keep in a cool dark place for 2 months before using to allow the flavors to develop.

**Makes one quart.**

## Cinnamon Potpourri Ornaments

¾ cup applesauce
1 package unflavored gelatin
9 oz. jar cinnamon
3 Tablespoons ground cloves
¼ cup cornstarch

In small saucepan mix applesauce and gelatin and let stand for 3 minutes. Heat applesauce and gelatin mixture over medium heat, stirring until it simmers. Remove from heat. Combine cinnamon, cloves and cornstarch in a separate bowl. Stir in applesauce mixture. Turn out onto counter and knead a few times. Divide in half and place between two sheets of plastic wrap. Roll dough between the plastic sheets to ¼ inch thickness. Remove top layer of plastic and cut out ornaments using 2 inch cutters. Use straw to cut holes for hanging. Dry ornaments on wire rack overnight. String with twine or ribbon.

*These ornaments can be made months in advance and smell great! Scent may last up to two years.*

## Blueberry Vinegar

1 large bunch fresh basil
1 lb. fresh or frozen blueberries
4 cups white wine vinegar
1 Tablespoon fresh chives, chopped

Tear basil leaves into small pieces. Mix blueberries and a dab of vinegar in a glass bowl. With a wooden spoon, crush berries to release their juices. Stir in vinegar, basil and chives. Pour into large glass jar and shake well. Place jar in a cool dark place for four weeks, shaking from time to time.

Sterilize about four small vinegar jars. Line a funnel with three layers of cheesecloth. Place funnel in each jar and strain the flavored vinegar through funnel. Garnish with fresh chive flowers and blueberries and seal tightly.

## Vegetable Garden Salsa

1 cup fresh or frozen corn, defrosted
1 cup tomatoes, diced
¼ cup fresh cilantro, chopped
2 Tablespoons red onion, chopped
1 small jalapeno pepper, seeded and chopped
¼ teaspoon sugar
½ teaspoon cumin
1 Tablespoon white vinegar
salt and pepper to taste

Combine corn, tomatoes, cilantro, onion, jalapeno, sugar and cumin in a small bowl. Toss gently, adding vinegar, salt and pepper to taste.

**Makes 2 generous servings.**

*A light refreshing appetizer or side dish.*

## Summer Salad Dressing

½ cup sugar
1 teaspoon salt
1 teaspoon dry mustard
1 teaspoon paprika
1 teaspoon celery salt
1 teaspoon grated onion
1 cup salad oil
¼ cup vinegar

Combine sugar, salt, dry mustard, paprika, celery salt and onion. Alternate adding first some oil and then some vinegar to dry ingredients until oil and vinegar combination are mixed with dry ingredients. Mix well.

*This is a wonderful salad dressing!*

## Jalapeno Salsa

12 green peppers
40 jalapeno peppers
12 medium onions
6 cloves garlic
6 qts. pureed tomatoes
2 cups white vinegar
2 Tablespoons salt
1 Tablespoon mustard seed
½ cup sugar
3 Tablespoons oregano
1 Tablespoon cumin
¼ cup oil
4 bay leaves
12 oz. can tomato paste
⅓ cup corn starch

In food processor, chop peppers, jalapenos, onions and garlic until finely chopped. Combine prepared vegetables with other ingredients except tomato paste and cornstarch. Simmer until slightly thickened in consistency (about 1 hour). Add tomato paste. Dissolve cornstarch with small amount of water. Stir into sauce if thicker sauce is desired. Remove bay leaves. Spoon into clean hot pint jars leaving ½ inch headspace and seal tightly. Process in boiling water bath for at least 10 minutes.

**Makes 18 to 20 pints.**

*Great to serve at parties or give as gifts.*

## Sicilian Zucchini Salsa

1 medium onion, chopped (½ cup)
1 clove garlic, minced
2 Tablespoons olive oil or cooking oil
2 medium zucchini or yellow summer squash, chopped (2 cups)
8 oz. can stewed tomatoes
8 oz. can tomato sauce
½ teaspoon dried oregano, crushed
½ teaspoon dried rosemary, crushed
½ teaspoon dried thyme, crushed
2 teaspoons fresh basil, chopped
dash of salt and pepper

Cook onion and garlic in hot oil in a medium saucepan until onion is tender but not brown. Stir in the zucchini or summer squash, undrained tomatoes, tomato sauce, oregano, rosemary, thyme, salt and pepper. Bring the mixture to a boil. Reduce heat. Cover and simmer 10 minutes or until vegetables are tender. Uncover and simmer about 20 minutes more until relish is desired consistency. Stir in fresh basil. Serve relish hot or cold over grilled chicken or meat. To store, cover and chill in refrigerator for up to 1 week.

**Makes about 2½ cups.**

## Copper Kettle Apple Butter

240 lbs. Jonathan apples
(about 9½ bushels), peeled, cored and quartered

30 lbs. sugar

7½ oz. ground cinnamon

4 gallons apple cider

*Equipment:*
30 gallon copper kettle with stand and stirring paddle, carpenter's level, firewood, apple peeler, paring knives, large pans, 180 clean pint jars, rings and flats, jar tongs, jar funnels, ladles, 2 very large pots for cooking, small pan for boiling flats, large saucepan

Prepare fire circle and sink bricks into areas for the feet of the kettle stand. Place stand with kettle in it and level with carpenter's level. Build fire. Pour 2 to 3 gallons of apple cider into kettle. Add apples until kettle is half full. Stir constantly and add more apples as the fruit cooks down. When apples are cooked to applesauce, add any previously cooked applesauce that has been preheated. Cook for 2 to 3 hours. Mix cinnamon with 10 lbs. of sugar. Add the cinnamon mixture and remaining sugar to pan.

Continue to stir and cook until it has a smooth texture and enough liquid has cooked off to pass the "weep test" (put a spoon of apple butter in clean, dry bowl and tip to see if liquid runs off or if it "weeps"). When butter doesn't "weep," use a large saucepan to ladle it into very large pots. Move pans to kitchen or canning area. Fill jars, wiping rims with a clean cloth then place a flat and ring and lid on each. Using jar tongs place jars in hot water bath for 10 minutes. Take out and set aside to seal and cool.

*Some apples may be cooked into applesauce the previous day if desired. Serve with Chewy Dunking Snaps (recipe follows). One midwestern family's yearly tradition. National Public Radio broadcasted a live production of this recipe process from Mrs. Neuenschwander's home in 1994.*

## Chewy Dunking Snaps

¾ cup shortening

1 cup sugar

1 egg

⅓ cup molasses

2⅓ cups sifted flour

2 teaspoons baking soda

1 teaspoon ginger

1 teaspoon cinnamon

½ teaspoon cloves

¼ teaspoon salt

Cream together shortening, sugar, egg, and molasses. Sift dry ingredients and add to creamed mixture. Mix well. Shape into 1 inch balls. Roll in sugar and place on ungreased baking sheet. Bake at 375°F for 12 to 15 minutes.

**Makes 5 dozen.**

For crisp cookies, store in loosely covered container. For soft cookies, store in an airtight container.

*These are perfect to dunk in hot apple butter.*

## Sweet Lime Pickles

7 lbs. cucumbers
2 cups household lime
2 gallons water
2 quarts vinegar
8 cups sugar
2 Tablespoons salt
1 teaspoon celery seed
1 teaspoon whole cloves
1 teaspoon mixed pickling spice
1 stick whole cinnamon
1 teaspoon alum
2 to 3 drops green food coloring

Slice cucumbers in ¼ inch slices. Soak in lime and water mixture for 24 hours. Wash and drain pickles and cover with clear water and let set 3 hours. Combine remaining ingredients except alum and food coloring. Drain and soak overnight in this mixture. Add alum and green food coloring. Bring to boil and simmer 35 minutes. Ladle into hot jars, leaving ½ inch headspace. Process in boiling water bath according to jar size. Process 20 minutes for quart jars, or 10 minutes for pint jars.

**Makes 6 quarts or 12 pints.**

## Fresh Fruit Pizza

2 cups sugar
1 cup butter
3 eggs
1 teaspoon salt
1 teaspoon baking powder
¼ teaspoon baking soda
¼ cup milk
1 Tablespoon vanilla
8 oz. cream cheese, softened
⅓ cup confectioners' sugar
fresh strawberries, kiwi, bananas and grapes, sliced

Cream together sugar and butter in large mixing bowl. Add eggs, salt, baking powder, baking soda, milk and vanilla. Mix dough until desired consistency (add more milk as needed). Press dough into pizza pan and bake at 350°F until brown, about 20 minutes. Mix cream cheese and confectioners' sugar together in a separate bowl. Allow cookie to cool for 10 minutes. Spread the cream cheese mixture evenly on baked dough. Arrange sliced fruit in rings on top of cheese. Serve immediately or cover and refrigerate. Keeps for several hours.

*This is a wonderful summer appetizer, snack or dessert.*

## Watermelon Pickle

2 lbs. watermelon rind
¼ cup pickling salt
4 cups water
2 cups sugar
1 cup vinegar
1 stick cinnamon, broken
1 teaspoon cloves, whole
½ lemon, thinly sliced
5 maraschino cherries, quartered

Trim dark green and pink from rind; cut white part of rind into 1 inch cubes. Soak 7 cups of rind overnight in the pickling salt and water solution. Drain; rinse rind. Drain again. In saucepan, cover rind with cold water. Bring to boil; simmer about 10 minutes or just until tender. Drain.

Meanwhile, combine the sugar, vinegar, cinnamon and cloves. Cover and simmer 10 minutes. Remove cinnamon and cloves. Add drained rind, lemon and cherries. Simmer about 10 minutes until rind is clear. Fill clean, hot pint jars with rind and syrup, leaving ½ inch at the top. Adjust lids according to package directions. Process in boiling water bath for 5 minutes.

**Makes 3 pints.**

## Cinnamon Cucumber Rings

1½ to 2 gallons cucumbers, cut into rings
2 cups household lime
8½ quarts cool water
1 cup vinegar
1 Tablespoon alum
1 small bottle red food coloring
2 cups vinegar
2 cups water
1 package red hot candies
10 cups sugar
8 sticks cinnamon

Peel, slice into rings, and remove seeds from cucumbers. Place in lime water. Soak for 24 hours. Drain and cover with cool water and soak for an additional 3 hours. Drain; add vinegar, alum, food coloring and enough water to cover. Heat and simmer for 2 hours. Drain and set aside.

Prepare syrup by combining vinegar, water, red hots, sugar and cinnamon. Bring to boil. Place rings in container with tight fitting lid and cover with syrup. Close container completely and let stand overnight. Drain, reheat syrup and pour over cucumbers once per day for 2 additional days. On the 3rd day bring all to a boil and ladle into hot pint jars with ½ inch space at the top. Process in a hot water bath for 20 minutes.

*Great side dish for summer gatherings.*

## Mustard Sauce

½ cup tomato soup
½ cup vinegar
½ cup salad mustard
3 egg yolks, beaten
½ cup sugar
¼ cup butter

ombine all ingredients and cook until thick, stirring constantly. A double boiler can be used. Refrigerate extra sauce and heat before reserving.

*Delicious on ham loaf, meat sandwiches or as a dipping sauce for appetizers.*

## Raisin Sauce

½ cup brown sugar
1 teaspoon dry mustard
2 Tablespoons cornstarch
2 Tablespoons lemon juice
1 Tablespoon vinegar
1⅓ cups water
½ cup raisins

n a small saucepan, combine brown sugar, dry mustard and cornstarch. Slowly add the lemon juice, vinegar, and water, stirring constantly. Add raisins and cook over medium heat until raisins are tender.

**Makes 6 servings.**

*This is a delicious sauce to serve with baked ham.*

## Saffron Cream Sauce

1½ cups dry white wine
½ cup shallots, minced
1 cup whipping cream
generous pinch of powdered saffron
1 Tablespoon olive oil
salt and pepper to taste

oil wine and shallots in small saucepan for about 12 minutes, until liquid is reduced to 2 Tablespoons. Add cream and saffron. Simmer about 10 minutes, stirring frequently, until liquid is reduced to ¾ cup. Strain into bowl, pressing firmly on solids with back of spoon. Season with salt and pepper.

*Serve over pan-seared or grilled salmon, beef steaks, or other meats.*

## Shiitake Mushroom Sauce

¾ cup shiitake mushrooms, sliced
2 Tablespoons shallot or onion, finely chopped
1 Tablespoon butter
1 Tablespoon all purpose flour
⅛ teaspoon salt
dash of pepper
2 drops hot pepper sauce
⅔ cup milk
½ cup sour cream
1 Tablespoon parsley, snipped

n a small saucepan cook the mushrooms and shallots in butter. Stir in flour, salt, pepper, and pepper sauce. Add milk all at once. Cook and stir until thickened and bubbly then cook and stir for 2 more minutes. Stir in sour cream and parsley. Serve immediately. Extra sauce can be covered and refrigerated overnight.

**Makes about 1⅓ cups of sauce.**

*Delicious on rare beef. Can also be used on pork.*

## Apple Tomato Chutney

n a large saucepan combine all ingredients. Bring to boil then reduce heat. Cover and simmer for 30 minutes, stirring occasionally. Uncover and cook for 15 minutes. Cool to room temperature. To store, cover and chill in the refrigerator up to 1 week.

**Makes about 3 cups chutney.**

2 medium cooking apples, cored and chopped
3 medium tomatoes (about 1 lb.), chopped
½ cup sugar
⅓ cup vinegar
¼ cup green pepper, chopped
¼ cup raisins
¼ cup water
1 Tablespoon lime or lemon juice
1 teaspoon ground cinnamon
2 cloves garlic, minced
¼ teaspoon salt
dash of freshly ground black pepper

*Serve cold with grilled meat or poultry, or warm with pork.*

## Fudge Sauce

½ cup butter
1 cup cocoa
1 lb. confectioners' sugar
1 cup milk
1 can evaporated milk

Melt butter in large sauce pan. Sift cocoa and sugar together, set aside. Mix milk and evaporated milk together then slowly add to sifted mixture, stirring to mix. Pour mixture into saucepan with butter. Bring to a boil, stirring constantly. Cool slightly before serving over ice cream. More milk can be added to thin. Remaining sauce can be refrigerated for several weeks.

*Delicious with homemade ice cream.*

## Sweet Carrot Honey

1 pint carrots, grated
1 lemon rind, grated
2 cups sugar
juice of 2 lemons
½ teaspoon nutmeg, optional

Grate carrots and lemon rind. Mix in sugar and lemon juice. Sprinkle with nutmeg and blend. Stir until well mixed. Simmer in a large pan until the mixture is thick and clear, stirring frequently, about 50 minutes. Immediately pack in hot jars and seal.

*Serve as a condiment with meats at picnics and pot luck dinners.*

## Home Canned Strawberry Preserves

2 quarts strawberries
9 cups sugar
¾ cup water

Prepare berries by washing and hulling. Heat sugar and water in a large kettle, stirring constantly until sugar is dissolved. Add berries and bring to a rapid boil. Continue to boil for 15 minutes until desired consistency, stirring constantly. Let stand uncovered for 12 hours, stirring occasionally to plump berries. Put in sterilized jars and seal.

*You can enjoy your strawberry harvest year-round with these wonderful preserves.*

## Marinade for Lamb

1 cup lemon juice
½ cup extra virgin olive oil
½ cup salad oil
2 cloves garlic, crushed
2 Tablespoons ground horseradish
drop of Tabasco
2 Tablespoons chili sauce
¾ cup chutney
1 cup barbecue sauce
¼ cup soy sauce
1 teaspoon freshly ground pepper
1 teaspoon Worcestershire sauce
¼ teaspoon rosemary
¼ teaspoon oregano

ombine all ingredients until well blended. Marinate lamb overnight. When ready to grill lamb, pour off marinade and place in saucepan. Heat thoroughly until sauce becomes thick. Baste lamb with sauce while grilling.

*May also be used for pork chops. Serve grilled meat with barley casserole.*

## Royal Marinade for Shrimp, Chicken, and Pork

32 oz. pineapple juice
¼ cup soy sauce
⅔ cup white wine
juice of 2 lemons
¼ teaspoon ginger, crushed
¼ teaspoon fresh garlic, minced
½ cup brown sugar
¼ teaspoon freshly ground black pepper

ix all ingredients well. Place in marinator or low, flat plastic container. Add meat. Marinate several hours or overnight. Be sure to turn meat several times to marinate both sides.

Grill meat whole or cube and put on skewers with carrots, mushrooms, turnips, peppers, onions, potatoes or pineapples.

**Makes 1½ quarts and will keep up to six weeks when refrigerated. Can use for 3 to 4 meals.**

*Serve with rice pilaf and white wine.*

## Marinade for Beef

¼ cup vegetable oil
¼ cup dry vermouth
¼ cup soy sauce
1 teaspoon dry mustard
1 teaspoon prepared mustard
1 clove garlic, minced
¼ teaspoon pepper
½ teaspoon salt
1 Tablespoon Worcestershire sauce

Mix all ingredients in food processor or blender for 2 minutes. Pour marinade over steaks. Refrigerate, turning steaks every hour for 4 hours. Best if refrigerated for at least 12 hours.

## Red Wine Marinade for Beef and Lamb

½ cup red wine
½ cup olive oil
juice of 1 lemon (about 3 Tablespoons)
1 to 3 garlic cloves, minced
1 teaspoon each oregano, thyme, marjoram and rosemary

Mix all ingredients well. Pour into meat marinator or shallow long plastic container with tight fitting lid. Add meat. Marinate 6 hours or overnight, turning at least 4 times to marinate both sides of meat.

Grill meat whole or cut up for shish-ka-bobs with potatoes, onions, peppers, tomatoes and mushrooms.

*This will keep up to six weeks in refrigerator.*

## Marinade for Pork Tenderloin

2 teaspoons thyme, crushed
2 Tablespoons dry mustard
½ cup dry sherry
½ cup soy sauce
2 cloves garlic, minced
1 teaspoon ground ginger
⅓ cup oil

Crush thyme in spoon to release flavor. Combine all ingredients except oil and stir well. Add oil. Pour over pork loin or pork roast and chill overnight. Turn occasionally.

Slice pork 1½ to 2 inches thick and grill.

## Fresh Dill Dip

½ pint (8 oz.) sour cream
1 cup mayonnaise
3 Tablespoons dill, fresh or crushed
2 Tablespoons Beau Monde
1 teaspoon onion, chopped
1 Tablespoon fresh parsley, snipped

ix all ingredients together and refrigerate overnight. Yogurt may be substituted for the sour cream, if desired.

*This is delicious as an accompaniment to fish as well as vegetables.*

## Coconut Strawberries

½ cup sweetened condensed milk
3 oz. box strawberry gelatin
7 oz. shredded coconut
1 Tablespoon sugar
1 teaspoon almond extract
red food coloring
artificial green stems

ix all ingredients together. Shape into strawberries and roll in red sugar. Put on green stems. Stems can be purchased where cake decorating supplies are sold.

*Decorative item for cookie trays and buffets.*

## Grilled Quesadillas

6 7 inch flour tortillas
2 Tablespoons cooking oil
¾ cup salsa
1½ cups (6 oz.) shredded Monterey Jack cheese (with or without jalapeno peppers)
cilantro sprigs
sour cream, guacamole, salsa

rush one side of 3 tortillas with cooking oil. Place tortillas, oil side down, on a large baking sheet. Spread salsa over each tortilla on baking sheet. Sprinkle each with cheese. Top with remaining tortillas. Coat top of tortillas with remaining oil.

Grill quesadillas on rack of an uncovered grill directly over medium coals for 3 to 4 minutes or until cheese begins to melt and tortillas start to brown, turning once.

Cut quesadillas into wedges. Top each with a dab of sour cream, guacamole, and salsa. Garnish with a sprig of cilantro.

## Date Strawberries

1 cup butter
1 cup sugar
2 eggs, beaten
8 oz. dates, pitted
1 cup flour
1 teaspoon salt
1 teaspoon vanilla extract
2½ cups crispy rice cereal
red sugar, optional
1 cup chopped nuts, optional
artificial green stems

elt butter in saucepan then add sugar and eggs to pan. Mix in dates. Beat with mixer while in pan. Cook for 5 minutes. Add flour, salt, vanilla, cereal and nuts. Mix well. Shape into strawberries while mixture is warm and roll in red sugar. Add stems; cool. Store and serve at room temperature. Stems may be purchased where cake decorating supplies are sold.

*A good snack or dessert for children.*

## Pierogi

1 cup water
1 teaspoon salt
3 cups flour, divided
3 eggs
2 to 2½ lbs. potatoes, cooked and mashed
4 to 6 oz. cheddar cheese (farmer cheese may be substituted)

ix water and salt together; bring to a boil. Add 1 cup flour to mixture and let cool. Add eggs to cooled mixture, one at a time; then add 2 cups flour; knead into dough. If dough seems sticky to work with, add flour, a little at a time. Let dough rest about ten minutes. Make filling by mixing cheese with mashed potatoes.

Roll dough thin on floured surface. Cut dough into 2-inch squares or with a pierogi cutter. Place one teaspoon potato mixture on each square and fold over. Seal edges tightly with fingertips or pastry roller.

Drop into boiling water and cook until pierogi float. Can be frozen for up to 2 weeks.

**Makes 6 servings, 72 pierogi.**

*Delightful traditional dish common to many different nationalities. Serve with beets, applesauce, or as a side dish in place of pasta or potatoes.*

Christmas dinner with all the trimmings is one of the most memorable, time honored traditions in Midwest homes. Holiday meals especially reflect our heritage and the foods served by the ethnic groups from which we come.

The Traditional Christmas Goose was served with the savory sweet dressing prepared by European grandmothers from the ingredients available to them. A handful of raisins, or two, or three. Whatever the proportions turned out to be, the goose and dressing were always hard to wait for as the aroma of roast goose, apples and spice filled the house. Although the composition and proportions of the dressing were dependent more on the mood of the cook or availability of ingredients than on any particular recipe, the goose and stuffing were always sensational. Now that many of these women are gone and families are spread out across the country, we pass these nearly lost traditions on to new generations.

After several years of celebrating Christmas in our home with turkey and sage dressing I prepared from recipes from my family, we were traveling to my husband's family home to celebrate Christmas. My children were initially relieved to hear Grandma was preparing a turkey breast in addition to her traditional goose. They knew they liked Mom's sage dressing, but weren't sure about Grandma's goose or dressing. One bite of the Traditional Christmas Goose and Sweet Dressing and the turkey was quickly forgotten, much to their grandmother's delight.

# Celebrations

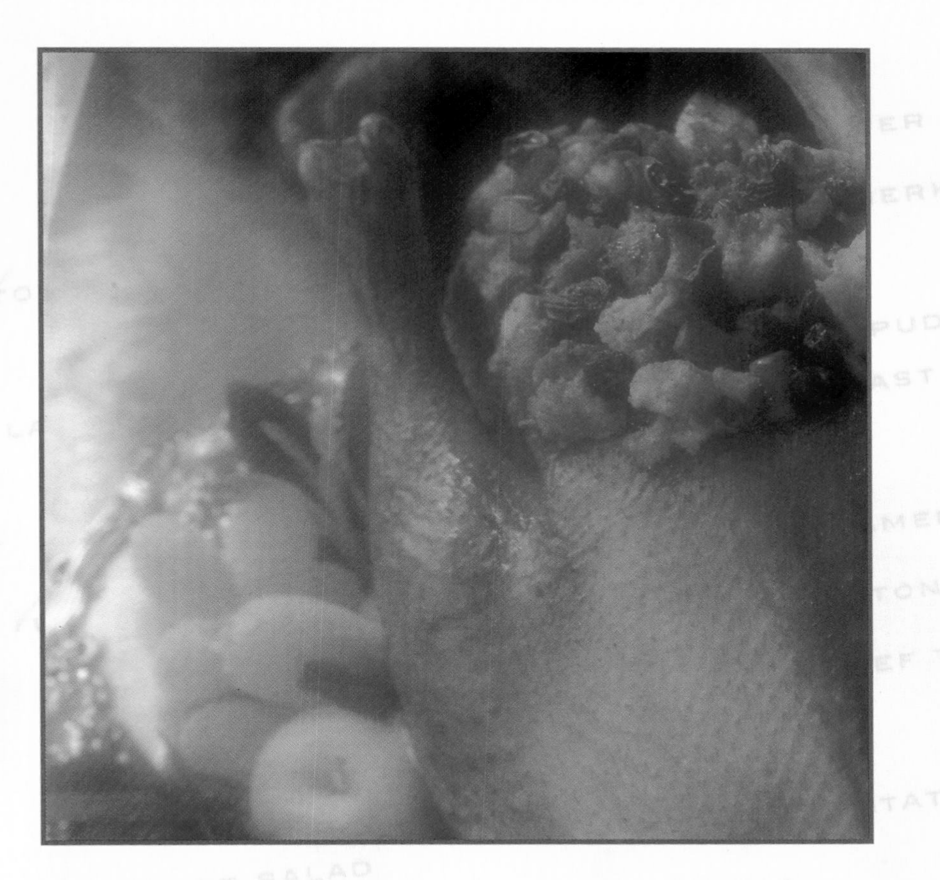

Pumpkin Soup

Traditional Christmas Goose with Sweet Dressing

Herbed Corn Pudding

Spiced Sweet Potato and Coconut Souffle

Garlic Green Beans

Parker House Rolls

Autumn Cheesecake

*Over the river and through the woods . . .*

A traditional family Christmas dinner

- 10 to 12 lb. fresh goose
- 8 cups day old bread, cubed
- 3 cups apples, chopped
- 2 cups raisins
- 6 Tablespoons sugar
- 1 teaspoon salt
- 1 Tablespoon cinnamon
- ¼ teaspoon thyme
- ¼ teaspoon ginger
- ¼ teaspoon mace
- ½ cup water
- ¼ cup melted butter, optional

## Traditional Christmas Goose with Sweet Dressing

ombine bread cubes, apples and raisins in large bowl. Set aside. In a small bowl mix sugar, salt and spices together then sprinkle over bread. Toss well. Stir in water and, if desired, melted butter. Set aside.

Prepare goose by removing excess fat from body cavity and neck skin. Prick thigh and leg area of goose well before roasting to allow fat to drain off goose during cooking. Stuff with sweet dressing. Roast, uncovered, breast side up for one hour at 400°F. Do not baste during cooking but use a bulb baster to remove accumulated fat every 30 minutes. Remove goose from oven; invert on rack so breast side is down. Reduce temperature to 325°F. Roast 1½ hours longer or until meat thermometer placed in center of inside thigh muscle registers 180°F. Let stand, breast side up, loosely covered with foil for 20 minutes before carving.

Serves 10 to 12.

## Pumpkin Soup

¼ cup margarine
1 medium onion, chopped
2 large shallots, chopped
1 medium baking potato, peeled and diced
3 celery ribs, chopped
2 medium carrots, chopped
¼ cup dry Madeira wine
6 to 7 cups chicken stock
1½ teaspoon dried thyme
¼ teaspoon paprika
3 cups pumpkin, pureed
½ cup evaporated milk
salt to taste
½ teaspoon pepper

Melt margarine over low heat in medium saucepan. Add vegetables and cook until softened stirring occasionally. Pour in Madeira and cook covered over low heat 5 minutes. Add 6 cups chicken stock, thyme, paprika and pumpkin and simmer 30 minutes. Puree soup in batches in blender. Pour milk, salt and pepper in pan and add pumpkin mixture. Use additional chicken stock if mixture is too thick. Heat and serve.

**Serves 8.**

## Herbed Corn Pudding

2 Tablespoons butter
1½ Tablespoons flour
1 cup milk
2 cups corn
1 Tablespoon sugar
1 teaspoon salt
1 Tablespoon parsley, minced
¼ teaspoon basil
¼ teaspoon marjoram
2 eggs, well beaten
pepper

Melt butter, add flour and blend well. Add milk and make a smooth sauce. Add corn, sugar, salt and herbs. Heat and blend. Remove from heat. Add a small amount of warm mixture to beaten eggs and mix well to temper eggs. Stir egg mixture into corn mixture then pour into buttered baking dish. Bake in a 350°F oven for 30 minutes or until firm.

This flavorful holiday favorite can easily be doubled to serve a party of 10 to 12. Bake 45 to 50 minutes, if doubled.

**Serves 6.**

## Spiced Sweet Potato and Coconut Souffle

*Souffle:*

3½ cups sweet potatoes, mashed

1 cup sugar

½ teaspoon salt

2 eggs

4 Tablespoons margarine, melted

1 teaspoon vanilla

1 teaspoon cinnamon

1 teaspoon nutmeg

½ teaspoon allspice

1½ Tablespoons Cointreau

*Topping:*

1 cup shredded coconut

⅓ cup flour

¾ teaspoon baking powder

1 cup brown sugar

1 cup chopped pecans

4 Tablespoons butter, melted

Mix all souffle ingredients with mixer and pour into buttered 2 quart baking dish. Mix topping ingredients and pour on top of souffle. Bake at 350°F for about 35 minutes.

Serves 10.

## Garlic Green Beans

1 lb. fresh green beans

pinch of salt

4 cloves garlic, thinly sliced

3 Tablespoons butter

Snap ends off beans but leave remainder of bean whole. Place beans in boiling salted water and boil for 5 to 10 minutes until beans are crisp-tender. Drain beans. Melt butter in a large skillet, add garlic and beans and saute over low to medium heat for 5 minutes. Place beans and garlic on a platter to serve.

Serves 4.

## Parker House Rolls

5 Tablespoons shortening or margarine
2 teaspoons salt
½ cup water
1 cup milk
½ cup warm water
2 cakes yeast
(6 packages dry yeast, 13⅓ teaspoons)
⅔ cup sugar
2 eggs
6 to 7½ cups all purpose flour

Place the margarine and salt in a mixing bowl. Combine ½ cup water and milk; scald. Pour scalded liquid over margarine and salt; let cool to lukewarm. Crumble yeast cakes into a separate bowl and add ½ cup lukewarm water to dissolve.

When margarine, salt, milk and water mixture is lukewarm, add yeast mixture. Add sugar, eggs and 2 cups flour, beating until smooth. Add 2 more cups flour, again beating until smooth. Stir in the final 2 cups flour, then turn out on counter and knead. Continue to add flour until dough forms and holds shape but is slightly sticky.

Put dough in a greased bowl, cover with a towel and refrigerate 6 to 8 hours. When ready, shape rolls* and place on greased baking sheets. Let rise 2 hours, then bake at 350°F for 15 minutes or until golden brown.

*To form Parker House shape: Divide dough in half. Working on a floured surface roll each half to ¼-inch thickness. Cut with a floured 2½-inch round cutter. Brush with melted butter. Make an off center crease in each round. Fold so large half overlaps slightly. Place 2 to 3 inches apart on baking sheet. Let rise and bake as directed.

## Autumn Cheesecake

1 cup graham cracker crumbs, finely crushed
½ cup ginger snaps, finely crushed
5 Tablespoons butter, melted
8 oz. cream cheese, softened
¾ cup sugar
16 oz. pumpkin
1 teaspoon cinnamon
¼ teaspoon ginger
¼ teaspoon nutmeg
dash salt
2 eggs
1 cup whipped cream
pecan halves, to garnish

Preheat oven to 350°F.

Combine crumbs and butter. Press into a 9-inch springform pan, pushing 1 inch up the side. Cream together the cream cheese and sugar. Mix in the pumpkin and spices. Add the eggs, one at a time, mixing well after each addition. Pour batter into springform pan with crust. Smooth and spread evenly. Bake for 55 to 65 minutes until tester comes out clean.

Loosen cake from rim of pan. Cool before removing rim. Chill. Serve with whipped cream. Garnish with pecan halves.

**Serves 8 to 10.**

## Cinco de Mayo—
## a Lively Mexican Fiesta

Fried Wonton Envelopes with Guacamole Dip

Mexican Fudge

Fajitas

Mexican Spoon Bread

Tequila Dip with Fresh Strawberries

Sopapillas

Margaritas

# Fajitas

¼ cup vegetable oil

2 Tablespoons lemon juice

2 Tablespoons soy sauce

2 Tablespoons green onions, chopped

1 clove garlic, minced

1 teaspoon black pepper, coarsely ground

1 teaspoon celery salt

1 Tablespoon jalapeno pepper juice

jalapeno pepper slices, optional

1½ to 2 lbs. lean flank steak, skirt steak, skinned chicken breast or boned pork loin

Combine all marinade ingredients and mix well. Remove any fat from steak and wipe well with paper towels. Place steak and marinade in shallow dish. Marinate for at least 6 hours, turning frequently. Broil over hot coals or in broiler. Broil steak 5 minutes on each side and chicken 4 minutes on each side or until desired doneness. Slice into thin strips.

Serves 4 to 8.

*Serve with sauted bell pepper and onion strips wrapped in heated flour tortillas. Top with grated cheese, guacamole, sour cream or salsa.*

## Fried Wonton Envelopes

8 oz. Monterey Jack cheese with peppers, cut into 1x1x½-inch pieces
24 small wonton wrappers
vegetable cooking spray
vegetable oil

lace one cheese cube in center of each wonton wrapper. Moisten edges of wrapper with water. Fold corners of wrapper to center, enclosing filling and overlapping edges slightly. Place on sheets of wax paper sprayed with cooking spray; cover with additional wax paper to prevent drying. Pour oil to depth of 3 inches in a Dutch oven; heat to 350°F. Fry wontons, 3 or 4 at a time, until golden brown on each side, turning once. Drain on paper towels. Serve immediately with Guacamole Dip.

**Makes 24 appetizers**

## Guacamole Dip

2 large ripe avocados, peeled, seeded and mashed
3 Tablespoons fresh lime juice
½ teaspoon garlic salt
1 Tablespoon chopped fresh cilantro or ½ teaspoon dried coriander
2 Tablespoons green onions, finely chopped
2 Tablespoons salsa

ombine all ingredients. Chill.

**Makes 1¼ cups.**

## Mexican Fudge

4 oz. jalapenos
1 lb. cheddar cheese, grated
6 eggs, beaten
¼ teaspoon Tabasco sauce
black olives

ightly grease an 8x8-inch glass baking dish. Drain jalapenos and spread over bottom of dish. Mix cheese and eggs and pour over jalapenos. Slice olives and place in rows on top of cheese mixture. Bake at 350°F for 30 minutes. Cool slightly and cut into small squares with olive slice centered on top of each square.

## Margaritas

12 oz. can frozen limeade, thawed
2 cans cold water or 1 can water and 12 ice cubes
6 oz. tequila
1 oz. Cointreau

ombine all ingredients in large pitcher.

**Makes six 4 oz. drinks.**

## Mexican Spoon Bread

1 cup cornmeal
1 cup flour
1 teaspoon salt
¼ cup sugar
1 Tablespoon baking powder
1 egg
1 cup milk
1 cup cottage cheese
½ cup margarine, melted
1 small can green chilies, chopped
grated cheese

reheat oven to 400°F. Grease a 9x12-inch dish.

Mix all ingredients except green chilies and cheese. Pour half of cornbread mixture into baking dish. Top with chilies and cheese. Spread remaining cornbread mixture on top. Bake for 35 minutes.

## Tequila Dip with Fresh Strawberries

2 cups sour cream
3 Tablespoons sugar
3 Tablespoons tequila
1 Tablespoon Cointreau
1 Tablespoon grated lime zest
1 Tablespoon grated orange zest
¼ teaspoon cinnamon
3 Tablespoons ground almonds
orange and lime zest for garnish

ombine all ingredients except garnish in medium bowl. Whisk until smooth and well blended. Cover and chill several hours (best if chilled overnight). Garnish with orange and lime zest. Serve with fresh strawberries.

**Makes 2½ cups.**

## Sopapillas

1 cake yeast (3 packages dry yeast)
¼ cup lukewarm water
1 egg
1½ cups lowfat milk
1 Tablespoon margarine, melted
1 Tablespoon salt
¼ cup sugar
6 cups flour
confectioners' sugar

ix together yeast, water and egg. Add milk, margarine, salt, sugar and 4 cups of flour. Mix well. Add remaining flour one cup at a time. Knead slightly. Let rise until doubled in size. Punch down and let rise again. Roll ⅛-inch thick. Cut into 4-inch squares and drop immediately into hot oil (425°F or higher) cooking only three to four at a time. Cook until puffy and golden, turning once. Drain on paper towels and dust with confectioners' sugar. Serve while hot. Excellent when served filled with honey or butter.

**Makes 2 dozen.**

Celebrating with Friends

A Bridal Luncheon or
a Ladies' Card Luncheon

Cold Avocado Soup
Imperial Chicken
Lemon Pilaf
Asparagus Vinaigrette
Cheddar Muffins
Raspberry Walnut Torte

## Imperial Chicken

8 whole chicken breasts, cooked, skinned, and cut into chunks
4 lbs. shrimp, boiled, peeled and deveined
3 14 oz. cans plain artichoke hearts, quartered
3 lbs. fresh mushrooms, sauteed
6 cups medium white sauce (recipe follows)
2 Tablespoons Worcestershire sauce
salt and white pepper to taste
2 Tablespoons fresh or ½ teaspoon dried thyme, marjoram or sage
1 cup sherry or dry white wine, do not use cooking sherry or wine
½ cup grated Parmesan cheese, divided

Divide chicken, shrimp, artichokes and mushrooms equally between 2 greased 3-quart casseroles. Prepare white sauce, add remaining ingredients except cheese. Pour over mixture in casserole dishes. Top with grated Parmesan cheese (¼ cup per casserole). Bake uncovered at 375°F for 40 minutes.

Serves 18.

*To save time, the chicken, shrimp and mushrooms may be cooked the day before. This dish is easily halved.*

## Medium White Sauce

¾ cup butter
¾ cup all purpose flour
1 teaspoon salt
⅛ teaspoon white pepper
6 cups milk

elt butter in a large saucepan over low heat. Blend in flour, salt and white pepper. Add milk all at once and whisk until smooth. Cook over medium heat, stirring constantly, until mixture thickens and bubbles.

**Makes 6 cups.**

## Cold Avocado Soup

8 very small avocados
2 medium green onions, with tops
½ cup sour cream
½ cup milk or cream
4 cups chicken stock, cooled
salt and pepper to taste
1 to 2 dashes Tabasco sauce
dill

ombine all ingredients in a large mixing bowl. Process in blender in 3 batches, as blender will not hold entire amount. Serve chilled in stemmed wine glasses with sprinkles of dill on top.

Add more chicken stock if consistency is too thick.

## Lemon Pilaf

1 cup sliced celery
1 cup green onions, sliced
2 Tablespoons butter or margarine
3 cups hot cooked rice
1 Tablespoon grated lemon zest
½ teaspoon salt
¼ teaspoon pepper

aute celery and green onions in butter or margarine until soft but not browned. Add rice, lemon zest, salt and pepper. Toss to blend well. Cook and stir over low heat 1 to 2 minutes or until heated through.

This recipe can be doubled or tripled to match the number of servings of Imperial Chicken being served.

**Serves 6.**

*This is a fitting accompaniment to veal or fish, as well.*

## Cheddar Muffins

2 cups flour
1 Tablespoon baking powder
1 teaspoon salt
½ teaspoon paprika
2 Tablespoons sugar
1 egg, beaten
½ cup milk
½ cup sour cream
⅓ cup butter, melted
1 cup cheddar cheese, grated
½ cup onion, chopped
2 Tablespoons butter
1 to 2 teaspoons dill

reheat oven to 400°F.

Stir flour, baking powder, salt, paprika and sugar together in bowl. Blend in egg, milk, sour cream, butter and cheese just until smooth. Be careful not to over stir. Saute onion in butter. Fold in sauteed onions and dill. Grease muffin tin and bake until golden or about 20 minutes.

**Makes 12 muffins.**

## Asparagus Vinaigrette

1 teaspoon salt
½ teaspoon pepper
½ teaspoon garlic, finely minced
¼ teaspoon sugar
½ teaspoon dry mustard
1 teaspoon Dijon mustard
⅛ teaspoon cayenne pepper
dash Worcestershire sauce
dash Tabasco sauce
3 Tablespoons tarragon vinegar
10 Tablespoons salad oil
2 Tablespoons whipping cream
2 teaspoons parsley, chopped
24 fresh asparagus spears, trimmed

o make sauce, combine all ingredients except asparagus in a large jar. Shake well and chill.

Steam asparagus until tender but still crisp. Drain and arrange on individual plates. Drizzle cold sauce over asparagus tips.

**Serves 4.**

## Raspberry Walnut Torte

1¼ cups flour, divided
⅓ cup confectioners' sugar
½ cup butter or margarine, softened
2 10 oz. packages frozen red raspberries, thawed
¾ cup walnuts, chopped
2 eggs
1 cup sugar
½ teaspoon salt
½ teaspoon baking powder
1 teaspoon vanilla extract

reheat oven to 350°F.

Combine 1 cup flour, confectioners' sugar and butter, blend well. Press mixture into bottom of a 9x13x2-inch pan. Bake for 15 minutes. Set aside to cool.

Drain raspberries, reserving the liquid for the sauce. Spread berries evenly over the crust using the back of a spoon. Sprinkle with chopped walnuts. Beat eggs with sugar in a small mixing bowl until light and fluffy. Add salt, remaining ¼ cup flour, baking powder and vanilla, blend well. Pour over walnuts. Bake for 30 to 35 minutes or until golden brown. Cool. Cut into squares and serve with whipped cream or vanilla ice cream and Raspberry Sauce.

Serves 18.

## Raspberry Sauce

½ cup water
reserved raspberry juice
½ cup sugar
2 Tablespoons cornstarch
1 Tablespoon lemon juice

ombine water, reserved raspberry juice, sugar and cornstarch in a saucepan. Cook, stirring constantly until thickened and clear. Stir in lemon juice. Cool slightly, then serve over Raspberry Walnut Torte or ice cream.

KC Crackers

Kansas City BBQ Shrimp

Dilly Red Skin Potato Salad

Minted Melon Balls

Raspberry Swirl Cookies

Spiced Cookies

Raspberry Rapture
Ice Cream

# *Hotter than the 4th of July*

A Patio or Poolside
Summer Celebration

1½ lbs. large shrimp, peeled and deveined
½ cup butter, melted (do not use margarine)
3 teaspoons garlic, crushed
2 teaspoons Worcestershire sauce
½ cup beer
½ teaspoon rosemary
½ teaspoon thyme
1 teaspoon basil
1 teaspoon onion powder
½ teaspoon garlic powder
1 teaspoon paprika
1 teaspoon black pepper
1 teaspoon creole seasoning

## Kansas City BBQ Shrimp

Layer shrimp in oven-safe dish. Mix other ingredients together in a large bowl and pour over shrimp. Bake at 325°F for 20 to 25 minutes. Test for doneness; may need additional time depending on size of shrimp. Serve in bowls.

**Serves 4.**

## KC Crackers

2 22 oz. jars pepperoncini salad peppers, drained

6 oz. Monterey Jack cheese with peppers, cut into 24 1½x¼x¼-inch rectangles

6 oz. chicken breast half skinned, boned, cooked and cut into 24 pieces

24 sheets frozen phyllo pastry, thawed

butter flavored cooking spray

48 fresh long chives, optional

Select 24 two-inch long salad peppers; set others aside for garnish. Remove and discard stems and seeds from peppers. Drain thoroughly on paper towels. Stuff each pepper with 1 piece Monterey Jack cheese and 1 piece chicken; set aside. Spray both sides of 4 phyllo sheets with cooking spray; stack. Cut stacked phyllo in half lengthwise and then in thirds crosswise. Place 1 pepper on each phyllo stack at the long end. Starting with long end, roll phyllo around pepper. Twist ends to seal. Place on a baking sheet. Repeat with remaining phyllo and stuffed peppers. Bake at 375°F for 20 minutes or until golden brown. Tie twisted ends of pastry with chives, if desired. Serve immediately.

You may slice the green portion of green onions lengthwise and substitute for chives. The unbaked crackers may be frozen in an airtight container for up to 3 months.

## Dilly Red Skin Potato Salad

2½ lbs. red skin potatoes

½ lb. fresh green beans

¼ large red onion

⅛ cup Italian dressing

¼ cup mayonnaise

1 cup sour cream

2 generous sprigs fresh dill, stemmed and chopped

salt and pepper to taste

Scrub and boil potatoes until easily pierced with a fork. Cut each potato into large chunks, refrigerate to chill. Blanche green beans, cut in halves or thirds. Cut red onion into large chunks. Mix chilled potatoes, beans, onions and Italian dressing. In a separate bowl mix mayonnaise, sour cream, and dill. Add dressing to vegetables and toss until evenly coated. Season with salt and pepper to taste. Chill well. Best if made several hours or even a day before serving. Keep refrigerated.

## Minted Melon Balls

1 large cantaloupe, ripe but firm
1 large honeydew melon, ripe but firm
⅓ cup Mandarin Napoleon brandy or Cointreau
⅓ cup chopped fresh mint leaves

Cut melons in half, seed and make into balls. Add brandy to melon balls, stirring well. Refrigerate until ready to use. Right before serving, sprinkle with mint.

## Raspberry Swirl Cookies

½ cup butter
1 cup sugar
1 egg
1¼ teaspoons vanilla extract
2 cups all purpose flour
1 teaspoon baking powder
¼ teaspoon salt
½ cup raspberry jam, seeds removed
½ cup flaked coconut, finely chopped
¼ cup walnuts, finely chopped

Preheat oven to 375°F.

Cream butter, gradually adding sugar. Beat well at medium speed of electric mixer. Add egg and vanilla; beat well. Combine flour, baking powder and salt in a separate bowl. Add to creamed mixture a few tablespoons at a time, beating well. Shape dough into 2 balls. Wrap in plastic wrap and chill 2 hours.

Combine jam, coconut and nuts in a small bowl and stir well.

On a floured wax paper, roll each dough ball to an 8x10-inch rectangle. Spread half of the raspberry filling on each rectangle evenly to within ½ inch of edges. Carefully roll dough, jellyroll fashion, starting at long end and peeling wax paper from dough as you roll. Pinch side seam to seal (leave ends open). Wrap dough in plastic wrap. Freeze before slicing. Unwrap roll and cut in ¼-inch slices. Place 2 inches apart on greased cookie sheets. Bake for 8 to 10 minutes or just until cookies begin to brown around edges. Cool on wire racks.

**Makes 3½ dozen.**

*A decorative cookie, especially good with Raspberry Rapture Ice Cream.*

## Raspberry Rapture Ice Cream

1 quart half and half cream
2 eggs, beaten
3 oz. package raspberry gelatin
½ cup boiling water
12 oz. frozen raspberries, thawed
3¾ oz. package vanilla instant pudding mix
¾ cup sugar
1 cup whipping cream
1 Tablespoon vanilla

Heat cream and eggs in a saucepan, stirring constantly until the temperature reaches 165°F. Let mixture cool to room temperature, stirring occasionally.

Dissolve gelatin in the boiling water. Puree the thawed raspberries in a blender. Slowly pour the gelatin mixture into the pureed berries while the blender is running. Combine pudding mix and sugar in a small bowl. Mix the half and half mixture, raspberry mixture, pudding mixture, whipping cream and vanilla in a large bowl. Pour into cylinder of ice cream freezer. Freeze according to manufacturer's instructions.

**Makes 2 quarts.**

*This recipe may be used with other berries or peaches as well. Adjust sugar as needed to taste.*

## Spiced Cookies

2½ cups sifted flour
2 teaspoons baking soda
½ teaspoon cloves
½ teaspoon allspice
½ teaspoon cinnamon
¼ teaspoon ginger
¾ cup butter, softened
1 cup sugar
1 egg
¼ cup light molasses
confectioners' sugar

Mix dry ingredients together. Set aside. Beat butter, sugar and egg until light and fluffy. Add flour mixture alternately with molasses starting and ending with flour mixture. Refrigerate for at least one hour with bowl covered. Lightly grease cookie sheet. Preheat oven to 375°F. Roll into balls and then roll balls in confectioners' sugar. Bake 8 to 10 minutes. Remove to rack to cool.

**Makes 3 dozen.**

# Acknowledgements

*We thank the following people for their generous gifts of time and talent...*

## Recipe Submissions

Mary Lou Allen
Karen Altobelli
Allison Armstrong
Jean Ann Atwell
Elizabeth Balsbaugh
Nancy Balsbaugh
Susan Bean-Ward
Vicki Benton
Karla Bergner
Judy Bornkessel
Alice Brentano
Sharon Brown
Rita Z. Brungardt
Berta Bunn
Kathy Burke-Thomas
Deb Burnham
Joan Buttler
Amy Byers
Lisa Campbell
Linda Canny
Pam Carder
Anita Carpenter
Becky Carter
Gregory G. Caspers
Mrs. R.W. Caspers
Sally Chew
Dee Childress
Lisa Coen
Christine R. Crippin
Arthurine Criswell
Susan Cumberland
Jan Daniels
Sally Dannov
Darlene Davies
Shannon Demaree
Stephanie Dembicki
Enid Dickson
Nancy Dillingham
Sandy Durick
Louise Dyche
Pam Dykes
Cindy Ecclefield
Aileen Eidson
Amber Eppinger
Julie Fiebiger
Janet Fike
Gina Foster
Julie Foster
Debbie Gasparovich
Stacie Gram
Theresa Grisham
Peggy Gustin
Julie Hainje
Sharon Hall
Alice Hawk
Katy Henschel
Marcia Herre
Dawn Hightower
LaVonne Hightower
Nancy Hobbs
Nedra Hobert
Barbara Holt
Kathy Huerter
Bill Humenczuk
Gwen Humenczuk
John Humenczuk
Margo Humenczuk
Miranda Iszory
Joan Jaska
Sally Jenkins
Julie Jones
Lucille Kiefer
Theresa King
Jo Kuckelman
Lisa Kurtz
Kathryn Laurans
Cathy Lindhorst
Lyllis Ling
Crystal Maguire
Susanne Mahoney
Linda Maness
Kay Martin
Gina McCord
Adele McGrath
Steve Meier
Mrs. John E. Meyer
Margaret Meyers
Rebecca Miller
Rene Morris
Charlotte Mueller
Karen Murphy
Cheryl Murray
Phyllis Nason
Cee Ann Neuenschwander
Jim Neuenschwander
Gregory J. Neville
Carma Nowak
Cynthia Ochs
Peggy Osborn
Louise G. Oyche
Marsha Oyer
Dorraine Palmer
Jan Peerson
Sarah Petz
Betty Phillips
Pat Pierson
Barbara Pond
Jill Quigley
Sonja Randall
Luci Slatter Reilly
Carol Robertson
Loralee Robertson
Jack Rose
Judy Rose
Linda Sands
Sharon Schaaff
Renee Scherer
Marilyn Schlosser
Janice Seibold
Kathy Serrano
Leigh Shreves
Sally E. Smith
Sally R. Smith
Mary A. Spann
Frances Speer
Barbara Spilker
Lana St. Clair
Karen Kilian Stafford
Margaret Steineger
Sandra Stogsdill
Laura Strattan
Ann Stubblefield
Kelly Taylor
Romona Tetzlaff
Dora Mae Thomas
Jill Thomas
Vicki Thomas
Christie Thurlow
Todd Thurlow
Betsy Vicknair
Joyce Vogel
Betty Weeks
Ed Weeks
Hellon Weeks
Joan Wescott
Karen White
Mildred Whiteside
Alice Wilhelmus
Susan Williams
Joan Wirges
Faye Wood
Mary Ruth Yulich
Elizabeth Zavora
Kay Zingsheim
Kellie Zych

## Recipe Testing

Mary Lou Allen
Marilyn Alstrom
Betsy Anderson
Ginny Ayer
Nancy Balsbaugh
Susan Beam-Ward
Gloria Bell
Debbie Bender
Peggy Boller
Gail Boos
Judy Bornkessel
Eadie Boyer
Cathy Breidenthal
Jenni Breidenthal
Judy Brennan
Alice Brentano
Angie Brown
Nancy Browne
Linda Brozenis
O.G. Bruce
Rita Z. Brungardt
Kathy Burke-Thomas
Deb Burnham
Lisa Campbell
Gayle Canfield
Linda Canny
Pam Carder
Becky Carter
Colleen Carter
Heather Carter
Joy Carter
Ron Carter
Gregory G. Caspers
Dawn Caspers
Gloria Castor
Carrie Cheatham
John Cheatham
Max Cheatham
Lisa Coen
Denise Davis
Cindi Day
Janie DeGoler
Shannon Demaree
Irene Dowler
Marilyn Dreas
Nancy Dunlap
Kathleen Eastwood
Sue Ann Fagerberg
Rae Fee
Lisa Fettes
Bertie Fisher
Lynette Fisher
Julie Foster
Debbie Freely-Hall
Iris Garzee
Debbie Gasparovich
Claudia Gibson
Karen Grantham
Angela Gupta
Deb Hachen
Vickie Hammons
Jane Hanson
Paula Harr
Amy Hathaway
Alice Hawk
Dawn Hightower
Mary Jane Hobbs
Brian Hobert
Carrie Hobert
Nedra Hobert
Connie Huerter
David Humenczuk
John Humenczuk
Margo Humenczuk
Marie Humenczuk
Miranda Iszory
Sally Jenkins
Michelle Jennings
Leslie Johnson
Julie Jones
Dianne Keller
Paula Kramer
Kathryn Laurans
Sandy Leonard
Kay Lloyd
Susan Masson
Mel McAnany
Laura McConwell
Marin McCrossen
Tiffany McDaniel
Adrienne Mickells
Rebecca Miller
Angie Mitchell
Barbara Mohr
Louise Moody
Rene Morris
Georgianna Mullin
Karen Murphy
Linda Murray
Nancy Murray
Phyllis Nason
Cee Ann Neuenschwander
Marcie Neuer
Elaine Norman
Cynthia Ochs
Kathy Onnen
Marsha Oyer
Ellen Pansing
Jean Pasieniuk
Janita Peterson
Jennifer Phelps
Martha Phillips
Jackie Prother
Chris Rada
Carol K. Reiling
Sharon Rhodes
Marjorie Riggin
Linda Rippetoe
Donna Robinson
Janet Robinson
Harry Salyer
Tanya Salyer
Linda Sands
Nancy Schafer
Renee Scherer
Beverly Seat
Darlyne Sheppeard
Helen Sherwood
Susan Shinkle
Marilee Shrader
Bette Smith
Richard Snook
Peggy Spake
Virginia Speck
Barbara Spiker
Laurie Stewart
Sandra Stogsdill
Mary Patricia Sullivan
Dora Mae Thomas
Jill Thomas
Jim Thomas
Vicki Thomas
Joyce Thompson
Cathy Thomson
Christie Thurlow
Todd Thurlow
Karen Thurston
Tonya Thurston
Virginia Trickett
Linda Truitt
Barbara VanMiddlesworth
Marsha Verbanic
Joyce Vogel
Becki Vohs
Janeen Walker
Claire Ward
Susan Watkins
Betty Weeks
Ed Weeks
Hellon Weeks
Joan Wescott
Tracie Wesson
JoAnn Wheat
Skip Wheat
Alice Wilhelmus
Susan Williams
Joan Wirges
Brad Wirths
Nancy Worth
Jane Young
Deana Zahnd
Carolyn Zarter
Marti Zickefoose
Kellie Zych

## Indexing

Susan Meier

## Focus Committee

**Gail Boos**
**Becky Guthrie**
**Therese King**
**Adele McGrath**
**Courtney Vialle**

## Sponsor Notes

*** Page 29 generously sponsored by Connie Grimes, Kathy Burke-Thomas, Debra Whited Burnham, Tudy Kennedy, Paula Kramer, Barbara McLaughlin, LeAnn Smith and Donna Uzzell**

*** Page 83 generously sponsored by Mary Jean Ellis, Carol Ellis Roberts, Connie Ellis Grimes and Christy Ellis Robertson**

# Index

# Notes

*1—When a dish is served "a la king" it really means that a cream sauce has been used. Not an ordinary cream sauce, but a glorified one. Mushrooms, green peppers, a dash of lemon and nutmeg, real cream and egg yolks are added to the sauce before it is combined with the meat or fish. In former days, sherry was always used in addition.*

in the temperature used for a butter cake.

### Sponge Cake.

The recipe for a genuine sponge cake is as follows:

6 egg yolks
1 c sugar
1 T lemon juice with grated rind
6 egg whites
1 c flour
¼ t salt

Beat the egg whites until stiff and dry, add lemon juice, rind and salt to the whites. Now in separate bowl beat the egg yolks until thick and lemon colored. Add the sugar still beating. Cut and fold the beaten whites into the egg yolks. When partially mixed, add the flour which has been sifted a number of times.

Use the cutting and folding motion, not a stirring one. Put into an ungreased sponge cake pan. Bake in a slow oven for one hour. When baking the cake divide the time in the regulation way. During the first quarter, the cake rises. It continues rising and starts to brown in the second quarter. Browning continues in the third division of time. The cake shrinks from the side of the pan in the last quarter.

### Using a Paper.

If the browning seems to be going too rapidly, cover the top of the pan with a paper. Some women put a small pan of water in the oven during the baking progress, but that practice is hardly to be recommended. The steam from the water changes the texture of the crust.

Those of you who saw the cakes at the show were impressed, I am sure, with the beautiful, uniformly brown crust of some of the cakes. They were perfect.

The grain of a sponge cake should be fine throughout. The crumb should be tender. When the crumb is pressed in with the finger, it should act just like a sponge, and spring back into the

The cheaper sponge cake is the one made with water. This recipe is a reliable one.

6 egg yolks
1 c sugar
[illegible] T hot water
1 c flour
1½ t baking powder
6 egg whites
¼ t salt
1 T lemon juice with some grated rind, or
1 t almond extract and
1 t vanilla extract

Beat the egg whites until stiff and dry. Add salt and lemon juice to the whites.

Beat the egg yolks until thick and lemon colored, add sugar, beating continually. Fold in half of the whites, then the flour and baking powder sifted together. Cut and fold this in, as well as the remainder of the whites. Add the hot water. Put in an ungreased tin and bake. As was said earlier in the article, this cake will take a little hotter fire than the one made without baking powder.

If the tin in which you put the batter is greased the mixture tries to cling to the sides, and can't do it. It keeps slipping down if the sides are too slippery. Many people cut a circle of paraffin paper to cover the bottom of the pan. When this is done there is no difficulty in getting the cake from the pan after it is baked.

A sponge cake is really more tender on the second day than it is when just taken from the oven. When it is properly served it is never cut, but is torn apart using two forks for the process. The pieces are uneven in size, and somewhat irregular in shape. But people who know consider that the proper way to serve it.

## Corner Letter Box

*For the best recipe contributed to the Daily Magazine Section, The Plain Dealer will pay a daily award of $1. Address Corner Letter Box.*

### Au Gratin Potatoes.

Put a layer of cold boiled, diced potatoes into a baking dish, sprinkle with salt, add grated cheese and diced pimentoes. Cover with white sauce and sprinkle with browned bread crumbs. Repeat until dish is full. Bake until thoroughly heated through and well browned. MRS. O. M. HARPER.
Forest.

This recipe wins the $1 prize.

oven.

### Yellow Angel Food.

Yolks of 4 eggs, pinch of salt, 1 tablespoon cold water, 1-2 cup boiling water, 1 1-2 cups sugar, 1 1-2 cups flour with 2 teaspoon of cream tartar

### Date Cake.

Take 1 cup boiling water, 1 package dates, 1-2 cup English walnuts, 1 cup sugar, 1 tablespoon each butter and lard, 1 egg, 1 1-2 cups flour, 1 tablespoon baking